MACMILLAN HISTORY OF LITERATURE

TWENTIETH-CENTURY ENGLISH LITERATURE

Harry Blamires

First published 1982 by
THE MACMILLAN PRESS LTD
Companies and representatives throughout the world

ISBN 0 333 27020 7 (hc)
ISBN 0 333 27021 5 (pbk)

Typeset by
Cambrian Typesetters, Farnborough, Hants
Printed in Hong Kong

Contents

List of plates

Acknowledgements

Grateful acknowledgement is due to publishers who have given permission for the use of quotations from copyright poems: to Duckworth (Gerald) & Co Ltd for 'Lord Heygate' from *Cautionary Verses* (1940) by Hilaire Belloc, to Cassell & Co Ltd for 'The Cool Web' from *Collected Poems* (1965) by Robert Graves, to John Murray Ltd for 'Devonshire Street W1' from *Collected Poems* (1970) by John Betjeman, to the Oxford University Press for 'Butterflies in the Desert' from *Stones of Emptiness* (1967) by Anthony Thwaite, and for 'A Given Grace' from *Selected Poems 1951–74* (1978) by Charles Tomlinson.

The author and publishers wish to acknowledge the following illustration sources and to state that they have tried to trace all copyright holders. In cases where they may have failed they will be pleased to make the necessary arrangements at the first opportunity.

BBC TV Stills Library 17, 18; British Library/David Higham Associates 16; Courtauld Institute of Art/Conway Library 5; Professor Ellmann/Harriet Shaw-Weaver 10; Grey Walls Press/The Late Mervyn Peake 15; Illustrated London News 12; Imperial War Museum 7; David Jones/Faber and Faber 14; London Express News and Feature Services 4; National Portrait Gallery 11; The Tate Gallery 13; Popperfoto 1, 2; Texas University at Austin/Humanities Research Centre 3; Mrs Julian Vinogradoff — from *Ottoline* by Sandra Jobson Darroch: Chatto and Windus 8; Wiltshire Historical Society 6

Editor's preface

THE study of literature requires knowledge of contexts as well as of texts. What kind of person wrote the poem, the play, the novel, the essay? What forces acted upon them as they wrote? What was the historical, the political, the philosophical, the economic, the cultural background? Was the writer accepting or rejecting the literary conventions of the time, or developing them, or creating entirely new kinds of literary expression? Are there interactions between literature and the art, music or architecture of its period? Was the writer affected by contemporaries or isolated?

Such questions stress the need for students to go beyond the reading of set texts, to extend their knowledge by developing a sense of chronology, of action and reaction, and of the varying relationships between writers and society.

Histories of literature can encourage students to make comparisons, can aid in understanding the purposes of individual authors and in assessing the totality of their achievements. Their development can be better understood and appreciated with some knowledge of the background of their time. And histories of literature, apart from their valuable function as reference books, can demonstrate the great wealth of writing in English that is there to be enjoyed. They can guide the reader who wishes to explore it more fully and to gain in the process deeper insights into the rich diversity not only of literature but of human life itself.

A. NORMAN JEFFARES

Introductory note

THE twentieth century is notable not only for its centrally outstanding writers on whom academic studies of the period have tended to concentrate, but also for a great range of lesser writers who have helped to make the age a richly productive one. A comprehensive attempt is made here to do justice to both categories proportionately. One historic upheaval, the First World War, and one literary group, the major figures of the Modern Movement, have been singled out for special treatment in separate chapters, but otherwise the survey runs in loosely structured chronological sequence, and a system of overlapping the decades, chapter by chapter, is adopted in order to keep the framework flexible. It is obvious that literary history cannot deal with writers in turn according to their dates of birth, for one writer dies at twenty-five while another, perhaps twenty years his senior, does his important work in his sixties or his seventies. Nor can the productivity of the succeeding decades be studied in strict sequence, for when a given writer comes under consideration his work as a whole must be at issue even though it may extend over several decades. The placing of writers in this survey generally depends on the date of their main impact on the public, or on the date of the historic event or literary development with which they are strongly associated. Within the limits of the space available, the aim is to indicate the distinctiveness of individual writers' achievements that may well extend over a lifetime, while at the same time reckoning fully with the changing movements, fashions, and emphases that give the succeeding phases of literary history their special character and flavour. Sub-headings indicate the central interest of succeeding sections but are not to be taken as defining exclusively what they contain.

In the case of plays the bracketed date is not always the

date of publication. It is the date of the play's first impact on the general public whether on the stage or in print.

I should like to express my gratitude to the Editor, Professor A. N. Jeffares, for his very helpful suggestions for improving the original typescript.

1
The new century
1900–1914

I Introduction

'HISTORY gets thicker as it approaches recent times: more people, more events, and more books written about them,' A. J. P. Taylor has observed. Literature too gets thicker: more writers, more works, and more books written about both. Moreover the sifting process which publicly identifies literature of quality works so slowly that the contemporary scene is always cluttered with writers who will not survive it, and therefore a survey of recent literature cannot be made without sometimes premature use of the critical sieve. Nevertheless a firm sense of the broad pattern of literary development in our century already exists. The period roughly coterminous with the reign of George V (1910–36) has been recognised as one of the great epochs of English literature. A few writers of the period have been granted the kind of status granted to Shakespeare and Milton, Wordsworth and Dickens, as giants under whose shadow the lesser writers of their age must be judged. In so far as the Modern Movement which they initiated spilt over into the reign of George VI (1936–52) the Georgian periods together contained the most crucial literary developments of the century.

In 1911 George V, as King–Emperor, with Queen Mary at his side, the two sitting crowned and robed on golden thrones, received the homage of the Indian Empire at the Durbar in the new capital of Delhi. From that point the two Georgian reigns witnessed the run-down of imperial power, the bleeding away of life and wealth in two world wars, and massive social upheavals such as strikes, slump, and unemployment: yet the reigns contain one of our richest literary epochs. Perhaps there is no direct correlation between national self-confidence and literary productivity. Is there an inverse relationship? It may be argued that national events so disturbing and disastrous as those of the years 1910 to 1950 will naturally stir the imaginations of artists and writers, that prosperity and power do not breed fine literature, that Dickens was great not because Victorian England was powerful but because it was wickedly scarred with injustice and inhumanity.

But the Georgian and Elizabethan decades have been years of social progress as well as of imperial decline. They have seen great developments in education, the breaking of the stranglehold of the public schools on government, bureaucracy, and the professions, and the rapid expansion of university provision. The socialisation of welfare services, the ironing-out of class distinctions, the emancipation of women, the more equitable distribution of wealth, and technological progress affecting work, mobility, and domestic comfort have no doubt offset the depressing psychological effects of imperial decline. Now that the United Kingdom is said to be among the 'poorer countries' of Western Europe there is far less of the widespread urban privation and squalor endured when it was the richest. At the time of Edwardian dominion over palm and pine there were two and a half million people in domestic service at home; a sixth of the babies born in Greater London did not live to be a year old; St Pancras Borough Council calculated 1151 'underground dwellings' (slum basements) inhabited by 5000 people during the day and by far more at night. In 1904, 1200 men were killed in the mines and 400 railway employees on the tracks.

Such were the conditions shortly after Queen Victoria died and King Edward VII succeeded to the throne. But political movements dedicated to the achievement of massive social reforms were already in their infancy. There was the Fabian Society which sought the advancement of socialist ideals without revolution and within the democratic parliamentary system. Founded in 1884, it had both G. B. Shaw and, for a time, H. G. Wells among a membership that reached over 3000 by 1914. Keir Hardie, the self-educated miner from Ayrshire and virtual founder of the modern British Labour Party, was returned as Member of Parliament for Merthyr Tydfil in 1900 and increased his majority in three subsequent elections. Meanwhile Emmeline Pankhurst founded her Women's Social and Political Union in 1903 and soon afterwards militant demonstrations in the cause of gaining full voting rights for women were leading to arrests and imprisonment. The voice of social protest was heard even in the theatre. In Shaw's *Major Barbara*, staged in 1905, the enlightened millionaire, Andrew Undershaft, declared: 'This is what is wrong with the world at present. It scraps its obsolete steam engines and dynamos; but it won't scrap its old prejudices and its old moralities and its old religions and its old political constitutions.'

Not that progressive social legislation was lacking in the early years of the century. In 1902 the Education Act of Balfour's government made the county and county borough councils responsible for both primary and secondary education. In 1908 old-age pensions were introduced and in 1911 Lloyd George's National Insurance Act set up the State system for financing workers' medical treatment by weekly contributions from employers and employees. Such political moves towards ameliorating modern man's lot were corroborated by discoveries and developments in technical fields destined to transform daily life. 1903 saw the first motor taxis on the London streets, the Automobile Association was founded two years later, and Bleriot flew the Channel in 1909. At the same time the expansion of the telegraph and telephone systems and the growing use of electric lighting and power were symptomatic of technological change that was going to free those two and a half million domestic servants without depressing the standard of home and public life.

But the spirit of an age which its literature embodies cannot be summed up simply in terms either of national wealth and power or of social justice and mechanical progress. There are securities of a profounder kind affecting man's sense of his place in the scheme of things. In the early years of the century Einstein's theory of relativity demolished the Newtonian principles on which the framework of the physical universe had seemed to depend. Meanwhile Freud disturbed man's confidence in the rational and moral framework within which human behaviour had seemed to be subject to regulation and control. Henceforward great movements towards emancipation and social reform were to gain ground alongside a weakening of religious faith and a tottering sense of man's ability to control his own destiny. The First World War seemed to confirm that man could not look after himself and that, when it came to the crunch, Christianity, the religion of the civilised West, did not work. Developments in the field of philosophy were also disturbing. The fortresses of metaphysical and idealist tradition were assaulted. G. E. Moore, the Cambridge philosopher, published his seminal *Principia Ethica* in 1903 and initiated a lifetime's work in ethical theory. His insistence on analysis of language and concepts used in philosophical discourse began a process which continued after the First World War under the influence of Wittgenstein. Philosophy began to abdicate its claims to anything more ambitious than analysis of the machinery of discourse. Great metaphysical systems, explicating the nature of being and the destiny of humanity, were to become museum pieces like other more expensive Victorian constructions.

A symbolic farewell to such grandeurs seems retrospectively to be detectable in the deep lamentation over the loss of the *Titanic* in 1912. The vessel had summed up the unsinkability of class, wealth, and the engineering triumphs they could well afford to purchase. The self-confidence which had built the Euston arch and netted the country in railway lines was geared to the transportation *en masse* of first, second, and third class passengers and suitable attendants. The packed liner and the packed railway train were representative social hierarchies on the move. By contrast, when the twentieth century constructed its motorways, it made provision for everyone to scurry about independently on his own business or pleasure, and the beetling mini could run rings round the limousine at points of congestion.

It will not do to over-simplify the changes brought by our century in terms of the collapse of a settled, traditional order, political and social, moral and cultural. The fashionable myth of escalating emancipation from traditional forms and disciplines will not survive serious study of our age's literature. In the work of the Moderns what looks at first sight like a disintegration of form very often turns out on closer inspection to be an extension of the range of perception and representation according to a logic inherent in traditional modes of expression. Nevertheless literature, and indeed the other arts, have experienced innovatory movements since the turn of the century which have made the 'twentieth-century' label a readily recognisable if not easily definable one. An air of excitement, often too of controversy, attended the first appearance of works which developing taste has gradually found less sensationally novel than at first they seemed. There was a storm of indignation in 1908 over the sculptor Jacob Epstein's nude 'Figures' on the British Medical Association's building in the Strand. Artists, of course, tended to challenge established *mores* by their personal conduct as well as established taste by their work. The colourful figure of the virile, nomadic painter, Augustus John, bestrides the pages of the diarists and chroniclers of the first quarter of the century. John, the dominant portrait-painter of his day, who was commissioned to paint the members of the Versailles Peace Conference, left memorable studies of Yeats and Hardy. But in the artistic field perhaps the most influential event of the pre-war period was the Post-Impressionist Exhibition organised in London in 1911 by Roger Fry, who succeeded in his aim of making the work of Cézanne accepted in Britain. Rejecting the evanescent appeal of the Impressionists to the observer's feelings, Cézanne sought to catch the permanent nature of things by emphasising form rather than atmosphere, and he exercised a crucial influence on Picasso.

While Roger Fry brought Cézanne to London, Sir Thomas Beecham, the conductor who had become lessee of Covent Garden Opera House in 1910, brought the Russian Ballet. Diaghilev and Nijinsky toured European capitals in 1911 to 1913, bursting upon the West with a company which put the male dancer back into the centre of things and, whilst giving impeccable performances of the established repertoire, also introduced choreography alive with new mimetic artistry and dramatic power. Igor Stravinsky's music for the ballets, *Petrushka* and the *Rite of Spring*, startled by its challenge to harmonic and rhythmic convention. But musically the period from 1900 to 1914 was also the age of Puccini's *Madam Butterfly* and of the *Sea Symphony* by Vaughan Williams, who cultivated a recognisably English idiom by drawing on the native folk-song tradition and on English Tudor music. Above all it was the age of Elgar's *Dream of Gerontius* and of those two symphonies whose broad nobility and brooding meditativeness voiced both the external grandeur and the inner apprehensiveness of the Edwardian Age.

II   Edwardian poetry

The death of Queen Victoria has come to be regarded as a dividing line in our cultural history, as the use of the term 'Victorian' indicates. Something of what it meant to leave 'Victorianism' behind can be illustrated from the work of writers whose productive careers overlapped the centuries and yet who continued to work at full stretch in their later years. Thomas Hardy (1840—1928) had lived through more than half the nineteenth century and might have been expected to belong to it inseparably, yet his late years produced work bearing the stamp of the new age. The last of Hardy's novels, *Jude the Obscure* (1895), had been bitterly denounced for its assault upon current social and moral attitudes, and, already long practised in verse composition, Hardy turned to poetry for relief. Chronologically, therefore, he is a nineteenth-century novelist and a twentieth-century poet. It is generally claimed that he is a twentieth-century poet in spirit as well as in chronology, and there are several volumes of poems to substantiate the claim. But Hardy also wrote *The Dynasts*, a *magnum opus* published in three parts (1904, 1906, and 1908), and a work essentially nineteenth-century in spirit and conception.

Hardy called *The Dynasts* an epic 'Spectacle . . . presented in the likeness of a Drama' but intended for 'mental perform-ance' (Preface). He planned his 'Iliad of Europe from 1789 to 1815' over many years. He chose his subject because it was a 'great historical calamity' whose events impinged on his own part of the country; for Weymouth held George III's summer residence during the wars with Napoleon, and the Wessex coastal district underwent desperate military preparations under threat of invasion. Hardy's vast panoramic sequence sweeps from country to country and takes in large-scale events such as the battles of Trafalgar and Austerlitz, Napoleon's retreat from Moscow, and his defeat at Waterloo. Super-imposed on the human action are scenes in an Overworld where 'certain impersonated abstractions, or Intelligences, called Spirits' overlook and comment upon earthly events.

> Thus doth the Great Foresightless mechanize
> In blank entrancement now as evermore
> Its ceaseless artistries in Circumstance . . . .

So the Spirit of the Years sums up the dire role of the controlling Immanent Will at the end. In grandiloquence of style, in scope and in purpose, the work seems to belong to the age of massive artistic monuments like Wagner's *Ring*.

The volumes of verse are a different matter. *Wessex Poems* (1898), *Poems of the Past and the Present* (1902), *Time's Laughing-stocks* (1909), *Satires of Circumstance* (1914), *Moments of Vision* (1917), *Late Lyrics and Earlier* (1922), *Human Shows, Far Fantasies* (1925), and *Winter Words* (1928) present a corpus of astonishing variety in metrical form, where the drive of spontaneous thought and feeling meets the mould of shape and stress, and constriction is lost in vibrancy and tension. The impact of form on feeling produces sometimes the quivering sense of a tussle with words in which the poet has only just come off best. Many of the lyrics bring sharply etched detail of the natural world broodingly but unpretentiously up against the realities of the human lot.

> When the Present has latched its postern behind my tremulous stay,
>   And the May month flaps its glad green leaves like wings,
> Delicate-filmed as new-spun silk, will the neighbours say,
>   'He was a man who used to notice such things'?   ('Afterwards')

Some of Hardy's finest poems sprang from the death of his first wife, Emma, in 1912. The marriage had deteriorated over the years, and Emma's death awakened remorseful memories of their earlier love and later alienation that issued in poems of deep poignancy and power, like 'Had You Wept', 'The Voice', 'The Going', and 'Your Last Drive'. Hardy spoke of them modestly to A. C. Benson at Cambridge in 1912 — 'The verses came; it was quite natural; one looked back through the years, and saw some pictures . . .' Hardy was given to nostalgia in less grave matters too, picturing in verse the memories evoked by a second-hand dress suit ('The sleeve bears still a print of powder / Rubbed from her arms . . .') or declaring his loyalty to the lost age of the polka and the quadrille, of *The Bohemian Girl* and *Il Trovatore* ('An Ancient to the Ancients'), yet as a poet he is justly claimed for our age. His austere respect for form coexists with utter clarity and with resolute insistence on speaking in his own voice.

> I need not go
> Through sleet and snow
> To where I know
> She waits for me;
> She will tarry me there
> Till I find it fair
> And have time to spare
> From company.   ('I Need Not Go')

Such directness, like Edward Thomas's, has come to represent for some poets and critics the most authentic tradition of English poetry in our century.

The Dynasts, in largeness of vision and vividness of detail, can hold and fascinate the reader, but changing taste has put the big poem, epic or philosophical, out of fashion. Nevertheless more than one poet tried early in the century to immortalise himself in a massive monumental work. C. M. Doughty (1843–1926), the explorer of Arabia who had published *Travels in Arabia Deserta* in 1888, turned to poetry to construct a thirty-thousand-line epic, *The Dawn in Britain* (1906), whose artifice-packed blank verse deters the would-be wrestler with its jumble of mythologies. Words like 'sith', 'wonne', 'gins', 'widewhere', 'rumerous', and 'immane' abound, as do laborious, stumbling rhythms of unique indigestibility:

> Aye, and lifting spear, me menaced, truculent,
> Send, gelt-god chained; like Briton hound to Rome . . . .

The epic was succeeded by several later poems of substantial dimensions, including finally *Mansoul or The Riddle of the World* (1920), whose stylistic quality may be savoured in the poet's vision of the Dream City:

> Of all this, gone there-up, I took account:
> Dedale, emailed, deviseful, gem-dight work . . . .

What is it that lures poets to exercise their imaginations so unimaginatively? Robert Bridges (1844–1930), whose output also spans the two centuries, belongs to the nineteenth century by virtue of his shorter poems. They reveal a rare mastery of rhythm and a virtuoso's control of tone and timbre, all of which accounts for the choice of Bridges as Poet Laureate in 1913. But Bridges belongs to our century by virtue of

Testament of Beauty (1929), a long philosophical poem, the culmination of experimentation with unrhymed Alexandrines measured by the number of syllables rather than by accentuation. There are some four or five thousand lines disposed in four books labelled 'Introduction', 'Selfhood', 'Breed', and 'Ethick', and they argue with a great deal of exemplification the testimony of Beauty that God is Love. The style is so self-consciously literary, so stripped of the cadence of living speech, that it reeks of verbal mummification.

> Wisdom hath hewed her house: She that dwelleth alway
> with God in the Evermore, afore any world was,
> fashion'd the nascent Earth that the energy of its life
> might come to evolution in the becoming of man.

Another poet who succumbed to the epic lure was Alfred Noyes (1880–1958), whose first volume, *The Loom of Years* (1902), and his larger-scale narrative poem, *Drake* (1906–8), launched him on a highly successful literary career. A handful of catchy ballad-style poems like 'The Highwayman' made him for long a useful poet for the school classroom, but Noyes's facile fluency irritated the cognoscenti. 'Don't talk of Noyes — he only cloys', Isaac Rosenberg wrote from the trenches in France in 1916. A visit to the Mount Wilson Observatory in California inspired in Noyes the ambition to celebrate science and reconcile it with religion in the three-volume epic, *The Torch-Bearers* (1922, 1925, 1930), whose flaccid blank verse gives us portraits and studies of men such as Copernicus, Kepler, Galileo, and Newton. Volume II includes a metrical version of the famous Oxford debate on Darwinism between Huxley and Bishop Wilberforce. John Buchan rashly proclaimed the work 'a great epic of faith, which I am convinced will be one of the most permanent things of our time'.

By contrast, Rudyard Kipling (1865–1936) knew what he was good at and stuck to it. After spending many years abroad, especially in India, Kipling settled at Burwash, Sussex, in 1902. He had behind him the larger part of his major output as a poet, an output rich in rolling balladry, in resonant rhetoric, and in that lower-deck lingo whose dropped consonants and back-street expletives constitute a kind of barrack-room Billingsgate, exhaling the honest down-to-earthness of the uniformed common man. But *The Five Nations* (1903), *Songs from Books* (1913), and *The Years Between* (1919) are collections of verse which justify the place often given to Kipling in anthologies of twentieth-century poetry, and many of his later volumes of stories were interspersed with verse. Kipling, the bardic sage of 'Recessional' ('Lo, all our pomp of yesterday / Is one with Nineveh and Tyre'), the racy rhymester of 'The 'Eathen', and the graceful troubadour of the antique verses between the chapters of the children's book, *Puck of Pook's Hill* (1906), is a master of the memorable, not only by virtue of his rhythmic facility and verbal control, but by virtue of his ability to be catchy without lapsing into doggerel, to be commonplace without being pedestrian.

Kipling's prose output is more versatile and often more sensitive than his popular reputation as a drum-beating imperialist would suggest. *Kim* (1901), the story of an Irish orphan's adventures in India, no doubt reveals that inability to plot which Kipling accepted as unfitting him to be a novelist. As a short-story writer, however, he surprises by his inventiveness and technical adroitness. The animal tales, *Just So Stories* (1902), belong in the nursery and are at times over-whimsically sugared with coy solecisms, cosy coinages ('jumpsome') and other arch babyisms ('the most beautifullest Mummy that ever was'). In the collections of stories for adults, which include *Traffics and Discoveries* (1904), *Actions and Reactions* (1909), *Debits and Credits* (1926), *Limits and Renewals* (1933), and *Thy Servant a Dog* (1938), there are many tales concerning men under stress which reinforce the Kipling ethic of stoicism under the unbreakable, if sometimes undefinable Law. Devices for heightening impact by framing a tale in the view of a narrator—observer or participant are skilfully managed, even if action is sometimes swamped under oblique and supercilious garrulities. To get a picture of Kipling's scope, it is only necessary to compare 'The Woman in His Life' (*Limits and Renewals*), a story of post-war strain and breakdown which involves multiple mutual life-saving by an officer and his former batman, with 'Aunt Ellen' from the same volume, a comic-strip sequence of high-jinks on the road between Grantham and London in the early motoring days, with a packed eiderdown in transit that looks embarrassingly like a corpse.

Kipling perhaps reached his biggest public through his gift for writing verses peculiarly apt for being set to music and sung or for being publicly recited, two forms of entertainment which found hungry audiences in concert-hall and drawing-room in the pre-1914 world. His 'The Road to Mandalay' and his 'If' were respectively sung and declaimed in every corner of the land. Sir Henry Newbolt (1862—1938) had the crafts-manship and flair to satisfy the same appetite. *Songs of the Sea* (1904) and *Songs of the Fleet* (1910) included 'Drake's Drum', 'The Old Superb', and others which many a sturdy baritone has rocked his shoulders and smacked his lips over in the settings by Sir Charles Stanford. Moreover Newbolt's verse tributes to the courage and self-sacrifice of the Britisher when desperately beset by foes or cornered by terrorists (see 'He Fell Among Thieves' and 'Vita Lampadai') proved emi-nently recitable, though to modern ears they assault the tear-ducts unmercifully in tracing the public school ethos from sunlit school close or rugger field to perilous imperial outpost.

Among the now more justly forgotten poets of the first decade of the century Sir William Watson (1858—1935) inclined over-much to meditative commonplaces and trite poeticisms, but his 'Ode on the Coronation of Edward VII' exudes the confidence of the age in the imperial greatness being brought to bear on the new monarch's head:

> Kingdom in kingdom, sway in oversway,
> Dominion fold in fold . . .
> So wide a girth this little cirque of gold.

Yet, for all the zeal of Watson as a ceremonial poet, it was A. C. Benson (1862—1925), Cambridge don, who left the unforgettable record of Edwardian grandeur in supplying the verses, 'Land of Hope and Glory', for the tune from Elgar's 'Pomp and Circumstance' march.

A poet more fruitfully attuned to the Kiplingesque vein than such lesser writers was John Masefield (1878—1967), who succeeded Bridges as Laureate in 1930. His *Salt Water Ballads* (1902) and *Ballads and Poems* (1910) contain a cluster of much-anthologised poems, rhythmically and rhetorically alive, some of them of the fresh-air-and-open-road variety, like 'The West Wind' and 'Tewkesbury Road', and some of them hailing the virtues of salt sea and saltier seamen in heartfelt acclaim or nautical bluster, like 'Sea-Fever' and 'A Ballad of John Silver'.

> I saw a ship a-sinking, a-sinking, a-sinking,
> With glittering sea-water splashing on her decks,
> With seamen in her spirit-room singing songs and drinking,
> Pulling claret bottles down, and knocking off their necks,
> The broken glass was clinking as she sank among the wrecks.
>
> ('An Old Song Re-Sung')

Masefield knew the sea at first hand. Born in Herefordshire, orphaned at an early age, he became a trainee seaman in 1891 and was soon in New York where he worked in a bar, then in a carpet factory, before returning to England and settling in Bloomsbury to write. A number of later autobiographical prose works shed light on these early days: *In the Mill* (1941), *New Chum* (1944), *So Long to Learn* (1952), and *Grace Before Ploughing* (1966). In Bloomsbury Synge and Yeats were among his friends in what he called

> Those hours of stricken sparks from which men took
> Light to send out to men in song and book.   ('Biography')

Masefield dedicated himself in 'A Consecration' to sing, not of the great and the proud, but of the scorned and rejected, 'the ranker, the tramp of the road . . . the sailor, the stoker of steamers'. Whether his long narrative poems, with their vivid but over-externalised romanticism, convincingly measure up to this radical aim may be doubted. *The Everlasting Mercy* (1911) records the conversion to Christ of a drunken poacher in vigorous octosyllabic couplets:

> I drank, I fought, I poached, I whored,
> I did despite unto the Lord.

It shocked by its bracing juxtaposition of the idiom of the bar-room ('You closhy put', 'You bloody liar') with outbursts of evangelical fervour. 'Incomparably the finest literature of the year', J. M. Barrie called it, yet it remains a work of verbal energy and vehemence rather than of imaginative pressure and emotional intensity. *Dauber* (1913) seems more deeply felt, no doubt because of its autobiographical content. Young Dauber prefers his mother's sketch-book to his father's farm and goes off to sea determined to learn how to paint sea and ships. His art makes him as much an outsider on board as he was at home, and he feels a failure; but he is proved in a month of severe storm and stress, before drowning in a gale. *Reynard the Fox* (1919) is Masefield's most effective narrative poem. He saw the hunt as a social event bringing local society together and doing for him what the Canterbury pilgrimage did for Chaucer. The vivacious couplets give a rollicking account of the chase from the point of view of hunters and quarry alike.

Masefield was involved with Yeats and with Gordon Bottomley in trying to establish poetic drama in the contemporary theatre, but he lacked theatrical sensitivity and the talent for writing effective dialogue. *The Tragedy of Nan* (1909) unhappily essays the convergence of the squalid and the mystical. The river Severn brings the soothing music of eternity to the ears of the broken heroine, daughter of an executed sheep-stealer, who stabs her fickle wooer. *The Tragedy of Pompey the Great* (1910), a prose play in three acts, and *Philip the King* (1914), a one-act play in rhymed verse, are too stilted and static for performance. As a novelist, Masefield has narrative prodigality rather than psychological insight or feeling for human relationships. *Sard Harker* (1924), a tale of testing adventure in South America, culminates in a riot of implausibilities.

In contrast to sturdy spirits such as Masefield and Kipling, there remained one of the decadent *fin-de-siècle* group who had not drunk himself to death by the turn of the century, Arthur Symons (1865–1945). He published *Poems* (1902), selecting from previous collections; and later volumes include *Lesbia* (1920) and *Jezebel Mort* (1931) as well as the revealing prose works, *Spiritual Adventures* (1905) and *Confessions* (1930), in which he analyses his own mental breakdown. Symons remained a poet of the nineties, under the spell of the Impressionist and Symbolist movements, given to preciosity of technique, to nebulousness of drift, and to enervation of tone, but capable of throwing off a memorable phrase:

> Ah, in these flaring London nights,
> Where midnight withers into morn . . .
>
> ('In the Meadows at Mantua')

Another lingering voice of the nineties was that of A. E. Housman (1859–1936), whose collection, *The Shropshire Lad* (1896), was followed years later by *Last Poems* (1922) and the posthumous *More Poems* (1936). 'Deliberately he chose the dry-as-dust, / Kept tears like dirty postcards in a drawer,' W. H. Auden has written of him. For Housman was a classical scholar whose methods and learning in that field epitomise the extremes of meticulous pedantry, and whose personal life was soured by early disappointments. But his verses achieved immense popularity. They are traditional in form, economic in diction, and express the emotions of young men at the transience of beauty and happiness, the sad contrariness of life, and the dominion of death.

> Far and near and low and louder
> On the roads of earth go by,
> Dear to friends and food for powder,
> Soldiers marching, all to die.
>
> ('On the idle hill of summer')

A gloomy preoccupation with young men who march away in the army to be killed or who stay at home and get hanged makes Housman highly susceptible to parody, but his best poems have a haunting wistfulness. Without sacrificing integrity as a craftsman, he fabricated an imaginatively authentic pastoral region out of a handful of emotive Shropshire place names and a sprinkling of simple ruralisms and archaisms.

III The Edwardian novel

Like Hardy, the novelist Henry James (1843–1916) enjoyed a productive Indian summer. James came of a well-to-do American family and became the apostle of cultivated cosmopolitanism. On visits to Italy, France, and England he immersed himself in the culture of the old world, and the contrast between the ingenuous vitality and roughness of America and the sophisticated poise and decadence of Europe became a pervasive theme in his early work. He returned to it in his twentieth-century novels with a maturity of observation, a subtlety of analysis, and a fastidiousness of style that made the last three novels a triumphant consummation of his artistic career. James had devised a superfine exactitude in phrase-spinning to catch the evanescent tentativeness, the ambiguities, modifications, and mid-career transitions that are the stuff of human thought and feeling. This experimentation has led critics to compare James with stream-of-consciousness novelists such as Virginia Woolf. But James's detachment, his preference for ironic distancing and oblique inference rather than for heart-to-heart disclosure, set him apart.

In *The Wings of the Dove* (1902) Kate Croy, a Londoner, conspires with the man she wants to marry, the journalist Merton Densher, to lay hands on the fortune of Milly Theale, an American heiress doomed soon to die. The plan is for Densher to make love to Milly, marry her, and inherit on her death. Milly is successfully wooed, but learns the truth and dies broken-hearted. Densher finally cannot bear to profit from his inheritance and Kate will not have him without it. The complex interweaving of the bogus and the genuine, the awakening of real feeling by the act of pretence and by the fruits of pretence, is finely articulated. The hinge of it all is the gullibility of the honest American, and this also is the theme of *The Ambassadors* (1903), but here the tone is altogether sunnier, the theme less grave. The innocent abroad is Strether, husband-to-be of a wealthy American widow. She has despatched him to Paris in search of her son Chad, supposedly at risk from an undesirable liaison. Strether is bemused by the charm and beauty of the relationship which he is supposed to find disreputable and has no equipment to break through the civilised veneer that veils it. The values of puritan, business America stand opposed in the background to those of decadent, self-indulgent Paris, yet the kindly ambassador treads a path on which delicacy can find no footing for getting to grips. The world of nuance and inference, of elegant camouflage and brittle masquerade, is investigated by James with an inimitably sly relish. *The Golden Bowl* (1904) is different again in tone. Here there is neither the sourness with which evil flavours *The Wings of the Dove* nor the refreshing ironic humour of *The Ambassadors*, for James probes a complex human situation more deeply than in the latter, more sympathetically than in the former. Maggie Verver, daughter of a wealthy American, marries an impoverished Italian aristocrat, Amerigo. Maggie's best friend,

Charlotte Stant, marries Maggie's widowed father. But, unknown to Maggie, Charlotte and Amerigo have previously been lovers and were discouraged from marriage only by lack of means. The game played by this quartet of kindly people, bent only on helping one another and sustaining two firm marriages, but with the current of unspent passion inwardly electrifying the most polite and 'innocent' endeavours of the one-time lovers, is masterfully managed.

Conrad's masterpiece *Nostromo* (1904) came out in the same productive year as *The Golden Bowl*. 'Born a Pole and cast upon the waters, he has worked out an English style that is more than correct, that has *quality* and ingenuity,' James wrote in supporting an appeal for Conrad to the Royal Literary Fund. Joseph Conrad (1857–1924), orphaned by the age of twelve, astonished his land-locked compatriots by his determination to go to sea. After four years in the French merchant navy, years whose excitements included smuggling arms into Spain, gambling, and attempting suicide, he began to serve on British cargo ships, learned English, and eventually qualified as First Mate and Master. Voyages to the East and a visit to the Belgian Congo supplied background and material for his novels. The publication of *Almayer's Folly* (1895) marked the end of twenty years' service at sea and the start of a literary career. Conrad married and settled down in England. A fruitful relationship with Ford Madox Ford began in 1897. Conrad and he found themselves equally dissatisfied with the traditional method of shaping fiction in a series of dramatic situations. Both wanted to renew the novel form, abolishing logical narration by the authorial voice and substituting a sequence of impressions which have the verisimilitude of real life and allow crucial facts in the plot to be conveyed obliquely and parenthetically in a progression of cumulative intensity. Ford was only half Conrad's age, but the pair collaborated in two novels, *The Inheritors* (1901) and *Romance* (1903). Their common indebtedness, not only to Henry James, but to Flaubert, Maupassant, and Turgenev, proved fruitful in their mature work, but the close intimacy came to an end in 1902 when Ford went abroad.

Conrad's central concern is with the response of men to danger and stress. He is fascinated by those who succumb to the pressure of an extreme test, whether in a sudden, unpremeditated lapse at a point of crisis or under the corrosive challenge of long-drawn-out isolation or victimisation in remote and sickening environments. *Almayer's Folly* and *An Outcast of the Islands* (1896) deal respectively with two Dutchmen, Almayer and Peter Williams, in turn settled under the patronage of Tom Lingard, 'King of the Sea', at a remote trading station in Borneo, both deluded by dreams of prosperity and succumbing, in their different ways, to their own illusions and the wiles of Arab traders. In *The Rescue* (1920), started soon after but taken up for completion only twenty years later, Lingard himself is tested, for the needs of a wealthy white couple, perilously stranded in a yacht, claim him at a moment when he should be wholly preoccupied with repaying a solemn debt of honour to an ousted native ruler. *Lord Jim* (1900) is a subtler study. Jim is a simple and sensitive soul. His ship, the *Patna*, is damaged in a storm. Members of the crew lower a boat and call out to Jim to jump. In the thoughtless panic of the moment Jim betrays his own nature and joins those who are apparently leaving their passengers, a thousand Moslem pilgrims, to drown. Jim alone has the decency to face the Court of Inquiry, and he loses his certificate. But after this 'fall' he rehabilitates himself as a trading manager in a remote tropical community and ultimately achieves the redemption of self-sacrifice. *Youth* (1902) includes, as well as the title story of a cargo fire at sea, the justly acclaimed story, 'Heart of Darkness', with its portrait of Kurtz (the 'Mistah Kurtz – he dead' of the epigraph to Eliot's *The Hollow Men*), agent at an isolated trading post in the Congo, rendered 'hollow at the core' by the dark corruption of the jungle.

Nostromo is a richly peopled study of an imaginary South American republic, Costangua, at a time of revolution. Charles Gould, the English owner of a silver mine, entrusts a consignment of silver to the universally respected Italian, Nostromo, for conveyance beyond the reach of the rebels. After a collision, Nostromo's boat is run aground on an island and he buries the silver there. The treasure is assumed to be sunk with the boat while Nostromo pays secret visits to the island to help himself to it. The fullness of the political, social, and topographical background is remarkable. The insidious corruption of men and society by selfish materialism is closely analysed in the influence of silver upon human virtue and idealism.

For all his emotional authority and moral thrust Conrad is in many ways a flawed writer, capable of stylistic overstatement, of moral over-simplification, and of sheer sentimentality in handling love. The foreign oddity of phrasing in his earlier books gave an adventitious angularity to his style which he lost when he gained in fluency. Among later novels *Under Western Eyes* (1911) is a story of assassination and betrayal in Tsarist Russia, *The Shadow-Line* (1917) harks back to an early experience at sea with a sick crew, and *The Arrow of Gold* (1919) carries memories of the gun-running days.

It is a far cry from the exotic locales and elemental tensions of Conrad's fictional world to the prosaic backgrounds of Arnold Bennett's. 'I am so *saturated* with impressions that I can't take in new ones . . . and here comes a man with his great voluminous books, dripping with detail — but with no scheme, no conception of character, no *subject* . . . everything perceived, nothing seen *into*, nothing related . . .' So Henry James spoke of Bennett's seemingly undoctored documentation of workaday life. The criticism is not just, but it shows how some refined sensibilities found Bennett too concerned with the externals of life.

Arnold Bennett (1867–1931) went up to London from Hanley, Staffordshire, in 1888 and worked his way into journalism. His professionalism enabled him to run a career as a popular entertainer alongside his work as a serious artist. After a first novel, *A Man from the North* (1898), the potboilers began with *Grand Babylon Hotel* (1902) and the worthier novels with *Anna of the Five Towns* (1902). The twin careers carried Bennett to the social apex where he revelled in yachts and expensive hotels. At the same time he gained the ear of the nation's reading public as book reviewer of the *Evening Standard*, where he shrewdly picked out for attention such new writers as Graham Greene, Evelyn Waugh, and Ivy Compton-Burnett.

The cream of Bennett's books have artistry, human awareness, and imaginative dimension that are the product of discipline and reflection. *Anna of the Five Towns* is a Potteries novel in which Bennett shows himself as much at home in recording intimate details of a women's sewing meeting as in cataloguing household furniture. From the start he puts his finger on the pulse of provincial life where every event has its public dimension as fuel for talk and for the taking up of attitudes. Against the grim background of the Black Country the young woman, Anna, is finally hit by the sudden realisation that she loves a broken young man and not her safe, reliable fiancé, but in dutiful prudence she marries the latter nevertheless. This first exploration of the unbreakable will of the ordinary Midlander prepares the ground for Bennett's *magnum opus, The Old Wives' Tale* (1908), which tracks the lives of two Potteries sisters, Constance and Sophia Baines, from girlhood to old age and death. Constance is equable and firm, Sophia passionate and impulsive, and their careers match their characters, Constance's at home where she marries a conscientious employee in the family drapery business, Sophia's in Paris, whither she is whisked in elopement with a showy commercial traveller. But the great theme of the book is the way time and mutability gradually bear down on two girls seen at first in the flower of youth. There is as much hidden drama in the life of the stay-at-home as in that of her wandering sister, abandoned abroad by her feckless husband. Bennett's detailed registration of the active world, the material environment, and the experience that makes up the fabric of physical life from day to day is impressive, and the psychological validity of the portraiture shows how acute his powers of observation were.

The trilogy which began with *Clayhanger* (1910) does not fulfil its early promise. The tensions of Edwin Clayhanger's boyhood and young manhood, and the historical canvas with its recall of events such as Gladstone's Home Rule Bill and Queen Victoria's Jubilee, give authenticity to the first novel, but the succeeding volumes, tracing respectively the history of Edwin's beloved, Hilda (*Hilda Lessways*, 1911) and the chequered course of subsequent marital domesticity (*These Twain*, 1916), are uneven. Of later novels *Riceyman Steps* (1923) is remarkable for its compelling economy and matter-of-factness. 'A bookseller crosses the road to get married,' said George Moore, slyly summarising the plot. And so he does; but Earlforward, the antiquarian bookseller, is a unique study of miserliness conjoined with decency and amiability. Humdrum quirkiness melts into tragedy when the wife he genuinely loves dies of malnutrition, the victim of his own miserliness. Less sombre, but no less overshadowed by disease and death, is *Lord Raingo* (1926), based on Bennett's experience at the Ministry of Information in 1918 during the last months of the war. The intrigue and in-fighting between Downing Street, Westminster, and Whitehall are shrewdly registered. Lloyd George is brilliantly portrayed as Andy Clyth, and his personal secretary—mistress, Frances Stevenson, as Rosie Packer.

Bennett had a reputation for personal moodiness and unpredictability, but H. G. Wells observed that he 'radiated and evoked affection to an unusual degree'. Sympathy between the two writers was perhaps natural. Both worked their way from provincial backgrounds to peaks of literary and social eminence. Both fictionalised their first-hand insights into the lives of humdrum working people. While James and Conrad served the cause of art for long unrewarded, Bennett and Wells filled their pockets and had the world at their feet. Yet neither was content merely to write pot-boilers, Bennett because he had the creative daemon, Wells because he oozed reforming zeal. Wells (1866–1946), after having lampooned his friend, Henry James, in *Boon* (1915), likening his stylistic method to the painful efforts of a hippopotamus to pick up a pea from the corner of its den, later tried somewhat lamely to explain away his insult in a letter. 'To you literature like painting is an end; to me literature like architecture is a means, it has a use.' Its use was to drag the people's minds into the age of socialistic equality and scientific advance.

Born in Bromley, Kent, son of a poor shopkeeper, Wells struggled from work in a draper's shop, through pupil-teaching, to a scholarship at the Normal School of Science, South Kensington, and some years of schoolmastering, before he broke successfully into writing with *The Time Machine* (1895). The novel takes the reader forward some 800,000 years to find the 'earth a garden' and 'humanity on the wane', the human intellect having committed suicide in pursuit of comfort and ease. It was the first of a series of essays in science-fiction which included *The War in the Air* (1908) and *The Shape of Things to Come* (1933). Quasi-scientific prophecy has built-in obsolescence by virtue of the pace of scientific development and the need for fictional inventiveness to keep ahead of it, but for all the ingenious refinements of the genre in the last seventy years, Wells's pioneering role in this kind of fantasy is unmistakable.

If scientific prediction dates, so does social radicalism, the other great theme of Wells's life-long crusade. The books of Wells's which have best stood the test of time are those in which the social message is least explicit and obtrusive. For Wells has an ebullience that can charm. A writer who cannot sit still and contain his hilarity will sometimes irritate, and jocular facetiousness easily stales. Nevertheless Wells's better social comedies have a winning verve and open-heartedness. They include *Love and Mr Lewisham* (1900), a study of the hero's struggle to educate himself, reflecting Wells's own experience, a book in which, for all its assaults on social corruption, the human substance remains central. *Kipps* (1905) takes the fairy-tale theme of sudden access to wealth and applies it to a young apprentice draper with a background like Wells's own, though Artie Kipps's modest attempts to better himself educationally are scarcely commensurate with Wells's. A serious point is made about the irrational distribution of money and its comparative irrelevance to happiness, but what gives the book its vitality is the authorial cheerfulness and the sportiveness with which the amiable hero is pictured — even when 'steeled to the high enterprise of marrying above his breeding'. In *Tono-Bungay* (1910) high jinks at the expense of ad-mad commerce scarcely redeem the general shapelessness, but *The History of Mr Polly* (1910) deserves attention because it launches on its twentieth-century career the theme of the lower-middle-class man who throws off the shackles of routine and convention and breaks out in middle life. The theme was to make a fortune for J. B. Priestley with *The Good Companions* in the 1930s and the break-out pattern was later to become a cliché of fiction in the 1950s. Mr Polly is a bankrupt shopkeeper: he sets fire to his shop and runs away from home and wife to become odd-job man at a country pub. The sense of an organised society wasteful of human energy and enterprise adds social dimension.

Ann Veronica (1909) is a break-out novel from the feminine side. Ann is a biology student of twenty-one, driven to desperation by suburban routine, parental tyranny, and conventional inter-sexual inhibitions. Intolerably provoked, she leaves home, and it is not long before she is hob-nobbing with Fabians and publicly demonstrating with suffragettes. But what stuck in the throat of the contemporary public was that Ann's final rebellion is against sexual inhibitions. She takes the initiative in claiming her unhappily married tutor for her lover. In the seven years since Bennett's *Anna of the Five Towns*, the sturdy-minded young woman has slipped the moral traces and fashioned a new code for her kind. Wells's gradual drift towards the propaganda novel is already evident here, and social theorising takes precedence over human interest in later works such as *The New Machiavelli* (1911) and *The World of William Clissold* (1926). *Mr Britling Sees it Through* (1916) has topical interest as a picture of the home front during the early years of the war. Wells's imaginative range as a writer was no doubt limited by his determination to sort the world out, but his output included over a hundred titles and his public impact as a political and social theorist was considerable.

IV Drama and controversy

One of Wells's polemical foes was G. K. Chesterton (1874–1936), journalist, novelist, poet, and biographer, whose buoyant personality stamped itself on the contemporary literary scene almost as bulkily as Johnson's on eighteenth-century London. Chesterton hated the progressive socialistic ideas of Wells and Shaw because he detected in them the menace of soulless corporatism; but this hatred was secondary to his detestation of the upper-class Tory establishment and those who boosted imperialistic self-aggrandisement in the name of patriotism and at the expense of other peoples.

> Though drunk with sight of power and blind,
>   Even as you bowed your head in awe,
> You kicked up both your heels behind
>   At lesser breeds without the Law;
> Lest they forget, lest they forget
>   That yours was the exclusive set.

Occasional verse, like this parody of Kipling's 'Recessional', proved a useful weapon in Chesterton's polemical armoury. His friend Hilaire Belloc (1870–1953) was also adept at light versification. The two literary allies were dubbed 'the Chester-belloc' and the link between them was strengthened by Chesterton's move from the Church of England to the Church of Rome in 1922. Belloc's own output included history, biography, and miscellaneous essays, the harvest of prolific journalism (*On Nothing*, 1908; *On Everything*, 1909; *On Anything*, 1910, etc.). Much of it has dated, but his light verse keeps its appeal:

> Lord Heygate had a troubled face,
> His furniture was commonplace —
> The sort of Peer who well might pass
> For someone of the middle class.
> I do not think you want to hear
> About this unimportant Peer.   ('Lord Heygate')

Belloc's exercises in rhymed couplets often have a sting neatly concealed in seeming throwaways. (See *Cautionary Tales*, 1907; *More Peers*, 1911; *New Cautionary Tales*, 1930.) The undemonstrative touch in his verse is notable because his weakness as a prose writer lies in the ease with which he lapses into overstatement and the kind of hectoring rumbustiousness that is calculated to project a larger-than-life authorial *persona*. But Belloc's name was a household word when he ran weekly articles on the military progress of the 1914—18 war in *Land and Water*.

Chesterton's serious poetry keeps its freshness. He was a master of flamboyant rhetoric and sturdy rhythms, as 'Lepanto' shows. *The Ballad of the White Horse* (1911), a long narrative of King Alfred's defeat of the Danes at Edington, is technically the best thing of its kind since Macaulay's *Horatius*, and it has added dimensions by virtue of the larger struggle between Christianity and paganism implicit in the conflict. Chesterton's ready knack of imprinting a hint of cosmic conflict between the powers of darkness and the powers of light upon human endeavours, whether they are heroic confrontations on a battlefield or humdrum encounters on top of a London bus, gives spice to his prose output for those who warm to that kind of thing. This is an aspect of his Catholic-mindedness. He lived mentally in a world lit by tokens of the divine order and under threat from the negations of human rebellion. But the scintillation which guaranteed popularity to theological works such as *Orthodoxy* (1908) and *The Everlasting Man* (1928), biographies and critical studies such as *Robert Browning* (1903) and *Charles Dickens* (1906), and above all to the fantastic novels, derives from Chesterton's mastery of paradox, an ability to stand facile prejudices and assumptions of the day on their heads. Such topsy-turvydoms may degenerate into stylistic gimmickry if their flow is not disciplined, but they can glitter when they illuminate paradoxes inherent in man's nature and his world.

For his prose fantasies Chesterton found themes that gave full play to this talent. In *The Napoleon of Notting Hill* (1904), set a hundred years hence, the London boroughs are reinstated in their ancient magnificence in fun, but the Provost of Notting Hill takes the matter seriously and goes to war against other boroughs in defence of Pump Street when it is threatened by a new through road. In *The Man Who Was Thursday* (1908) Gabriel Syme is caught up in an anarchist conspiracy and given the name 'Thursday' as member of a seven-strong controlling group. It gradually emerges that, Sunday excepted, these members are police infiltrators each spying on the body. Such ingenious situations enable Chesterton to keep up his running battle with materialistic modernism and to litter his text with aphoristic insights into a more imaginative metaphysic. His 'Father Brown' detective stories, whose volumes include *The Innocence of Father Brown* (1911), *The Wisdom of Father Brown* (1914), and *The Incredulity of Father Brown* (1926), continue to hold the public. The innocent-faced priest, with his deep knowledge of human nature and his spiritual detachment from the fads and follies of the day, is the ideal Chestertonian vehicle for turning the tables on evil.

A writer closely associated with Chesterton and Belloc was Maurice Baring (1874–1945). Aristocrat, Catholic convert, diplomat, war-correspondent, he was an all-round man of letters, highly productive in work which presupposes a cultivated readership. The output includes plays and novels of high life that are over-fully documented and rich in intellectual discussion on aesthetic and cultural topics (like *C*, 1924; and *Cat's Cradle*, 1925). Baring also made numerous sportive ventures into literary tomfoolery. *Dead Letters* (1910) includes such pieces as 'Nero Interviewed' ('The Emperor said that the

Empress Mother would have seen me only she was suffering from one of her bad attacks of indigestion') and 'Letters from Lord Bacon to his Literary Agent' ('I received the printed copies of my four plays as arranged by Mr Shakespeare . . .'). Bacon resists such proposed changes as marrying off Juliet to Paris and reconciling Romeo with Rosaline at the end of *Romeo and Juliet*. The slump in Baring's appeal as a writer is no doubt due to his donnish lack of the common touch.

When Chesterton published his witty study, *George Bernard Shaw*, in 1909, Shaw observed handsomely, 'This book is, as everyone expected it to be, the best critical study I have yet produced.' Controversy between Chesterton and Shaw was a running public entertainment. It was not Shaw's socialism as such that offended Chesterton, but Shaw's puritanism, the outer sign of which was his teetotalism and vegetarianism, the inner substance of which was an earnest moralism disentangled from roots in Christian supernaturalism. Shaw (1856–1950) was born in Dublin ('I am a typical Irishman; my family came from Yorkshire') and, like other Anglo-Irish writers under consideration here, he is given complementary treatment in A. N. Jeffares's *Anglo-Irish Literature* (in this series). He moved to London in 1876 where his long and hard struggle for literary success began. A crucial influence on his career was the meeting with William Archer (1856–1924), the dramatic critic who translated the plays of Ibsen into English and who obtained reviewing work for Shaw in such journals as the daily *Pall Mall Gazette* and the weekly review, *The World*. Later Shaw became leader-writer, then music critic, for the *Star*. When he saw Ibsen's *A Doll's House* in 1889 he was moved by the sight of an audience not held by 'the conventional lies of the stage' but gripped by the searching out of vital truth. He turned playwright, he said, in order to carry on Ibsen's work, and in *The Quintessence of Ibsenism* (1891) he firmly lined himself up with the theatrical revolt against the 'well-made' nineteenth-century play conventionally adjusted in theme and tone to entertainment devoid of intellectual demand or social challenge. Hence his first play, *Widowers' Houses* (1892), assaulted slum landlordism, and *Mrs Warren's Profession* (produced New York, 1892) was banned in England for its exposure of the brothel industry. Its essentially Shavian purpose was 'to draw attention to the truth that prostitution is caused, not by female depravity and male licentiousness, but simply by underpaying, undervaluing, and maltreating women so shamefully that the poorer of them are forced to resort to prostitution . . . . Society, and not any individual is the villain of the piece.' (Preface.) Hence the exposure of the unreality of idealism in war and in love entertainingly worked out in the comedy, *Arms and the Man* (1894), whose spirited hero, or 'anti-hero', is a disillusioned mercenary caught up in Serbo-Croatian conflict in 1885. *Candida* (1904) gave an ironic twist to the conventional domestic-triangle plot in whic h solid, respectable clergyman husband, Morell, and impractical young poet, Marchbanks, find themselves rivals for the love of Morell's wife, Candida. In the upshot Candida opts for fidelity on the distinctly Shavian grounds that the efficient, hard-working husband is the 'weaker' and therefore the needier of the two needy contestants for her womanly support.

The capacity to up-end currently accepted valuations on the basis of seemingly more profound or subtle criteria is the mark of the sage when those new criteria prove under examination to be valid, of the hoaxer when they are shown to be bogus. Shaw's ambiguous status in the world of letters derives from his enigmatic footing at the junction of this dichotomy. Paradox is powerful when it illuminates hidden truth at the expense of established prejudice: but it is only mildly entertaining when it projects the obvious at the expense of the generally discredited. What always redeems Shaw's comedies from the vapidity inherent in ideological shadow-boxing is the fluent and fertile argumentativeness, the comic topsy-turvydoms, and the unfailing Irish wit. *You Never Can Tell* (1900) was a hilarious box-office success, and the social message is swamped in humour. Mrs Clandon, a 'veteran of the Old Guard of the Women's Rights movement', has brought up her daughter, Gloria, as the emancipated New Woman, but she is emotionally mastered by the skilful wooing of an impecunious dentist.

Shaw remains a powerful social commentator, at his most vital with issues that call neither for philosophic divination nor for moral acuity but for insight into the structure and workings of society and the capacity of the political animal for self-deception. *John Bull's Other Island* (1904), which was intended for Yeats's Irish Literary Theatre but whose scope was beyond the resources of the Abbey Theatre, makes a shrewd analysis of English and Irish attitudes, the illusions of each people about the other and of each about themselves. It was a real issue, and still is. So was the issue of *Major Barbara* (1905), where the conflict 'between real life and the romantic imagination' springs from the fact that the Salvation Army's work for the poor is in fact financed by donations from brewers and arms-manufacturers. Major Barbara's discovery that there is no wickedness but poverty causes her to sever her connections with the Army. The dilemma explored in *The Doctor's Dilemma* (1906) lies in which of two dying invalids to save — an unscrupulous but gifted artist or a modest but worthy General Practioner — when logistics allow the addition of only one more to a group of patients under a new treatment for consumption. The baiting of the medical profession gives the play its sparkle. *The Shewing-up of Blanco Posnet* (1909), a lively romantic melodrama of conversion set in the American Wild West, presents the trial of a worthless thief who has been stirred by human misery to a sense of his rottenness and to an act of generosity that has led to his capture. When the censor banned it for its references to God, Yeats urged that it should be put on at the Abbey Theatre, Dublin, where the Irish Players performed it in 1909 before taking it to the United States and playing it in Boston in 1911. *Pygmalion* (1914) shows a professor of phonetics turning a cockney flower-girl from the streets into a seeming duchess in the drawing-room by a few months' work on her accent, and failing fully to control the new being he has created. *Heartbreak House* (1921), in the form of a dream, portrays the leisured middle class whose lack of social conscience and political purpose caused the drift of Europe to the First World War.

Any survey of Shaw's work will leave the impression of literary versatility and prodigality of a rare degree, and yet to search for a masterpiece comprehensively representative of his genius is vain, for the lasting comic qualities seem to emerge as by-products of energetic attempts to pose as social reformer or artist—sage. *Man and Superman* (1903), a study of the life-force in action, in the shape of Ann Whitfield's sexual chase after the Shavian radical, John Tanner, has a

cohesion that is not at all enhanced by the insertion of a
massive dream-debate on the topic in question. *Back to
Methuselah* (1921), a five-act parable of Creative Evolution
which takes a whole day to perform and surveys mankind
from the Garden of Eden to a time thirty thousand years
hence in the effort to prove man's span of life too short,
in the event proves chiefly that a play can be much too long.
St Joan (1924), on the other hand, is a lively reconstruction
of the career and trial of Joan of Arc in which the saint,
faced with the cruel logic of the Inquisition, emerges as a
Protestant from history's womb untimely ripped.

A milestone in Shaw's career and in theatrical history was
the production of *Candida* at the Royal Court Theatre in
1904 under the management of Harley Granville-Barker and
J. E. Vedrenne. It inaugurated a phase in which the partnership gave London notable productions of plays by Shaw,
Ibsen, Yeats, Galsworthy, and others. Granville-Barker
(1877–1946), an actor as well as a producer, himself wrote
plays that had their place in the movement to compel
audiences to grapple with real issues of contemporary life. In
The Voysey Inheritance (1905) a young man is due to
succeed to a seemingly prosperous family business as a
solicitor, and learns that it relies on embezzlement. The
moral dilemma is complex because, on his father's death, he
finds that to bring the facts to light will mean personal
disaster for trusting clients. *Waste* (1907) is a political
tragedy in which a statesman's promising career ends in
disgrace and suicide because a woman with whom he has had
a brief liaison dies after illegal abortion. *The Madras House*
(1910) foresees the effect on a millinery business of female
emancipation and the new mass-market in fashion. The rag-
trade is made symbolic of an unjust society that exploits
women's sex.

Another writer whose career impinged oddly on Shaw's
was the journalist Frank Harris (1856–1931), editor of *The
Saturday Review* which employed Shaw and Max Beerbohm
successively as theatre critic. Harris left his *Life of Bernard
Shaw* (1931) incomplete at his death and Shaw finished it.
A raffish adventurer with a hair-raising career behind him,
Harris brazened his way into the London literary world in the
1880s. His play, *Mr & Mrs Daventry* (1900), shows a long-

suffering wife breaking away from a brutish husband. Harris
got the plot from Oscar Wilde who had already sold it to
various other writers. Harris's biography, *Oscar Wilde: His
Life and Confessions* (1918), has been called his best work,
but his most notorious is his five-volume autobiography,
My Life and Loves (1923–27), with its candid record of
sexual exploits of larger-than-life prodigality.

An amusing piece in Harris's fourth series of *Contemporary
Portraits* (1924) deals with the colourful personality Wilfrid
Scawen Blunt (1840–1922), the Victorian sonneteer, an
aristocrat who married Lord Byron's granddaughter.
Diplomat, traveller, and translator of Arabic poetry, Blunt
came to detest British imperialism and to champion nationalist causes including Irish Home Rule. His *Poetical Works*
were published in two volumes in 1914. It was characteristic
of Harris to warm to Blunt's own larger-than-life, self-
cultivated image as the man of all parts. 'The Admirable
Crichton is a part of the consciousness of the best Englishmen; "a good all-round man" . . . is their ideal,' he observed.

When James Barrie (1860–1937) called the butler 'Crichton' in his play *The Admirable Crichton* (1902) and revealed
him indeed, in a dire crisis, as the natural all-round leader of
the aristocratic family who in normal conditions gave him his
orders, he was indulging in a Shavian paradox; but, though it
is a lively play, the humour exudes relish of human vagaries
rather than judgment on a defective social structure. Barrie
was the son of a Scots weaver, and his early fiction linked
him with the Kailyard School that sentimentalised rural
Scotland. He dramatised one of his novels in *The Little
Minister* (1897), and *Quality Street* (1902) followed, a play
of quiet feminine domesticity set in Jane Austen's period.
After *The Admirable Crichton* came *Peter Pan* (1904) or 'The
Boy who would not grow up', a sentimental journey into
fantasy land whither the young children of the Darling family
are wafted one night by Peter and the fairy Tinker Bell. And,
alas, it would never have happened, had not Mr Darling in a
fit of temper chained up the children's 'nurse', Nana, a much-
loved Newfoundland dog and their loyal protector. Small
wonder that, on the children's safe return home, they find
their penitent father now living in Nana's kennel. 'O for an
hour of Herod!' the novelist Anthony Hope observed after

seeing a production. The riot of whimsy has kept London audiences enthralled annually at Christmas ever since.

What Every Woman Knows (1908) is tougher in spirit and free of mawkishness. Its Scots heroine, Maggie, is a woman who knows what she is about. Her menfolk strike a bargain with an aspiring but needy young man. They will finance his education and she will then have first refusal of him as a husband. The marriage takes place, and Maggie is victorious when it comes under threat. The plot is neatly managed, the characters carry conviction, and the humour is engaging. But Barrie's subsequent dramatic output was marred by unctuous sentimentality. *Dear Brutus* (1917) concerns a group of people regretful for the might-have-been lives they have bypassed. A midsummer eve's dream gives them a second chance, and they fare no better. The moral is that 'the fault, dear Brutus, lies not in our stars but in ourselves . . .'. *Mary Rose* (1920) is *Peter Pan* for grown-ups. Mary Rose disappears for twenty days on a Hebridean island in her childhood, and repeats the magic pilgrimage in adulthood, this time for twenty years. She returns briefly and meets her now grown son, but nothing in reality can again detain her from the 'home' to which the island's voice finally summons her back.

V The Irish Movement

While the London public was occupying itself theatrically with *Mr & Mrs Daventry* and *Quality Street*, and politically with the events of the Boer War, Dublin was seeing the infancy of the Irish Literary Theatre whose opening performances of Edward Martyn's play, *The Heather Field*, and Yeats's *The Countess Cathleen* were given in 1899. In *The Heather Field* an Irish landowner ruins himself through an uncontrollable passion for reclaiming land, and Martyn's subsequent play, *Maeve* (1900), concerns a doomed effort to rescue an impoverished Irish family by marrying into English money. George Moore (1852–1933), not relishing the imperialistic mood of wartime, forsook London for Dublin in 1901, and for ten years' immersion in the Irish movement. Moore, the heir to a large but heavily mortgaged Mayo estate, had studied painting in Paris in his twenties and had been a distinctive figure in the London cultural scene of the 1880s and 1890s, achieving great success with his novel *Esther Waters* (1894). His incursion into the Irish literary movement bore fruit in three volumes of autobiographical reminiscence covering the Dublin years, *Hail and Farewell* (*Ave*, 1911; *Salve*, 1912; *Vale*, 1914). They contain portraits of Martyn and Yeats, A.E. (George Russell) and James Stephens, Lady Gregory and Douglas Hyde, all key figures in the Irish renaissance more fully treated in A. N. Jeffares's *Anglo-Irish Literature*. A.E. (1867–1935), a poet himself (see *Collected Poems*, 1926), was zealous and generous in the encouragement of new young writers. As journalist and thinker, editor and enthusiast for Irish mythology, he was a dominant force in Dublin's literary life. Douglas Hyde (1860–1949), scholar and writer, and later first President of Ireland, was the prime initiator in the revival of interest in the Irish language and literature, and he founded the Gaelic League in 1893.

The curious relationship between Moore, the man of the world, and his foil Edward Martyn (1859–1924), devout Catholic and connoisseur of church music and architecture, is hilariously documented in *Hail and Farewell*. It had been Oscar Wilde's quip that Moore conducted his education in public, book by book, and certainly his flair as a gossipy raconteur made his works of autobiographical reminiscence engagingly infectious in spirit. (They include *Memoirs of My Dead Life*, 1906, and *Conversations in Ebury Street*, 1924.) *Hail and Farewell* is the work of a shrewd, ironic commentator on the human scene. Moore puts his friends at the mercy of his wit and his unsparing eye for littlenesses of character, but he exploits his own *persona* no less candidly. He is master of the denigratory nuance. And yet so constant is the bubble of good humour that laughter submerges malice. And the unity of this superficially sprawling cascade of chatter and reflection, polemic and meditation, resides in a masterful imaginative cohesion controlling the prodigality of memory and dream.

Moore's technical achievement as a prose stylist was immense. The transitions between portrait and anecdote, recollection and reverie, are smooth and natural by virtue of his superb verbal craftsmanship. His method of folding dialogue, thought, and description within narration was to leave its mark on the literature of the century, and Moore did it with a cleanness of outline, a lack of fuss, a rhythmic fluency, and a syntactic limpidity that are finely sustained. It is illuminating to trace the full maturing of this sensitive verbal instrument from the quiet novel, *The Lake* (1905), about a priest who leaves his parish, through the sparkling pages of *Hail and Farewell*, to the late historical novels, *The Brook Kerith* (1916) and *Héloise and Abélard* (1921). The former tells the story of a Jesus who is rescued alive from the cross by Joseph of Arimathea. Both here and in the eleventh-century background of *Héloise and Abélard* Moore contrives to drench his story in detail and colour without sacrifice of flexibility in presentation.

A unifying spirit behind the odd conjunction of Moore, Martyn, and Yeats was Lady Augusta Gregory (1852–1932), a member of the Anglo-Irish gentry who put her energies behind the Irish Theatre movement and was instrumental in founding the Abbey Theatre. Her one-act comedy, *Spreading the News*, was performed along with Yeats's *On Baile's Strand* on the opening night of the theatre in 1904. *Spreading the News* is a comic piece showing how coincidence, misunderstanding, and the Irish talent for factual embroidery magnify humdrum events to the scale of sensational criminality, at a country fair. *The Rising of the Moon* (1906), another popular piece, is set on the quay of a seaport town, where a prisoner who has broken gaol persuades a policeman to forego the price on his head and connive at his escape. Such events, illustrative of homely Irish character, were neatly parcelled up by Lady Gregory into brief dramatic episodes.

One of the great Abbey dramatists, J. M. Synge (1871–1909), was studying in Paris when Yeats came across him and urged him to immerse himself in the culture of his own land by going to the Aran islands. There Synge observed and absorbed the characters of the islanders, and he found in peasant humour and resourcefulness, toughness of spirit and intensity of feeling, the material for dramatic studies of great charm and vitality. In the events of the islanders' lives, the dangers from the sea, the vagaries of their sexual partnerships, and the fun of their escapades, he found his plots. And by transposing into English their Gaelic expressions and syntactical constructions he moulded an idiom supple in rhythm and spicy in phrase.

In *The Shadow of the Glen* (1903) an Ibsenesque heroine, Nora, is imposed piquantly on an Aran folk tale of a suspicious husband who feigns death in order to bring his wife's infidelity to light. The diversion of sympathy to the guilty party and of antipathy to the husband who keeps her caged put Synge from the start at loggerheads with the moralists. But *Riders to the Sea* (1904) gives universal status to its heroine, Maurya, in her grief for the loss of her sixth son to be claimed by the sea. (Vaughan Williams used its text almost verbatim for his opera of that name.) *The Well of the Saints* (1905), a three-act play, neatly dramatises a folk-tale of a cheerful old blind couple who are given back their sight by an itinerant saint, and are made miserable by the discovery of each other's ugliness. Synge's masterpiece is *The Playboy of the Western World* (1907). Christy Mahon arrives at an inn on the Mayo coast, fleeing from what he believes to have been his murder of his own father. His reception by the innkeeper's daughter, Pegeen, and by a local widow is so warm and adulatory that he blooms under their competitive admiration from a good-for-nothing into a garrulous and aggressive athlete. The new image is shattered by the appearance of Mahon senior with nothing worse than a bandaged head. But the tables are turned again when Christy persists in his new-found manliness in spite of Pegeen's disillusionment, and swaggers off, leaving Pegeen bereft of her own creation. Undoubtedly one of the great comedies of our century, the play nevertheless provoked a storm of opposition when it was first put on at the Abbey Theatre, for it seemed to defame Irish womanhood and to mock the native character which it was the duty of the nationalist movement to fortify.

A lesser name among the first generation of Abbey playwrights was Lord Dunsany (1878–1957), whose plays include *The Gods of the Mountain* (1911), a fable about beggars who pretend to be gods, and *The Golden Doom* (1912), a fable about the sacrifice of royal pride to childhood innocence, in which a boy and a girl pray for a lost hoop and are rewarded by the king's crown and sceptre. In these short plays Dunsany uses a stylised rhetoric and develops his own invented mythology used also in his short stories, *Time and the Gods* (1906).

A remarkable literary partnership flowered between Lady Gregory's cousin, Violet Martin (1862–1915) and Violet's own cousin, Edith Somerville (1858–1949). The joint authoresses collaborated under the names Somerville and Ross, Violet taking the pseudonym 'Martin Ross'. A sequence of largely comic stories of Irish life, *Some Experiences of an Irish R. M.* (1899), had been so successful that two more volumes followed, *Further Experiences of an Irish R. M.* (1908) and *In Mr Knox's Country* (1915). Major Sinclair Yeates, the Resident Magistrate, half-English and half-Irish, but newly arrived in Ireland and therefore something of an innocent abroad, brings a bold if repeatedly frustrated determination to impose reason and order on a region where chaos and hilarity are normative principles. Yeates is English enough to try hard and Irishman enough to relish the human agencies of his own failures. Though Violet Martin died in 1915, Edith Somerville, who dabbled in spiritualism, made what she believed to be contact with the deceased that enabled her to continue the partnership for the rest of her own long life. Of later work *The Big House at Inver* (1925), chronicling the downfall of a dynasty, is a spacious story written with leisure for stylistic graces.

VI Various prose writers

Among books of autobiographical interest published in the first decade of the century the posthumous *The Way of All Flesh* (1903) by Samuel Butler (1835–1902) is an early instance of the autobiographical novel of rebellion against social convention and parental pressure which has been so important in subsequent literary history. Butler's parents intended him for a career in the Church but he rejected Christianity. *Father and Son* (1907), the autobiography of Edmund Gosse (1849–1928), the author of several literary biographies, who exercised considerable critical influence on the literary life of his day, records a different kind of early struggle against the religious fanaticism of a father, Philip Gosse, who was both an eminent zoologist and a fervent Plymouth Brother rigid in biblical fundamentalism. Oscar

Wilde's posthumous autobiographical book, *De Profundis* (1905), was a selection by Robert Ross from the manuscript Wilde wrote in the prison cell. Ross's selection was perhaps an influential document historically. By picking out passages of genuine lyrical beauty in which Wilde strove to purge bitterness by chastened reflection on love and on Christ, Ross no doubt contributed to the subsequent reassessment of Wilde's downfall in terms of 'martyrdom' and helped to prepare the way for change in legislation against homosexuality.

A writer whose homosexuality brought a decline into depravity, Frederick Rolfe (1860–1913), a Londoner by birth and a Roman Catholic convert, aspired to the priesthood, was expelled from Scots College, Rome, and passed his days in embittered refusal to come to terms with his own failed vocation, with the benefactors who tried to help him, or with the world at large. An obsession with self-justification spilt over from life into literature. *Hadrian the Seventh* (1904) fictionalises Rolfe's urge to revenge himself on the Roman Catholic establishment that had rejected him. Twenty years after having been turned down as an ordinand, the hero is called to Rome to be recompensed and rehabilitated. In the event he is chosen as Pope and makes the most of the powers and dignities put at his disposal. A somewhat idiosyncratic Supreme Pontiff, he happily meets the Kaiser and manages the nations, and equally happily strolls about Rome dropping in for tea.

Rolfe had aristocratic as well as sacerdotal pretensions. He passed himself off as 'Baron Corvo' and he used the form 'Fr. Rolfe' as a writer. *Hadrian the Seventh* apart, his novels lack discipline of form and restraint in substance. *Chronicles of the House of Borgia* (1901) and *Don Tarquinio* (1905), however, recapture the Renaissance scene with some vividness of detail. *Nicholas Crabbe* (1958), published only posthumously, fictionalises Rolfe's early years as a writer even to the extent of rehashing actual acrimonious correspondence with publishers. *The Desire and Pursuit of the Whole* (1934) fictionalises events in the later years of decline in Venice, projecting frustrations and animosities relieved by an idealised passion for a girl with a 'muscular boyish breast'.

Hadrian the Seventh belongs to what looks like one of the century's publishing *anni mirabiles*, 1904, the year of

Nostromo and *The Golden Bowl.* So does *Green Mansions* by W. H. Hudson (1841–1922). Hudson, born in Argentina of American parentage, had settled in England in 1875. A field-naturalist, he wrote notably on bird-life, but his novel *Green Mansions,* set in South America, was widely acclaimed. It is a romantic tale of idealised love and tragic loss. The lovely heroine, Rima, a fantastic creation in whom the natural and the intelligent are uniquely unified (her garment is made 'out of the fine floating lines of small gossamer spiders'), was represented in the Hudson memorial statue by Epstein in Hyde Park. *A Shepherd's Life* (1910) gives an affectionate account of rural life on the South Wiltshire Downs; but far and away Hudson's best non-technical book is *Far Away and Long Ago* (1918), an autobiographical work about his early life on the pampas. It is peopled with fascinating characters, vividly sensitive to the natural world, and packed with such lore as how to cure shingles by rubbing a toad on the skin until it secretes in anger.

Peter Pan first confronted the world in the same year as Rima, the bird-woman. And this was when Edith Nesbit (1858–1924) published the third book in her comic children's series about the Bastable family, *New Treasure Seekers* (1904). Here, as in *The Wouldbegoods* (1901), there is a sturdier vein in writing for children, far removed from Barrie's whimsy and from patronising adult indulgence of postured childishness. Here there is the cheerful, earthy commonsense of children who have no time for romantic tosh. And while schoolchildren were beginning to read about the Bastables, their younger brothers and sisters were being introduced to Peter Rabbit, Benjamin Bunny, Tom Kitten, and the rest of the considerable animal mythology created by Beatrix Potter (1866–1943) in tellingly economic prose and delicate water-colours. The numerous stories began with *The Tale of Peter Rabbit* (1902) and *The Tale of Benjamin Bunny* (1904). Beatrix Potter too eschews whimsy and sentimentality. Here are dressed-up animals with their own way of life in a world of chairs and tables, pans and plates, made to size and judiciously accommodated down rabbit holes or under floorboards. Another pioneer in what was to become the vast twentieth-century industry of children's literature was Kenneth Grahame (1859–1932). In *The Wind in the Willows*

(1908) a river-bank society, a happy 'paternal squirearchy' including Rat, Mole, Badger, Otter, and others, is under threat because Toad of Toad Hall becomes enamoured of modern gadgetry and lets the side down. How the stoats and weasels of the Wild Wood take Toad Hall and are thence cast out presents something of a social parable.

The best work of Sir Arthur Conan Doyle (1859–1930) was done before the turn of the century, but *The Hound of the Baskervilles* (1902) and *The Return of Sherlock Holmes* (1905) belong to this era. So also does the historical novel *Sir Nigel* (1906). Doyle was inclined to rate it more highly than the detective stories which have had such a crucial influence on that popular twentieth-century genre. A. E. W. Mason (1865–1948) scored a resounding success with *The Four Feathers* (1902) and *The Broken Road* (1907). The former tells how a young English officer evades dangerous military service and receives four white feathers from disgusted friends, including his fiancée. His self-redemption by acts of notable courage is traced with deft exploitation of the maximum emotional tug and thrust. Mason's later career as a writer of detective stories was inaugurated by the publication of *At the Villa Rose* (1910). M. R. James (1862–1916), a palaeontologist, brought biblical scholarship and some awareness of the preternatural to bear upon his stories in two volumes, *Ghost Stories of an Antiquary* (1904 and 1911). Arthur Machen (1863–1947), a Welshman immersed in Celtic legend, indulged a somewhat less judicious interest in the preternatural in the autobiographical novel, *The Hill of Dreams* (1907) and in stories collected posthumously in *Tales of Horror and the Supernatural* (1949).

2

Hors de combat
The 1910s and 1920s at home

I Introduction

IT is often said that the First World War put an end to a way of life, but it did not, like the Second World War, engulf the home country, peppering the cities with bombs at night, filling their streets with air-raid wardens, fire-fighters, and ambulances, littering them next morning with debris, shrapnel, hose-pipes, holes in the road, charred handbags, and human remains. The munitions factories up and down the land hummed day and night, special constables trod the streets, open-topped charabancs and horse-drawn drays carried the new soldiers from the villages, troop trains transported them to the Channel in their thousands and brought them back wounded, still in their thousands. But the civilian did not find his train held up outside a city because an air raid was in progress; nor did stray enemy planes dive out of the blue to pump gunfire into a passenger coach. The civilians had to cope with shortages and rationing by day, but they had not spent their nights in air-raid shelters or in stations on the London Underground. The massive disturbances to daily life in the United Kingdom effected by the evacuation of children from cities, the training of the Home Guard, and the Air Raid Precautions were not experienced in the First World War.

This does not mean that the First World War was less cataclysmic or less agonising than the Second. The reverse is true. No doubt men and women throughout the land in the years 1914—1918 would gladly have exchanged the daily flood of yellow telegrams streaming into every hamlet of the land with news of men dead or missing for a closer personal encounter with blast and possible bloodshed. But

certainly the First World War did not prevent the continuance
of civilian life in many areas and many circles in a routine
from which the smell of the battlefield was remote indeed.
It became a theme of books written by combatants that
their wartime experience cut a gap of mutual incomprehension and incompatibility between themselves and their fellow
countrymen at home. Thus, although there is a literature of
the home front, including such books as Wells's *Mr Britling
Sees It Through* and Bennett's *Lord Raingo*, there is also a
richer stream of continuing literary productiveness which
bypasses the war.

The war, of course, was not the only event of its time to
cast a shadow over the British mind. 1917 was the year of the
Russian Revolution, when the Bolsheviks took control.
Nearer home, in the Easter Rising of 1916 in Dublin, a group
of Irish patriots proclaimed an independent republic and the
British responded harshly, crushing the rebellion and execut-
ing the rebel leaders. The subsequent civil strife and the
Anglo-Irish struggle that ensued after the war culminated in
1921 in the establishment of the 26 southern counties as the
independent Irish Free State, with its parliament in Dublin.
The six northern counties, with their parliament in Belfast,
remained part of the United Kingdom.

The end of a war fought in part for the rights of small
nations could not but lead to the fatally delayed granting of
Home Rule to Ireland. In other spheres developments halted
by the war were resumed at a quicker pace as peace returned.
The loosening of moral conventions and the weakening of
social stratifications were accelerated by the war and
especially by the role women were compelled to play in it
in the factories and in nursing. 1919 saw Lady Astor, the first
woman Member of Parliament, elected to Westminster. In
1920 Oxford University admitted women students and in
1921 a Birth Control Clinic was opened in London.

There are sombre and ironic contrasts between the
activities of war and the literature of peace. 1917, the year of
the bloody struggle at Passchendaele, was also the year of
Barrie's *Dear Brutus* and Norman Douglas's *South Wind*. And
throughout the years of slaughter in Europe work was
steadily progressing there on two of the century's most
monumental literary achievements. Marcel Proust was at

work on his *A la recherche du temps perdu*, of which the first part was published in 1913 and the second part in 1919, while James Joyce was at work on *Ulysses*. Though there was nothing afoot at home to match this making of masterpieces of French and Irish life, several thoughtful writers were casting a critical eye on the English social scene.

II Society under judgment

R. H. Mottram once described John Galsworthy (1867–1933) as the 'pure central type Englishman'. Galsworthy acquired this image partly from his personal inheritance as a member of a wealthy family of yeoman stock, educated at Harrow and Oxford, called to the Bar, and rich enough to live without work. It also derives from the scope of his significant work in fiction and drama. *The Forsyte Saga* traces the course of a solid English upper-middle-class family between 1886 and the 1920s, while the drama expresses the awakenings of conscience in the same class, Galsworthy's own, in the face of the evident social injustice and tension its ascendancy involved. Galsworthy had published three novels and two books of short stories when, in 1906, the play *The Silver Box* was performed and the novel *The Man of Property* was published, and the twin careers of the earnest commentator on English life were launched.

Galsworthy was soon classed with Shaw and Granville-Barker as a dramatist who tackled living issues. In *The Silver Box* the young gentleman and the unemployed husband of a servant both come back drunk in the early hours and end up with property in their hands that is not their own, but in the upshot there is one law for the rich and another for the poor. In *Justice* (1910) a young clerk alters a cheque in a desperate attempt to get a woman he loves out of difficulty and the majestic law bears down on him so heavily that he kills himself. At the time of this production Galsworthy was visiting prisons, consulting with the Prison Commission and even with the Home Secretary, Winston Churchill, and he was later judged to have been an influential advocate of penal reform. The victims of industry as well as of the law gained his sympathy. *Strife* (1909) is a powerful study of a strike at a Welsh tin-plate works, and its emphasis on the sheer doggedness of fighting employer and fighting employee brings forcefully home the sufferings of the latter. In *The Eldest Son* (1912) Galsworthy tackles the double standard of sexual morality affecting the gentleman's son and his game-keeper. In *The Skin Game* (1920) the conflict is between conservationist country gentleman and new-rich manufacturer who threatens to ruin local amenities with a factory. Galsworthy's plays neither turn into debates nor degenerate into propaganda. Sympathy for the underdog comes through portraiture that is sensitive to the complex interrelationships of class with class and man with man. Essentially human factors remain the core of the matter.

The Man of Property grew gradually into *The Forsyte Saga* by the accretion of two subsequent novels, *In Chancery* (1920) and *To Let* (1921), and some connecting pieces. The chronicling of the fortunes of the Forsyte dynasty from Victorian days pivots on the central studies of Soames Forsyte and Jolyon Forsyte. Soames is the man of property, symbol of wary possessiveness, but Jolyon, his more in-cautious and open-hearted cousin, breaks out of the rigid Forsytean mould to become a painter. Irene, Soames beautiful wife, brings into Soames's life something that he can neither understand nor bear to free from his grip. The theme is pursued through the life of the next generation. Galsworthy traces the gradual encroachment upon the Forsytean mind and life-style of those events that transformed Victorianism into modernism — the assertion of womanhood, the changing political consciousness, and the arrival of the motor-car. A significant moment in history is authentically reported on in the *Saga*; but Galsworthy did not enhance his reputation in his two later trilogies, *A Modern Comedy* (1929) and *End of the Chapter* (1934).

The Englishness of the upper-middle-class which Galsworthy at once celebrated and brought under judgment from within was more devastatingly assailed by E. M. Forster (1879–1970) who, though he belonged to the class by birth and upbringing, rejected its values with withering contempt. A crucial influence on Forster's thinking was the cultured liberal hedonism of the Cambridge scholar, Goldsworthy Lowes Dickinson, a devotee of the Greek spirit whose detached sweet reasonableness during the war was to irritate

simple souls like John Masefield when he was scraping the
mud and blood off human wrecks behind the lines in France.
('Goldie and those other eunuchs with their messy points of
view simply make me sick . . . . God deliver me from
talkers. . . .') If Galsworthy's critical vein was the product of
conscience disturbed by injustice and of sensibility offended
by materialism, Forster's was the product of outrage at
natural instinct defied and at emotion smothered by conventions of propriety. Forster's homosexuality no doubt lay at
the root of his protest, and his revolutionary hedonism
assaulted root and branch the society whose decline Galsworthy pictured with melancholy nostalgia. Moreover
Forster's radical personalism set a value on human relationships which challenged established objectivities with
seemingly anarchic thoroughness. ('I hate the idea of causes,
and if I had to choose between betraying my country and
betraying my friend, I hope I should have the guts to betray
my country.')

Forster patterned his novels so as to put representatives of
the values he hated — middle-class respectability, snobbery,
solidity, prudence, and efficiency — into conflict with
representatives of the Forsterian ethic whose native spirited-
ness, zest for life, frank sensuousness, and imaginative vitality
are intended to highlight the cramping pettiness of what they
are up against. The Herriton family of Sawston in *Where
Angels Fear to Tread* (1905) have the requisite rations of
priggishness, narrow-mindedness, and self-righteousness to
symbolise the English Aunt Sally. The widowed daughter-in-
law Lilia, a rather silly girl who is out of place in the milieu,
escapes the Herriton tyranny on a visit to Italy, marries
rashly, and dies in childbirth. The baby's future becomes the
issue in a complex working-out of the basic conflict between
those for whom human love matters and those in whom the
development of the heart is frustrated by hollow notions of
morality and respectability. *The Longest Journey* (1907)
explores a similar dichotomy in the studies of Rickie Elliot
and his bastard brother, Stephen Wonham, the one a product
of the public-school world, incapable of discovering reality,
the other altogether cruder but in touch with life. A neater
and more companionable book is *A Room with a View*
(1908) in which Lucy Honeychurch's choice between the

false and the true is healthily made when she determines to marry the railway clerk and not the conceited intellectual at the end. *Howards End* (1910) presents the familiar conflict through two families, the English Wilcoxes and the half-German Schlegels. For the latter there exist the inner life, imagination, culture, and deep personal need: for the former there do not. The contrast is powerfully made. Those for whom Forster's message catches fire claim it as a masterpiece, the last word in condemnation of people whose life is determined by catchwords and who sin against passion and truth. But the artifices of the assault upon artifice have always offended others. 'I came across a copy of *Howards End* and had a look into it,' Katherine Mansfield wrote in her *Journal* in May 1917. 'But it's not good enough. E. M. Forster never gets any further than warming the tea-pot. He's a rare fine hand at that. Feel this tea-pot. Is it not beautifully warm? Yes, but there ain't going to be no tea.'

Forster had been in India in 1912 and again in 1922 when for six months he was secretary to the Maharajah of Dewas. His account of this experience in *The Hill of Devi* (1953) sheds light on his last novel, *A Passage to India* (1924), in which his probing exploration of Anglo-Indian relations shows the local British administrators insulated in their offices and clubs and by their incorrigible public-school attitudes from the people they are supposed to be governing. The attempt by a college principal to bridge the gap issues in tragic misunderstanding. 'Only Connect' was Forster's motto for *Howards End*. The ultimate failure to connect in British India is not laid exclusively at the door of imperialistic stupidity, but the implicit critique of the book had obvious topical relevance.

Forster was fitfully associated with the Bloomsbury Group, a coterie of artists, thinkers, and writers who set a high value on aesthetic experience and on love, who rejected the moribund conventions of Victorian respectability, and were scornful of the vulgar and the philistine. The group originally centred around the two daughters of Leslie Stephen, Vanessa and Virginia, and their husbands, Clive Bell and Leonard Woolf. Lytton Strachey, Duncan Grant the artist, J. M. Keynes the economist, and G. E. Moore the philosopher, belonged to the group. Its importance in literary history lies rather in the convenient label it supplies for certain attitudes evident in the work of those who belonged to it or succumbed to its influence than in any specific declaration. Its values necessarily came under challenge when the First World War brought evidence of a threat to civilisation with which its sophisticated code could not grapple, and the post-war depression produced among intellectuals an outburst of social commitment to which Bloomsbury's aestheticism was repellent. Bloomsbury's cultivated indulgence of states of mind seemed to bypass moral judgment and social need alike. Addiction to gossip and assumption of superiority helped to give the 'Bloomsbury' tag a pejorative ring. Katherine Mansfield (1880–1923), who evoked in Virginia Woolf's diary the admission that hers was 'the only writing I have ever been jealous of', confessed to hating the group for their profession to live by feeling when they showed such feelinglessness for others.

Katherine Mansfield was one of two women writers from down under who had settled in England and were producing fiction at this time. The elder woman, Henry Handel Richardson (pseudonym of Ethel Florence Richardson) (1870–1946), born in Melbourne, was the daughter of an expatriate Dublin doctor who had joined the gold-rush, became a store-keeper, returned to medicine, failed, and went insane. She studied music in Leipzig, lived in Germany until the turn of the century, and came to England in 1903, having married John G. Robertson who was Professor of Germanic and Scandinavian Languages at London University. Her novel, *Maurice Guest* (1908), is a sensitive record of growing up based on her Melbourne and Leipzig years. Her major work, the trilogy of novels, *The Fortunes of Richard Mahony*, comprises *Australia Felix* (1917), *The Way Home* (1925), and *Ultima Thule* (1929). It is based on the events of her father's career, and traces Mahony's early struggles, his successes, and the subsequent decline that steadily isolates him from his family and from others. The sense of alienation from Australian and English society alike has its spiritual dimensions.

Katherine Mansfield's full name was Katherine Mansfield Beauchamp. Born in New Zealand, she settled in London in 1908 and kicked over the traces of her middle-class upbringing so violently that she crammed into a few years a series of liaisons which resulted in much inner torment. In so far as she found any kind of stable relationship it was with John Middleton Murry (1889–1957) whom she joined in 1912 and married in 1918. Katherine Mansfield was Chekov's literary disciple. Her first collection of short stories, *In a German Pension* (1911), were satirical sketches of German life. The arrival in London of her loved brother Leslie *en route* for France in 1915 and his death there the same year sparked off a series of stories of New Zealand life, fragments of her own family chronicle, most of them seen from the angle of a growing girl, many of them representing the exile's nostalgic transmutation of her past and yet also consciously designed to portray the 'undiscovered country' to the Old World. Katherine Mansfield's eye for detail, her neat use of symbolism, and her evocative sense of place are aspects of a remarkable talent; and she worked passionately to polish her technique, carefully weighing each measured sentence, developing her own line in interior monologue, and making deft transitions between authorial voice and her characters' own inner voices. She published two further collections during her lifetime, *Bliss* (1920) and *The Garden Party* (1922), and Murry edited *The Dove's Nest* (1923) post-humously.

Circumstances conspired to give adventitious interest to Katherine Mansfield's story. The shadow of consumption that haunted her and brought her early death, the violence of her sexual adventures, the ambiguities of her relationship with Murry, and the entanglement of the two of them with the domestic intimacies of Frieda and D. H. Lawrence (who used Katherine and Murry in portraying Gudrun and Gerald Crich in *Women in Love*) — all these are matters relevant to the study of her case. Crucial to the story is the role of Murry, the influential critic who started the *avant-garde* magazine, *Rhythm*, in 1911 while he was still at Oxford and by 1913 was editor of the *Athenaeum*, drawing upon such contributors as Eliot, Forster, Strachey, Russell, the Woolfs, and even Lawrence. Katherine Mansfield's death transmuted Murry into his late wife's literary idolator. His numerous writings about her, his editions of her *Letters* (1928), her *Life* (1933), and her *Journal* (1954) created a legend, for

Murry played down the unattractive excesses of Katherine
Mansfield by selective editing. Her personality and her fate
supplied all the needful ingredients for turning her into a cult
figure representative of passionate rebelliousness and doomed
frailty.

Though Murry eventually worked at the War Office during
the war and rose to be Chief Censor in 1919, he and
Katherine spent one of their happier phases living the
peaceful life of writers at Bandol in the early months of 1916
while the Battle of Verdun was raging. This literary detachment from the war they shared with Bloomsbury. Lytton
Strachey (1880–1932) proclaimed himself a conscientious
objector though he was anyway unfit for service. A central
Bloomsbury figure, Strachey, like Forster, had encountered
G. Lowes Dickinson at Cambridge and was a rabid homosexual. A disappointed would-be Cambridge don, he turned
professional writer, and his talent was a refined if limited
one. ('I am afraid you have little feeling for nature,' Virginia
Woolf told him.) His *Eminent Victorians* (1918) portrayed
the hitherto greatly admired pillars of Victorian England –
Cardinal Manning, Florence Nightingale, Dr Arnold, and
General Gordon – in a civilised, graceful manner and at the
same time accumulated ironies at their expense. The total
effect is one of irreverent denigration. There was enough
evidence of human weakness in the lives of these revered
figures for Strachey's witty, deflationary, and not always
accurate pen to achieve its purpose of malicious debunking
and to shock the public. Yet the next venture into this new
brand of biography reliant upon post-Freudian awareness of
unconscious motivation, *Queen Victoria* (1921), lacked the
cynical acerbity of its predecessor, for entry into Victoria's
mind evoked in Strachey an unexpected current of sympathy
and sentiment.

III   Decadents and others

Strachey had 'the wittiest mind of the age', Max Beerbohm
(1872–1956) told the artist William Rothenstein, but when
the two writers met, Strachey found Beerbohm coldly
remote. 'Formed as he was by unworldly Cambridge and
bohemian Bloomsbury, he was unused to the more mannered

and formal style of social intercourse which Max had learned from Oxford and Oscar Wilde.' So David Cecil has described the meeting in *Max: A Biography* (1964). A gifted caricaturist, Beerbohm had been associated with the decadents and a contributor to the *Yellow Book* in the nineties. His dual talent for graphic and verbal wit was unique. A fastidious stylist, a master of mannered felicities, he brought an aura of elegant breeding to his exercises in leisured trifling and diverting rumination. *The Works of Max Beerbohm* (1896) assembled early essays for premature historic recognition. Later volumes of essays included *Yet Again* (1909) and *And Even Now* (1921). In these, and in *Zuleika Dobson* (1911), a fantastic tale of mass-suicide by Oxford undergraduates infatuated with the ravishing grand-daughter of a college warden, Beerbohm sustains a discreetly postured irony that gives spice to his urbane wit.

Beerbohm was acquainted with many of the literary celebrities of the day and almost universally liked by them. For his parodic and satiric vein was rarely calculated to give offence. His insight into the quality and character of his contemporaries' work can be measured by reference to *A Christmas Garland* (1912) in which he presents parodies of seventeen well-known writers including James, Kipling, Wells, Chesterton, Shaw, and George Moore. Each of these is mocked in a piece of discerning mimicry. Here perhaps Beerbohm is at his funniest, here and in *Seven Men* (1919), in which imaginary important figures in society and letters are portrayed with rollicking penetration into vanity and pretension. In ' "Savanarola" Brown' L. Brown leaves behind him the unfinished manuscript of his tragedy, *Savanarola*, when he is killed by a bus in Piccadilly. The text of the play is a riotously comic burlesque of Elizabethan and neo-Elizabethan drama.

Beerbohm's elegant trifling is heavy-weight stuff when compared with the frivolous febrility of the novelist Ronald Firbank (1886–1926), who in his early days collected choice literature of the nineties, enshrining copies of Wilde, Beerbohm and the like in expensive bindings. Firbank had known Rupert Brooke and Vyvyan Holland (Wilde's son) at Cambridge, where his room was rich with silks, flowers, and statuettes, and where Maeterlinck and Huysmans were among his favourite authors. He published a first unimpressive tale, *Odette d'Autrevergnes* (1905), he travelled, lived the exquisite life of the dilettante, and impressed everyone by the feminine delicacy of his physique, his acute sensitivity, and his unlimited capacity for sauntering through life. The war put an end to his way of life, though he was not fit for service, and drove him to take up his pen and create an imaginative world which, in its total unreality, is itself a rejection of the war. *Vainglory* (1915), *Inclinations* (1916), *Caprice* (1917), and *Valmouth* (1919) are novellas, which is to say that neither in length nor in human substance do they deserve to be called 'novels'. If they have an English ancestry, it is to be found in Peacock for structure, in Wilde for tone, and in Meredith for dialogue. Certainly Firbank, like Aldous Huxley after him, learned from the nineteenth-century novelist, Thomas Love Peacock, whose method was to eschew plot, to assemble a group of individualistic, even eccentric personalities, and to record their conversation. In so far as there is a story in *Vainglory*, it concerns the efforts of Mrs Shamefoot to achieve commemoration in a cathedral stained-glass window. *Caprice* has more narrative shape. Sarah Sanquier, a clergyman's daughter, runs away to London to be an actress and succeeds in getting herself accidentally killed on an empty stage in a mouse-trap. The scene of *Valmouth* is a health resort which has become the refuge of well-to-do cranks and fritterers. Firbank's presentation is impressionistic: the human substance is largely externalised in dialogue, passages and fragments of which float unanchored before the reader's eyes. Thus the chatter of Edwardian society impinges upon the reader as upon an eavesdropper behind a curtain, who has to identify speakers and apportion snatches of talk as best he may. The method allows of the maximum wit and malevolence, but the target is scarcely the real world. Firbank's capricious preciosity inevitably limits his appeal and his later, post-war stories delighted only Firbankian enthusiasts.

'He was a decadent of the school of Wilde but lacking Wilde's intellect,' said Forrest Reid, Firbank's contemporary at Cambridge. 'I see him hovering between Wilde and Norman Douglas.' The link is valid. Norman Douglas (1868–1952), a frank hedonist, assayed the Peacockian method, but without the Peacockian discipline or the Firbankian economy, in his major novel, *South Wind* (1917). Douglas, born in Austria of Scots parents, lived most of his life in Italy and his main reputation was as a travel writer. *Siren Land* (1911), *Old Calabria* (1915), *Alone* (1921), and *Summer Islands* (1931) are travel books about Italy. They reveal a mind, effervescent in its varied enthusiasms, that makes the most of momentary distractions. They abound in natural detail and are vitalised by scraps of conversation and by musings on people and their ways. Douglas records in his autobiographical *Looking Back* (1934) how Lytton Strachey wrote to him in praise of *Alone*. 'Your books are so full; there is so much of so many things in them — so much experience, so much learning, so much art, so much humour, so much philosophy . . .' and when Douglas tried his hand at fiction in *South Wind* there proved indeed to be too much of everything. The multiplicity that vitalised the travel books paralysed the novel. The setting is a Mediterranean island, Nepenthe. A thin thread of plot traces the impact of the island on an Anglican bishop whose former convictions are undermined by the pagan light of the Mediterranean and by what Douglas called 'the joyful immoderation of everything and everybody'; but the theme is swamped under the accumulation of talk.

Another writer who had certain affinities with Firbank was the short-story writer, Hector Hugh Munro (1870–1916), who used the pseudonym 'Saki'. Satirical sketches that he contributed to the *Westminster Gazette* were collected in *Reginald* (1904). They record the cynical chatter of a frivolous young man. ('I know some perfectly virtuous people who are received everywhere.') The series was extended in *Reginald in Russia* (1910) where the curiously detached musing makes a game of human interests and affections in general. The *Chronicles of Clovis* (1911) and *Beasts and Super-Beasts* (1914) were further volumes of short stories, but the novel, *The Unbearable Bassington* (1912), is accounted Saki's best work. Here as elsewhere his target is the upper class. Their shallow, pleasure-seeking ways are satirised in a blasé, cynical tone. The epigrammatic wit, the humorous paradoxes, and the vapid flippancy bring now Wilde, now Firbank, now Coward to mind. The chatter of malicious, empty-headed women is often deliciously voiced:

'I fancy he [St Paul] wrote in Hebrew or Greek,' objected
Francesca . . .
'So dreadfully non-committal to go about pamphleteering in those
bizarre languages,' complained Merla.

But the hilarity is not tethered to any moral anchorage or
social judgment, and consequently an undertone of almost
nihilistic bitterness is detectable. Indeed an angry, aggressive,
misogynistic streak made Saki an unlovable personality and
cast its shadow on his work. A later novel, *When William
Came* (1914), imagines the reaction of London society to a
German invasion and occupation. Saki himself, though forty-
four in 1914, enlisted in the army, stubbornly refused to be
commissioned, rejoiced in the trenches at the remoteness of
'all the thousand and one horrors of civilisation', and was
killed.

There was an Englishwoman at work during the war years
whose innovatory method in fiction, had she deployed her
gifts more effectively, might have gained for her the kind of
following that turned Katherine Mansfield into a cult figure.
As it was, her failure to make adequate concessions to her
reader in the way of narrative structure and dramatic impact
condemned her to be valued by the *cognoscenti* and generally
unread. Dorothy Richardson (1873–1957), having taught in
Hanover and London, began to work for a Harley Street
dentist and turned her mind to writing and to the simmering
socialist and feminist movements of the day. Her relationship with H. G. Wells led to pregnancy and a miscarriage
before she eventually settled down as the wife of an artist.
Dorothy Richardson's importance is that in her massive series
of thirteen linked novels, which began with *Pointed Roofs*
(1915) and were together eventually called *Pilgrimage* (1938),
she brought the stream-of-consciousness method into English
fiction out of determination to match the masculine novel of
objective reality with a feminine subjectivity. Dorothy
Richardson transmuted her own experience into fiction by
projecting herself in her heroine, Miriam Henderson. A con-
tinuous life story passes before the reader in *Pointed Roofs*
and the volumes that succeeded it over the next twenty
years, but the work suffers from lack of selectivity, of
cohesion, and of intensity.

Dorothy Richardson portrays H. G. Wells as Hypo Wilson,

a manipulator of other people in his own interests. The way Wells's sexual prowess stamped itself on literary history may be further illustrated in the case of Katherine Mansfield's cousin, Mary Annette Beauchamp (1866–1941), who married Count von Arnim in 1890 and published as 'Elizabeth' her account of bringing up their three children on their Pomeranian estate in the Edwardian best-seller, *Elizabeth and her German Garden* (1898). E. M. Forster, who had served as the children's tutor, used her as model for Mrs Failing in *The Longest Journey*. Soon after the Count's death in 1910, Elizabeth had a two-year affair with Wells ('that coarse little man', she called him retrospectively), then married Earl Russell in 1919. Her lively novel, *Vera* (1921), is based on the unhappy marriage to Frank Russell.

Russell's younger brother, Bertrand, was the distinguished scholar who collaborated with A. N. Whitehead in *Principia Mathematica* (1910), who devised the mathematical and philosophical system known as 'Logical Atomism', and who presented in English translation the work of the Viennese-born philosopher, Ludwig Wittgenstein, *Tractatus Logico Philosophicus* (1921). This seminal book, questioning the traditional status of metaphysics and locating philosophical problems essentially in the area of linguistics, was to be the basis of 'Logical Positivism'. Russell, who made enemies by his pacifism during the war, had a long love affair with Lady Ottoline Morell, whose role as hostess to artists and writers put her for some time at the hub of the country's cultural life. In pre-war days her salon in Bedford Square was visited by such distinguished persons as Asquith and Henry James, Nijinsky and Diaghilev, Beerbohm and Yeats, Arnold Bennett and Wyndham Lewis, not to mention the Bloomsbury figures on whose group Ottoline's circle impinged through her life-long friendship with Lytton Strachey. Later her country house, Garsington Manor, near Oxford, became a congenial wartime refuge for pacifists as well as for serving soldiers such as Siegfried Sassoon and Robert Graves. Ottoline's numerous love affairs included one with Augustus John and one with Axel Munthe, the Swedish doctor whose nostalgic book of reminiscences, *The Story of San Michele* (1929), proved a runaway best-seller. The distinguished names linked by her friendship or patronage include also D. H. Lawrence,

Aldous Huxley, T. S. Eliot, Edmund Blunden, L. P. Hartley, Jacob Epstein, the sculptor, and Philip Heseltine, the composer who wrote as 'Peter Warlock'. Ottoline's patrician flamboyance and her passionate involvement with literary and artistic contemporaries evoked adoration and envy. Lawrence modelled Hermione Roddice on her in *Women in Love*, Aldous Huxley used her for Priscilla Wimbush in *Crome Yellow*, and Virginia Woolf represented her husband, Philip, as Hugh Whitbread in *Mrs Dalloway*.

IV Ireland, the North, and Wales

Ottoline's liberality was catholic. Lytton Strachey left an account of a tea-party she gave in London in 1928 when Aldous Huxley and Yeats were present and when he felt that conversation was annoyingly impeded by the unrestrained garrulity of 'a little gnome-like Irishman'. This was James Stephens (1882–1950), a product of the Dublin slums and one of A.E.'s protégés. He published a volume of verse, *Insurrections* (1909), and his first novel, *The Charwoman's Daughter* (1911), is a powerful evocation of the physical privations of tenement life in Dublin and of the inner dreams which can make them almost bearable. He then made a big hit with *The Crock of Gold* (1912). In this prose fantasy Stephens harnesses the magic and machinery of Irish folk-lore to his purpose of bringing philosophy and laughter to bear upon the rich jumble of life – a jumble embracing preternatural beings and talking animals as well as peasants and policemen. The method works by virtue of Stephens's torrential vitality and inventiveness, his single-mindedness, and his wit. There is a pungent earthiness about Stephens's fairies that puts his work at the opposite extreme from the whimsicality of Barrie. He captivates by feeding the mind, not drugging it. His volumes of short stories include *Here are Ladies* (1913) and *Etched in Moonlight* (1928). His *Collected Poems* (1926) evidences reliable craftsmanship over a wide diversity of moods and subjects.

Stephens, a diminutive, poker-faced, large-eyed fellow, was said to resemble a leprechaun. He somehow matches up to a Tourist Board image of an Irish writer. 'Where are you, Spirit, who could pass into our hearts and all / Hearts of little

children, hearts of trees and hills and elves?' Oliver St John
Gogarty asked of him. Gogarty (1878–1957), who briefly
shared lodgings with Joyce in the Sandycove Martello tower
in 1904, was mocked as Buck Mulligan in *Ulysses*. But there
was more to Gogarty than the manufacturer of devastating
epigrams and indecent limericks, though the wit was certainly
pungent. When Yeats went in for rejuvenation treatment,
Gogarty observed, 'He has reached the age when he can't
take "Yes" for an answer.' As a poet, Gogarty had a polished
equipment derived from Greek, Latin, and Elizabethan
models. His two books of reminiscences, *As I Was Going
Down Sackville Street* (1936) and *Tumbling in the Hay*
(1939) are the ramblings of a high-spirited raconteur. His
social conscience was evident in his first play, *Blight*, which
was put on at the Abbey Theatre in 1917 and focused
attention on Dublin's overcrowded tenements and slum landlordism. *A Serious Thing*, staged in 1919 at the time of the
Black-and-Tan excesses, deals ostensibly with Roman rule in
Galilee and contains telling topical shafts. ('I'm thinking it's
an extraordinary thing that every country we occupy seems
to be inhabited exclusively by rebels.')

A rising dramatist at the Abbey at this time was Lennox
Robinson (1886–1958) whom Yeats made manager in 1910.
Robinson's domestic comedies, though he fitfully dips his
toes in the shallows of prescribed psychological amateurism
(in *The White Blackbird*, 1925, for instance), are not distinguished, but he eventually gave in *The Big House* (1926) a
moving episodic presentation of the way the First World War
and the subsequent unrest impinge on a once wealthy Anglo-
Irish family in County Cork. Robinson was temporarily
replaced in 1915 and 1916 as manager of the Abbey by
St John Ervine (1883–1971), Ulster-born dramatist and
critic, who then went from the Abbey to the war and lost a
leg. Ervine wrote several novels, but his plays have stood up
better in the long run. *Mixed Marriage* (1911), *Jane Clegg*
(1913), and *John Ferguson* (1915) are naturalistic problem
plays with a firm didactic thrust. John Ferguson, an Ulster
Protestant farmer afflicted by illness and bereavement, clings
to his biblical faith with Job-like tenacity while he sees his
family life ruined by rape and murder which would never
have occurred had not a letter from his brother in America

missed the mail and arrived a fortnight too late. Ervine was successful in London during the inter-war years with thoughtful dramatic explorations of English middle-class domestic dilemmas like *The First Mrs Fraser* (1929) and *Robert's Wife* (1938).

Ervine's *Jane Clegg* was actually first produced at the Gaiety Theatre, Manchester. Miss A. E. F. Horniman, a wealthy Londoner, turned patroness of drama and provided financial support for the new Abbey Theatre from 1904 until her subsidy was withdrawn after a fuss over the theatre's failure to close in mourning on the death of Edward VII. Miss Horniman had turned her attention in 1907 to Manchester, where she rebuilt the Gaiety Theatre and started a repertory company to popularise the new 'drama of ideas' and to encourage new playwrights. A group of northern dramatists emerged, sometimes called the 'Manchester school'. Their emphasis was on the theatrical potential of ordinary people and of day-to-day life at a time of changing moral and social attitudes. Stanley Houghton (1881–1913), a critic and reviewer on the *Manchester Guardian*, wrote *The Dear Departed* (1908), *The Younger Generation* (1910), and *Hindle Wakes* (1912), the last a neat exploration of domestic turmoil in the families of two Lancashiremen united by friendship from boyhood and socially divided by the rise to wealth of one of them. They are now boss and humble employee respectively. Son and daughter of the two spend a week-end together 'for a bit of fun' and cause an inter-family to-do with intense moral and social ramifications. Houghton's dialogue wears well and his plays are still performed. Not so those of Allan Monkhouse (1858–1936) from Durham, who also worked for the *Manchester Guardian* and wrote plays for the Gaiety like *Mary Broome* (1912) and *The Conquering Hero* (1923) as well as several novels. A third *Guardian* journalist, Harold Brighouse (1882–1958), achieved a notable and still resounding success with *Hobson's Choice* (1916), a homely study of a domestic tyrant and Salford bootmaker who is finally brought to heel by the wit and will of his elder daughter.

While these Manchester men were manufacturing out of Lancashire phlegm, pig-headedness, and sour ironic humour a stage northern-ness that could hold up its head alongside stage Irishness, there was a Welshman at work who seemed more anxious to do for his nation than to extol it. Caradoc Evans (1878–1945), a draper's assistant from Cardiganshire, worked his way into journalism in London, then published collections of short stories — *My People* (1915), *Capel Sion* (1916), and *My Neighbours* (1919) — for which he devised a powerful, concise style on the basis of Old Testament diction coupled with translation of Welsh idiom. The style and the accompanying technique of conveying crucial facts by eloquent omission provided a venomous weapon for assaulting the crude brutalities of country life in west Wales. Farmers, labourers, and shopkeepers score off each other by low trickery and profit smugly from each other's most tragic miseries. They seduce the young womenfolk, trade them in marriage, conceal debts, bait local idiots, exploit the simpleminded, and beat wives into slavery and madness. And the greater the selfishness and savagery, the more likely it is that the villain is a pillar of the capel, eloquent in prayer.

By 1934, Glyn Jones averred, Evans 'was regarded in Wales as the enemy of everything which people of my class and generation had been taught to revere; he was held to be a mocker, a derider of our religion, one who by his paraphrasings and his fantastic translations made our language appear ridiculous and contemptible.' Evans's comedy, *Taffy*, produced at the Royalty Theatre, London, in 1923, so angered Welsh people that it was taken off, though Mrs Asquith, with her memories of how Lloyd George displaced her husband, reputedly delighted in its picture of the corruption and jockeying and hypocrisy involved in choosing a new village minister for the chapel in rural Wales. Of Evans's novels, *Nothing to Pay* (1930), *Wasps* (1933), and *Morgan Bible* (1943), the first is an impressive study of a miser. It draws movingly and vitriolically on Evans's early experience as a draper's assistant.

V Georgian poetry

Evans was one of those who early recognised and tried to publicise the talent of the Welsh-born poet, W. H. Davies (1871–1940). Davies turned tramp, lost a leg while jumping a freight train in the United States, then settled in England to live in doss-houses, peddle, and write poetry. When he sent a copy of his first volume, *The Soul's Destroyer* (1906), to Bernard Shaw, requesting half-a-crown or the book's return, Shaw appreciated the commonsense of the man and the promise of his work, and he wrote a preface for Davies's very successful *Autobiography of a Super Tramp* (1908). Davies married, settled in Gloucestershire on his Civil List pension, and poured out verse with indiscriminate prodigality. Among it there is poetry of quiet affection for the natural world which has ingenuous freshness. Davies has neither intensity nor passion, but his best work has an engaging spontaneity. 'Leisure' —

> What is this life if, full of care,
> We have no time to stand and stare? —

stands as a symbol of his tranquil spirit, though rural meditativeness is by no means his only vein. There is self-mockery in 'I am the Poet Davies, William', shrewd knowledge of the heart in 'One Thing Wanting', and quiet deflation of social antipathy between queueing mothers in 'The Hospital Waiting-Room':

> This woman said, though not a word
> From her red painted lips was heard —
> 'Why have I come to this, to be
> In such a slattern's company?'

Davies's unsophisticated idiom and his unexacting reflectiveness mark him as a Georgian. The Georgian movement began when Edward Marsh, a civil servant, had the idea of publishing an anthology to focus public attention on new talent. *Georgian Poetry 1911—12* was so successful that four further anthologies were published in the next ten years. Among poets represented in the first volume were Abercrombie, Bottomley, Brooke, Chesterton, Davies, de la Mare, Drinkwater, Flecker, Gibson, Lawrence, Masefield, Monro, and Stephens. The Georgians reacted against Victorian stateliness in manner and substance. Homely topics, but topics of ready-made 'poetic' appeal, attracted them. The effort to achieve emotional directness in easily assimilated verses sometimes had great charm but often led to banality.

There was often no sense of grappling with words, no teasing of imagery in the attempt to see the world afresh. In consequence the label 'Georgian' eventually came to denote slackness of observation, imprecision of statement, flaccidity of sentiment, and the sacrifice of intellectual stimulus to picture-postcard charm.

Georgianism as a phenomenon, however, was one thing: 'Georgianism' as a label has proved to be a very different thing, a tag to be applied to certain writers at their worst. Poets like Robert Graves and Siegfried Sassoon, who appeared in Marsh's volumes only to develop later into major literary figures, are generally described as having outgrown their 'Georgianism'. This use of the term as the definition of a kind of literary virus which sturdier constitutions happily throw off makes it difficult to do justice to those few poets for whom Georgianism was a chronic condition. They are not all negligible writers.

Walter de la Mare (1873–1956), for instance, made something unique out of Georgian simplicity of glance, gentleness of pressure, and quietness of voice. The world he fixed in his gaze at once veiled and half-disclosed a realm beyond sense and time. In de la Mare's poetry the meaning and the reality of things lie off-centre, off-stage. What delights and moves him, what mystifies and disturbs him, derives its beauty and power from the unseen and the unknown. De la Mare is not a philosophical poet for he conveys no message. Yet he has the philosophical poet's power to penetrate the surface of things and leave the reader dissatisfied with the opacity of a world seen by less piercing eyes. The philosopher explains and interprets. De la Mare does neither. He *de*lucidates the seen into the mysterious, the observed into the inexplicable.

De la Mare's mastery of elusiveness and trance-like mistiness evokes a realm of spellbinding wonder and sometimes of undelineated terror. The fantasy world is a world of moonlight and mystery, of grotesque creatures and dreamlike incongruities, a world of shadowy presences and even shadowier absences, of strange whispers and even stranger silences. There are fairies and goblins, elves and ghosts. There are children like Jenny, who pays sailormen with her golden locks to sail out to sea and drown, or like Jim Jay who got stuck fast in Yesterday and no amount of tugging could free him. But there are also beings more sombre and awesome who crash through the frontiers of the familiar and the comprehensible in fantasy unflavoured by playfulness or mischief. There is the ancient Coachman, glum and mum, mute and hunched, who drives his last coachload of travellers out of time ('The Last Coachload'). There is the knight of 'The Song of Finis' who sat on his steed 'at the edge of all the Ages', his soul freed from sorrow, his face all skin and bone. His horse whinnied, but no bird sang and no wind breathed.

> 'Lone for an end!' cried Knight to steed,
>   Loosed an eager rein —
> Charged with his challenge into Space:
>   And quiet did quiet remain.

De la Mare issued the first of many volumes of poetry in 1902 (*Songs of Childhood*) and *Collected Poems* in 1942. There were two later long poems, *The Traveller* (1945), a mythic account of a horseman's pilgrimage through the strangeness of life to the liberation of death, and *Winged Chariot* (1951), an exploration of the mystery of time. De la Mare's prose output began with *Henry Brocken* (1904). A constant theme in his creative thought makes its first appearance when Henry rides on horseback out of the familiar into the byways of life where characters from fiction are to be met with. In *The Three Royal Monkeys* (1910), a children's story, the three monkeys, orphaned and dispossessed, go questing for the land where their royal uncle reigns. *The Return* (1910) is a novel of demonic possession. But De la Mare's reputation as a prose writer rests mainly on his collections of short stories like *The Riddle* (1923), *The Connoisseur* (1926), *On The Edge* (1930), and *The Wind Blows Over* (1936), where refined craftsmanship is brought to bear upon situations of teasing oddity, of tragic loss, and of preternatural mystery. Evil impinges sometimes with a matter-of-factness that is quietly unnerving. The technique of seeing adult grief through the eyes of a child is tellingly employed in 'In the Forest' and 'The Almond Tree'.

Representative of those poets for whom the term 'Georgian' has been used pejoratively is John Drinkwater (1882–1937). His poetry had neither the imaginative intensity nor the verbal discipline to give it permanence. He was somewhat more effective as a dramatist. His loosely constructed chronicle plays, *Abraham Lincoln* (1918) and *Oliver Cromwell* (1921), proved stageable and popular for all their essential triteness. But Drinkwater's place in literary history is that of an insurance clerk who spiritedly broke out to become instrumental in forming the Pilgrim Players and later the Birmingham Repertory Company under the leadership of Barry Jackson.

Crucial to the success of *Georgian Poetry* was the work of Harold Monro (1879–1932) who opened the Poetry Bookshop in Devonshire Street in June 1913, when Henry Newbolt gave the inaugural address. *Georgian Poetry* was published under its imprint. The shop became a centre of poetry readings and a place of resort for rising poets. 'Hard-up poets and others were lodged at a nominal rent of 3/6 a week (often unpaid) in two attics above the bookshop,' Ruth Tomalin writes in her Preface to the 1970 edition of Monro's *Collected Poems* (1933). When Robert Frost had some poems accepted for Monro's paper, *Poetry and Drama*, 'he took it out in rent, finding Jacob Epstein, his wife and his latest block of stone next door.' Here Wilfrid Gibson lived briefly and so did Wilfred Owen and T. E. Hulme. 'Here, in a midnight quarrel, Frieda hurled D. H. Lawrence through a partition into the next room.' Here the great read their own work, Eliot, Ford, Edith Sitwell, W. H. Davies, Brooke, de la Mare, and Yeats among them. Here one evening, Rhys Davies recalled, Anna Wickham (1884–1947), whose collections included *The Man With a Hammer* (1916) and *The Little Old House* (1921), read verse of heartfelt feminine belligerence. An 'early beatnik', she chalked 'Good Stabling for Poets' on a board outside her house, the house where she was to hang herself. She was surely no 'Georgian' in spirit.

Nor was Monro himself. Disillusioned, haunted by lack of faith, he found no permanent consolation in pastoral escape or even, ultimately, in love. Alcoholic addiction tormented him. His poetic voice was a lonely and often anguished one. 'He is at the same time very intimate and very reticent,' T. S. Eliot wrote of him. 'He does not express the spirit of an age; he expresses the spirit of one man . . .' 'Bitter Sanctuary' represents the acute suffering of the addict in imagery of searing pathos. But Monro was equally master of the subtlety that hides anguish under surface whimsicality or ingenuousness.

> It is not difficult to die:
> You hold your breath and go to sleep;
> Your skin turns white or grey or blue,
> And some of your relations weep.
>
> ('Strange Meetings')

More recognisably representative of the 'Georgian' spirit was the work of Ralph Hodgson (1871–1962). Hodgson, a boxing enthusiast who bred bull-terriers and judged at dog shows, earned the reputation of being a recluse. He severely restricted his poetic output. The three volumes, *The Lost Blackbird* (1907), *Poems* (1917), and *The Skylark* (1958), together with *Collected Poems* (1961), reveal the animal-lover for whom the natural world stands as representative of an innocence and beauty which man is only too ready to corrupt and deface. Hodgson's lyrics hark back to the eighteenth century in their formal neatness, their crispness, and their satiric bite. His outcries against maltreatment of animals by hunting and caging, by exploiting them for work or entertainment, touched a responsive nerve in the British public, and lyrics like 'The Bells of Heaven' and 'Stupidity Street' became known as widely as any poetry written this century. 'Hymn to Moloch' is scathingly ironic:

> O Thou who didst furnish
> The fowls of the air
> With loverly feathers
> For leydies to wear,
> Receive this petition
> For blessin an aid
> From the principal Ouses
> Engaged in the trade.

Hodgson's longer poem, 'The Bull', which enters into the supposed consciousness of an aging bull, and his dynamic poem, 'The Song of Honour', appeared in *Georgian Poetry 1913–15*, the second anthology, which broke records by selling over 19,000 copies. Pride of place in this volume was given to *King Lear's Wife*, a verse drama by Gordon Bottomley (1874–1948) about the death of Lear's wife, which was performed by the Birmingham Repertory Company in 1915. It is thin in substance and in characterisation and reliant upon verbal decorativeness. While other Georgians have been deprived of their title because they broke through to something post-Georgian in their work, there is a case for depriving Bottomley of the title on the grounds that he harked back to Victorian grandiloquence against which the movement had initially set its face. Rossetti was his model and inspiration. A later play, *Gruach* (1921), shows Macbeth carrying off another's bride on her wedding night to make her Lady Macbeth. Bottomley's reliance upon stateliness of rhythm and contrived comeliness of phrase marks a degeneration of drama into rhetoric. There is indeed a discrepancy between the creative energy and critical thinking which exercised writers like Bottomley and Lascelles Abercrombie (1881–1938), not to mention Masefield and Drinkwater, while engaged in the attempt to revive poetic drama, and the actual quality of the work they produced.

In the second anthology of *Georgian Poetry* there were only three poems dealing with the war and one of them was Flecker's 'The Dying Patriot' ('Day breaks on England down the Kentish hills'). James Elroy Flecker (1884–1915) was already dead. He held diplomatic posts in the Middle East until consumption overtook him, and he made use of his experience to enrich Georgian mellifluousness with a dash of colour and spice from the east in *The Golden Journey to Samarkand* (1913). 'He has set out to make beauty, and has made it . . .' Marsh wrote to Brooke, unintentionally summing up the weakness of 'Georgianism'. When Marsh read aloud some passages to D. H. Lawrence, Lawrence warned, 'Remember skilled verse is dead in fifty years.' Flecker's *Hassan* (1922), a play about a Bagdad confectioner who rescues the Caliph from revolutionary captors, is polished and mannered in diction, and the verse choruses are orientally lush and haunting.

The third volume, *Georgian Poetry 1916–17*, included war poets such as Rosenberg, Sassoon, and Graves. It also included J. C. Squire (1884–1958), who wrote under the pseudonym 'Solomon Eagle' as Literary Editor of the *New Statesman* and founded the *London Mercury* in 1919. As editor of it he continued to champion the Georgian Poets after the publication of the last anthology in 1922, and the term 'the Squirearchy' was used to denote a group of conventionally minded poets who resisted modernist trends. Certainly Squire's own poetry is often imaginatively vague, verbally diffuse, and emotionally inert. Yet John Betjeman, introducing Squire's *Collected Poems* (1959), finds them 'far less escapist and stooky and wainy than we supposed' and rightly praises 'The Stockyard', a stomach-turning account of a visit to the Chicago Slaughterhouse.

Among those unwisely excluded from *Georgian Poetry 3* was Charlotte Mew (1869–1928). Hardy recognised her as 'the best woman poet of our day' and Harold Monro wanted Marsh to include the title poem of her first collection, *The Farmer's Bride* (1916), but de la Mare was against it. It is a disturbingly intense poem, a novel in miniature, in which a farmer speaks uncomprehendingly yet with touching affection of his young wife's sexual rejection of him. The Poetry Bookshop published Charlotte Mew's second collection, *The Rambling Sailor* (1929), soon after her death with a note on a life saddened by family bereavements, poverty, and madness, and ended by suicide. Miss Mew's slender output is deeply felt. The solemnity and poignancy of the dirge, 'Beside the Bed', the finely distilled emotion of 'A Quoi Bon Dire', and the totally unsentimental simplicity of 'Old Shepherd's Prayer' are representative of one of those rare minor poets precluded from 'greatness' only by quantity. She has understandably been compared with Emily Brontë.

> Because all night you have not turned to us or spoken
>   It is time for you to wake; your dreams were never very deep;
> I, for one, have seen the thin bright, twisted threads of them
>   dimmed and suddenly broken.
>   This is only a most piteous pretence of sleep.   ('Beside the Bed')

Such writing makes it difficult now to be indulgent to celebrated contemporaries like Lascelles Abercrombie and Thomas Sturge Moore (1870–1944) who strove too hard to manufacture beautiful lines. Current taste can more happily accommodate the writer who runs the risk of banality in pursuit of directness. Wilfrid Wilson Gibson (1878–1962), for instance, the Northumbrian poet, devoted a lifetime to simple versification, much of it narrative. Reviewing one of his earlier works, *Fires* (1912), Edward Thomas questioned whether the poet had merely embellished 'what would have been more effective as pieces of rough prose. . . . The verse has added nothing except unreality, perhaps not even brevity.' Gibson gathered his best work in *Collected Poems 1905–1925* (1925) and, for all the lack of intensity and verbal firmness, there is a freshness and transparency in poems like 'Flannan Isle' and 'The Drove-Road' that disarms criticism.

3

The first world war
(1914–1918)

I Introduction

GREAT Britain declared war on Germany on 4th August 1914. Behind this climactic event lay a long story of national, commercial, and colonial rivalry among the European powers. Germany's militaristic rulers were intent on enhancing the country's prestige by conquest and securing its industrial future by obtaining guaranteed sources of raw materials and guaranteed outlets for its products. Germany's determination to expand its Navy, an essential instrument of colonial expansion, was seen as a potential threat to British sea-power. As early as 1903 Erskine Childers (1870–1922), an Englishman whose mother was Irish, had written *The Riddle of the Sands*, an exciting novel of yachting and espionage around the German coast in which the long-term threat of German naval preparations for possible invasion of England was spelt out with prophetic accuracy. The 'Entente Cordiale', established between the British and French governments in the same year, was a defensive compact in the face of the growing menace. The immediate excuse for the outbreak of hostilities was provided when the Austrian Archduke Francis Ferdinand, the emperor's nephew and heir, was assassinated in Sarajevo by a Bosnian student. Germany promised support for Austria–Hungary in any retributive demands that might be made in consequence. Austria–Hungary began the attack on the Serbian capital, Belgrade. Russia mobilised in support of Serbia. Germany prepared for conflict with Russia and France. Britain and France were both guarantors of Belgian neutrality, and when Germany moved into Belgium British involvement was inevitable.

Historical causes, however long-standing, deep-rooted, or

various, seem to hindsight totally inadequate to account for the stubborn reality that followed. A battle-line was stretched across Europe, troops dug themselves into trenches on either side of no-man's-land, and as one side and then the other tried to break through the enemy's forces to victory, the line wavered this way and that through four years of bloodshed. The slaughter matched in scale the gigantic forces involved, as men were mobilised by the million and nations committed their total resources to the struggle. The back-up system required to keep the male youth of Europe, while thus occupied, fed, posted, equipped, rested, when wounded retrieved and treated, and when shell-shocked restored, was a monstrous and often clumsily inadequate network. The chronicle of the battles, in which costly offensives often achieved little or nothing, but in which always casualties were reckoned in their thousands, makes a sombre roll-call even today when men who remember are hard to come by: Mons, the Marne, Ypres, the Somme, Verdun, Passchendaele. And in addition there was a frustrated attempt in 1915 and 1916 to force a passage through the Dardanelles, to land troops on the Gallipoli peninsula, defeat the Turks, and relieve the pressure on Russia. This costly assault on difficult terrain under heavy fire from well-prepared defenders terminated in withdrawal after the attackers had achieved feats of courage and endurance that acquired epic status in the public eye. Though the war had its naval battles and its hard struggles in other fields, it is above all the Western Front and Gallipoli which today still seize the imagination through our literature for the way they sucked the country's manhood out of modern city and village, office and factory, field and garden, into an organised anti-civilisation where the machinery of slaughter was refined by the highest technological ingenuity, and the other circumstances of life, including the care for life itself, seemed savage in their crudity.

It is a matter for some astonishment that there are writers such as J. B. Priestley who served on the Western Front throughout the war and yet whose subsequent work seemed untouched by it. For the war laid its hand on all the arts. Augustus John became official war artist to the Canadian Corps and designed the memorial cartoon, 'Canadians opposite Lens'. Paul Nash, the landscape artist, became an official artist on the Western Front and held an exhibition of battlefield paintings in 1918. Stanley Spencer joined the Royal Army Medical Corps in 1915 and then volunteered for infantry service in 1917: his war experience was to inspire perhaps his greatest work, the murals in the memorial chapel at Burghclere. Among composers Vaughan Williams was claimed for war service and it inspired his powerful choral work, *Dona Nobis Pacem*. Gustav Holst, now in his fifties, produced in 1915 the orchestral work that first fully established him, *The Planets*; but even he was later packed off to Salonica and Constantinople to organise music for the troops.

II The war poets

Rupert Brooke (1887–1915) is a complex figure in literary history. He was the man who in conversation with Edward Marsh sparked off the idea for *Georgian Poetry*. He was a pre-war representative of social and cultural protest against Victorianism. He became a socialist and joined the Fabians. His studies of English Literature at Cambridge turned him into an enthusiast for the then little known poetry of Donne and for Elizabethan and Jacobean drama. He was horrified when he visited America to find Noyes regarded as a great poet and he told Marsh that Yeats was worth a hundred of Bridges. The first volume of *Georgian Poetry* which he did so much to inspire was hailed by D. H. Lawrence in Middleton Murry's *Rhythm* as a big breath of fresh air. Yet when Georgianism became associated in critical circles with amateurishness, escapism, lukewarmness, and conventional respectability, Brooke suffered from the same prejudice, and his popularity became suspect.

The irony which metamorphosed the radical reformer into the idol of the respectable was matched by the myth which transformed the poet of peace who died of blood-poisoning *en route* for Gallipoli into the symbol of heroic self-sacrifice. The legend that gathered round Brooke's memory turned him in the popular mind into the first of the war poets. Two kinds of poetry subscribed to the legend and the idolatry. In Germany in 1912 Brooke dashed off some rhyming octosyllabics while sitting at a cafe table. This was 'The Old

Vicarage, Grantchester', a flippantly devised poem not apparently much valued by Brooke but immediately appreciated by Marsh and others. The celebration of England seen from afar captured aspects of national character in felicitous couplets:

> Here tulips bloom as they are told:
> Unkempt about those hedges blows
> The English unofficial rose.

The hint of native self-mockery rescued the poem from sentimentality. This piece and poems like 'The Great Lover', with its celebration of household crockery and wet roofs, woodsmoke and raindrops, the 'cool kindliness of sheets' and the 'rough male kiss / Of blankets', established Brooke as the lover of innocent English rural homeliness and intensified the pathos of his early death.

In five war sonnets Brooke expressed the mood of public exultation in which the country entered the war.

> Now God be thanked Who has matched us with His hour,
> And caught our youth, and wakened us from sleeping . . . .

For Brooke personally the war supplied a central moral purpose and a focus for self-transcendence that rescued him from complex neurotic conflicts. Thus his rhetoric distanced human sacrifice from the realities of the battlefield and was seized upon by a public hungrier for heady heroics than for nearer acquaintance with grief. The final sonnet, 'The Soldier' ('If I should die, think only this of me'), summed up a mood of dedication to England which the poet's early death rendered poignantly unanswerable. Dean Inge quoted it in an Easter sermon at St Paul's.

Within a month of Brooke's death in April 1915, Julian Grenfell (1888–1915) was killed and *The Times* published his verses, *Into Battle*, celebrating the fighting man's share in the warmth, vitality, peace, and fullness of the natural world. The stars hold him in their comradeship, the trees stand to him as friend, the blackbird bids him sing, the horses teach him noble patience.

> And when the burning moment breaks,
>   And all things else are out of mind,
> And only joy of battle takes
>   Him by the throat and makes him blind,
>
> Through joy and blindness he shall know,
>   Not caring much to know, that still
> Nor lead nor steel shall reach him, so
>   That it be not the Destined Will.

The character of trench warfare on the Western Front made it impossible for serious poets to sustain such moods. Charles Hamilton Sorley (1895–1915), killed in the Battle of Loos in October 1915, disliked the glorification of sacrifice in Brooke's war sonnets. He had volunteered for service with eyes fully open and refused to poeticise death. It is neither triumph nor defeat, 'Only an empty pail, a slate rubbed clean, / A merciful putting away of what has been'. When his kit bag was sent back to England from the front, a famous sonnet was found in it.

> When you see millions of mouthless dead
> Across your dreams in pale battalions go,
> Say not soft things as other men have said . . .

Isaac Rosenberg (1890–1918) enlisted as a private also without illusions. 'I never joined the army for patriotic reasons,' he wrote. A diminutive man from a poor immigrant Jewish family, he was put in the Bantam regiment and killed near Arras in 1918. Rosenberg had studied painting at the Slade School of Art. In his Foreword to Rosenberg's *Collected Works* (1937) Sassoon called him a 'painter-poet. Adjectives and images involving colour abound, and the sharp, observant eye of the draughtsman is everywhere apparent.' His acquaintance with poverty left him with no motive to lament the lost delights of England at peace which Brooke celebrated so touchingly. His situation in the ranks gave him no intellectual companionship such as was sometimes open to those with commissions. He delineated the physical and emotional realities of war with unsparing accuracy. Nowhere are the immediacies of trench life more sharply particularised than in his 'Break of Day in the Trenches':

> Only a live thing leaps my hand —
> A queer sardonic rat —
> As I pull the parapet's poppy
> To stick behind my ear.

The rat will touch English and German hands indiscriminately
with its natural 'cosmopolitan sympathies'. The squalor and
indignity of slaughter are vividly registered in 'Dead Man's
Dump', the hideousness of trench life in 'Louse Hunting'.
Gordon Bottomley edited Rosenberg's *Selected Poems*
(1922) to which Laurence Binyon contributed an Introduc-
tory Memoir.

While Rosenberg came to poetry from painting, Ivor
Gurney (1890–1937) came to it from music. His education
at the Royal College spanned two musical generations, for in
1911 he was the pupil of Sir Charles Stanford, and in 1919
he returned to take up his studies again under Vaughan
Williams. Volumes of his songs, posthumously published,
include settings of poems by Yeats, de la Mare, Edward
Thomas, Graves, and Masefield. But Gurney was confined to
asylums from 1922 to his death. Edmund Blunden contributed a Memoir to *Poems of Ivor Gurney* (1954), noting traces
of the influence of Housman, Hopkins, and Edward Thomas
in Gurney's 'search for the shrewdly different in phrasing and
in metring'. Gurney's sufferings at the front were not the
direct and sole cause of his mental collapse and his bewildered
sense of intolerable injustice done, but awareness of war's
aftermath in slow and lingering damage adds poignancy to
poems like 'The Bohemians', 'War Books', and 'Strange
Hells'. Poems where the mind moves on the edge of sanity are
the most searing of all.

> Why have You made life so intolerable
> And set me between four walls, where I am able
> Not to escape meals without prayer, for that is possible
> Only by annoying an attendant.   ('To God')

The poet who did most to tear away false literary wrap-
pings from the reality of the war was Siegfried Sassoon
(1886–1967). His disillusionment with the war ultimately
drove him in 1917 to make a public protest against its
continuance that could well have resulted in court-martial;

but influential people had him sent instead to Craiglockhart
Hospital for shell-shocked officers near Edinburgh. Both
before and after his protest Sassoon distinguished himself by
remarkable gallantries. Robert Graves knew him at the front
as a ferocious warrior and recorded his heroism in *Goodbye
to All That*:

Siegfried distinguished himself by taking, single-handed, a battalion
frontage which the Royal Irish Regiment had failed to take the day
before. He went over with bombs in daylight, under covering fire
from a couple of rifles, and scared away the occupants.

This was Sassoon in the Somme offensive of July 1916. After
further heroic actions in the Battle of Arras, he came home
on leave to issue his public protest.

Something of the complexity of Sassoon's personality
emerges in two autobiographical trilogies, the first fictional,
the second factual. The first is *The Complete Memoirs of
George Sherston*. In *Memoirs of a Fox-Hunting Man* (1928)
Sassoon projects a picture of himself ('me with a lot left
out'), recapturing nostalgically the youth and young
manhood of a well-to-do lover of the hunt and the cricket-
field. In *Memoirs of an Infantry Officer* (1930) Sherston goes
through Sassoon's experience of front line warfare in 1916
and 1917 and his subsequent protest. *Sherston's Progress*
(1936) recounts Sherston's recovery and his voluntary return
to the trenches. Sassoon gives Sherston an awareness of the
multiplication of selves studied and, in particular, the
contrast between the 'happy warrior' and the 'professional
ruminator'. Both in evoking the pre-war rural scene and in
interweaving battle scenes with restless inner cerebration,
Sassoon's prose proves a highly sensitised instrument.

The third volume of the parallel, factual trilogy, *The Old
Century* (1938), *The Weald of Youth* (1942), and *Siegfried's
Journey 1916–1920* (1945), spells out the personal agony
from which the powerful war poems sprang. For Sassoon had
started his poetic career against the background of comfortable, cultured gentility remote from any consciousness of
current social problems and tensions. He discovered his talent
for biting epigram and plain speaking under the emotional
impact of war experience which shattered conventional
notions of nobility in battle. He hit upon the forceful tech-

nique of setting the brutal facts of trench warfare cheek-by-jowl with the clichés and slogans with which civilians comforted and deceived themselves at home. The chatter of two proud fathers of serving officers in their club ('The Fathers'), jingoistic religiosity about 'the boys' in a bishop's sermon ('They'), a war correspondent's report ('The Effect' — 'One man told me he had never seen so many dead before'); such shallow observations are picked up, folded neatly in the bloody bandages of reality, and returned to the speaker and his audience for further inspection.

In this way Sassoon turned the tables on a centuries-old tradition of evasion in poetic representation of war. *The Old Huntsman* (1917), *Counter-Attack* (1918), *The War Poems* (1919), and *Picture Show* (1919) contain powerful studies of war's real effects which make no concession to delicacy or refinement.

> The place was rotten with dead; green clumsy legs
> High-booted, sprawled and grovelled along the saps
> And trunks, face downward, in the sucking mud,
> Wallowed like trodden sand-bags loosely filled;
> And naked sodden buttocks, mats of hair,
> Bulged, clotted heads slept in the plastering slime.

That is Sassoon the artist of the battlefield in 'Counter-Attack'. And he was equally adroit at turning the phrases of the tommies and the jargon of battle orders into the stuff from which sharply etched portrayals of the tragedy, the irony, and the terrible humour of the slaughter could be sketched.

His example inspired an aspiring would-be poet, Wilfred Owen (1893–1918), whose devout Anglican upbringing had left him with scruples that added tension to his sufferings at the front. He had enlisted in 1915 and was sent out to the Somme battlefield in January 1917. Soon he was writing home vivid accounts of going over the top and seeing behind him 'the ground all crawling and wormy with wounded bodies'. But the carnage unhinged him and by June 1917 he was at Craiglockhart and writing to his mother:

I have just been reading Siegfried Sassoon, and am feeling at a very high pitch of emotion. Nothing like his trench life sketches has ever been written or ever will be written. Shakespeare reads vapid after them.

Soon after, he knocked on Sassoon's door and the celebrated friendship began. The two were both to return to the battle-field and distinguish themselves, Owen to be killed a week before the Armistice.

Unlike Sassoon, Owen had had his social conscience disturbed by experience of the miseries of the poor in pre-war days, when he planned to take Holy Orders and did lay pastoral work in Oxfordshire. But it was the war that gave focus to his compassion. A Preface he sketched out for future publication of his poems identified his purpose bleakly:

> This book is not about heroes. English poetry is not yet fit
> to speak of them.
> Nor is it about deeds, or lands, nor anything about glory, honour,
> might, dominion, or power except War.
> Above all I am not concerned with Poetry.
> My subject is War, and the pity of War.
> The Poetry is in the Pity.

The poetry is also in the technique, the uncanny precision in transferring physical hardship and emotional strain to the printed page.

> The poignant misery of dawn begins to grow . . .
> We only know war lasts, rain soaks, and clouds sag stormy.
> Dawn massing in the east her melancholy army
> Attacks once more in ranks on shivering ranks of gray,
> 　　　But nothing happens.　　　　　　　　　　('Exposure')

Owen's use of assonance contributes powerfully to the dis-concerting impact of a world awry. His rhythmic effects underscore the sense of laborious monotony. In 'Dulce et Decorum est' he annotates the ancient motto that it is fine and noble to die for your country by a searing account of a sudden gas attack overtaking men marching to rest, limping through sludge, bootless, blood-shod, blind, drunk with fatigue. One man is too slow in getting his gas-mask on. They fling him in the wagon to watch the white eyes writhing in his hanging face.

> If you could hear, at　　　jolt, the blood
> Come gurgling up from fi　th-corrupted lungs,
> Obscene as cancer . . .

If you could hear, you would think twice about repeating to children 'the old lie' of the title motto.

Sassoon used to claim that of the poets who survived the war Edmund Blunden (1896–1974) was the most permanently obsessed by it. Yet Blunden has been so treated by some anthologists that he is often regarded as a tranquil spirit annotating the rural scene with loving precision, musing nostalgically on old dears who pass their declining days between garden and fireside ('Almswomen') or on ancestral countryfolk whose homespun virtues left us our heritage ('Forefathers'). And indeed there is ripeness of thought and deftness of touch in such quietly contemplative studies. Yet Blunden's prose reminiscences, *Undertones of War* (1928), are a scathing record of experience on the Western Front. Blunden joined up in 1914 and between 1916 and 1918 he saw action on the Somme and at Ypres. Unlike Sassoon, Blunden makes no attempt to frame war experience and to contrast its agonies with the delights of a norm called 'peace'. He focuses on the war exclusively. Experiences of leave are as significant as the intervals are to a dramatist. Direct expression of outrage and horror is generally eschewed. The book relies on understatement and oblique irony. Anger and anguish smoulder off-scene, smothered by cool, sometimes even humorous, reportage. Blunden speaks phlegmatically of 'the best wire-netting bunks I had ever seen', of a 'sack of potatoes spouting blood', of a 'pair of boots still containing someone's feet'. Corpses are used as doorway blocks: living men are entombed in mud. Frightening things are said in semi-flippant throw-aways with sinister undertones. The voice is not raised: outrage at the chasm between HQ planning and the carnage is implicit: the quiet voice is deafening.

Blunden's poem, 'Third Ypres', is a mosaic of impressions, catching moments of hideous action and destruction. 'Concert Party: Busseboom' is an exercise in Sassoon's vein, describing an evening's entertainment put on for the troops, charming generals and privates alike until, the show over, the men face the chill sunset and hear guns opening 'another matinée' and calling to a different kind of dance.

> To this new concert, white we stood;
> Cold certainty held our breath;
> While men in the tunnels below Larch Wood
> Were kicking men to death.

Blunden's *Poems of Many Years* (1957) gathers material from forty years of publishing which began with *Poems* (1914) and which included numerous works of literary biography and criticism.

III Other soldier poets

Matching Blunden in clean poetic integrity and in rootedness in the English countryside was the older writer, Edward Thomas (1878–1917), who came to poetry in his last years only after nearly twenty years of productivity as a prose writer of topographical, literary, and biographical books, and as supplier of reviews and articles for journals. A Londoner of Welsh extraction, Thomas married Helen Noble, the daughter of a professional writer and critic, and determined to earn his living as such himself. The toil involved in thus supporting a wife and a young family was arduous and unremitting. Financial pressures bore heavily on him and he suffered from melancholy too. If the long years of producing books and articles to publishers' and editors' deadlines provided an incubation period for his latent poetic talent, enlisting in the army in 1915 no doubt provided the requisite time free of literary commitments that might otherwise have crowded out poetic composition.

Thomas was already thirty-eight when he volunteered for service in France, and he was killed in the Battle of Arras in April 1917. The late flowering of his poetic gift was thus entangled with the onset of war, but, unlike the 'war poets', Thomas never tried to portray the outer events of the battle-field or to voice the indignation of war's victims against the machinery of violence that entrapped them. The pathos of his death at the point of the full discovery of his poetic gift is deepened by the personal loss recorded by his widow, Helen Thomas, in two moving books of reminiscence, *As It Was* (1926), a record of their love, their marriage, and the birth of their son, and *World Without End* (1931), which spells out the joy and the sadness of Thomas's last home leave.

Some of Thomas's literary friends, Robert Frost among them, had urged him to turn poet. When he finally did so he was already prepared by a long-standing critical disapproval of 'artificers in verse', of the decorators who tried to work in the tradition of Keats without Keats's genius. Hence he adopted a spare forthrightness of expression which owed nothing to the cultivated graces of the conscious word-tasters. Eschewing all verbal finery, all ready-made rhythmic cadences, he moulds the phrases of authentic speech into verse whose body is vibrant with sincerity. R. S. Thomas, in a Preface to *Selected Poems* (1964) of his namesake, has remarked how Edward Thomas's poetry came at a time when the established attitude to poetry was about to be proved inadequate. 'The easy, glib rhythms, the complacent sweet-ness, the elegant phrasing — all these were to be rejected and held up to obloquy. It was Edward Thomas's scrupulous, self-searching honesty that was to make him something of a bridge between the older and the newer verse.'

There is nothing quite like Thomas's matter-of-fact record of conversation with the ploughman in 'As the Team's Head-Brass':

> 'Have you been out?' 'No.' 'And don't want to perhaps?'
> 'If I could only come back again, I should.
> I could spare an arm. I shouldn't want to lose
> A leg. If I should lose my head, why, so,
> I should want nothing more . . . .'

And Thomas's mastery of the cleanly sculptured lyric for voicing moods of love, of tension, or of doubt, is just as sure as this touch in conversational blank verse. The shorn lucidity of poems like 'Parting', 'Addlestrop', and 'Light's Out' is as far from banality as it is from decorativeness.

> There is not any book
> Or face of dearest look
> That I would not turn from now
> To go into the unknown
> I must enter, and leave, alone,
> I know not how.　　　　　　　　('Light's Out')

The quality of Thomas's poetry was only slowly recog-nised. In 1929, in his autobiography, *Goodbye to All That*, Robert Graves (1895–) declared Rosenberg, Owen, and Sorley 'the three poets of importance killed during the war' and made no mention of Thomas. Yet Graves has been one of the most intelligent poetic craftsmen of our age. He was the son of an Irish poet, A. P. Graves, by his second wife, a German of the von Ranke family to which the historian belonged. At the time when he should have gone from Charterhouse to Oxford he was caught up for five years by the war. In 1916 he was seriously wounded in the Battle of the Somme, was mistakenly reported dead, but lived to read his own obituary in the *Times*. Graves had gallantry but no illusions. He hated the war and the civilian jingoism, but he discouraged what he considered to be negative gestures and came to Sassoon's rescue when he was in danger of sacrificing himself under the influence of Ottoline Morrell's friends. Yet the war scarred Graves for life. The 'Goodbye' of his autobiography is a farewell to the social and cultural stabilities which the war undermined. He shared the returning soldier's sense of isolation from his fellows; his mind was littered with ineffaceable memories of horror and suffering; he underwent treatment for shell-shock; he sought fulfilment in love. 'The main theme of poetry is, properly, the relations of man and woman,' he wrote in his mythographic study, *The White Goddess* (1948). From 1926 to 1940 he lived with the American poet, Laura Riding, and forsook England for Majorca.

What made possible a continuing and lifelong devotion to poetry was the success of Graves's work as a historical novelist, in particular his two accounts of imperial Rome, *I Claudius* and *Claudius the God* (1934), in which the Emperor Claudius, who ruled from AD 41 to 54, recounts events in the reigns of his immediate predecessors and in his own. The detail and vitality of this reconstruction, its inside portrayal of corruption and scandal, and its easy readability made it a long-term best-seller. Graves's prose output includes other historical fiction such as the Byzantine *Count Belisario* (1938) and the eighteenth-century *Sergeant Lamb of the Ninth* (1941), as well as critical works.

But Graves has remained primarily a poet in outlook and in personal dedication. He has spoken of poetic composition as a matter of peeling off layers of self-obtuseness in the effort to get at the unpalatable truth. The Foreword to *Collected Poems* (1938) declares his 'furious reaction against the anodynic tradition of poetry . . . . To manifest poetic faith by a close and energetic study of the disgusting, the contemptible, and the evil is not very far in the direction of poetic serenity, but it has been the behaviour most natural to a man of my physical inheritance.' And in *The Crowning Privilege* (1955) he asserted the poet's duty to treat poetry 'with a single-minded devotion which may be called religious' in that it takes precedence over every other concern. Graves's output has been prolific. The earlier volumes were given titles: *Over the Brazier* (1916), *The Pier-Glass* (1921), and *Whipperginny* (1923), but Graves's subsequent practice has been to issue dated volumes like *Poems 1965–1968* and periodically to intersperse them with successive volumes of *Collected Poems* which sift previous collections and add to them.

Graves is not a poet of public commitment but of private engagement. His technical craftsmanship is sure and subtle. No one can more tellingly articulate the inner wrench of love's death or of personal displacement suddenly sensed amid the irrationality and mystery of life. Yet it is impossible to do quick justice to Graves by sampling. Sampling could evidence his talent, not his range. War poems like 'Dead Boche', 'The Leveller', and 'The Morning Before the Battle' set him alongside Sassoon and Rosenberg. But the poems of metaphysical self-analysis often seem to uncover emotional dilemmas peculiar to his own vexed and battered sensibilities. The honesty shines through more often than the feeling is shared. The reader's sense of Graves's isolation is deepened by the unyielding tartness of the temperament he projects. Yet his power to fold meaning with meaning in compact stanzas at once compelling and clean of pretence is a rare one.

> Children are dumb to say how hot the day is,
> How hot the scent is of the summer rose,
> How dreadful the black wastes of evening sky,
> How dreadful the tall soldiers drumming by.

> But we have speech, to blunt the angry day,
> And speech, to dull the rose's cruel scent,
> We spell away the overhanging night,
> We spell away the soldiers and the fright.

> There's a cool web of language winds us in,
> Retreat from too much joy, or too much fear . . .
>
> ('The Cool Web')

Survey of the reactions of writers to the First World War uncovers a new ethic responsive to the institutionalised mass brutality. The ethic of gallant and zestful commitment to fight with relish for a good cause against an evil foe is discredited. Yet pacifist idealism which resists involvement, though tepidly respected cerebrally, arouses a gut contempt. Maximum emotional approval is accorded to those who detest and despise the whole machinery of war, who reject every attempt to represent fighting as noble, and yet who fling themselves into the fray with illusionless determination to act and have done with it. The combination of scorn for those who fight because they believe in it with scorn for those who do not fight because they do not believe in it is an expression of deep psychological ambivalence in an age of disturbed allegiances and forsaken values. Thus Herbert Read (1893–1968), a veteran of the First World War, in 'To a Conscript of 1940', issues an exhortation to stoical acceptance of pointlessness. The gist of it is that brains and blood were given in vain in 1914–1918. The young soldier is urged to go,

> Knowing that there is no reward, no certain use
> In all your sacrifice.

A cleansing force is discerned in the acceptance of purposelessness.

> To fight without hope is to fight with grace,
> The self reconstructed, the false heart repaired.

Such thinking is related to the spread of philosophical relativism, existentialism, and nihilism. As the extent of the lunacy as well as the horror of 1914–1918 sank home in the inter-war years, the comforting practice arose of calling the First World War 'the war to end wars' and indeed of publicly insisting that, if there were ever to be another war, then the heroes of the trenches would have sacrificed themselves in vain. Public speakers tended to imply that men had streamed to the front, not with the purpose of killing the Kaiser, but with the determination to put an end to war once and for all.

Read's poem, 'The End of a War' (1933), deals with a fifteen-year-old memory. On the day before the Armistice Read's battalion was lured unsuspectingly into a fatal machine-gun ambush in the middle of a village. A wounded German soldier, found on the outskirts, had assured them that the retreating Germans had left the place. After the bloodshed, an English officer found the mutilated naked body of a girl. Read consigns this dramatic narrative to a prefatory note, while the poem itself consists of three sections, 'Meditation of a Dying German Officer', 'Dialogue between the Body and Soul of the Murdered Girl', and 'Meditation of the Waking English Officer'. The work sacrifices all indulgence in the emotions of outrage or revulsion to metaphysical brooding on ultimate questions of existence. Read's autobiographical reminiscences of childhood in rural Yorkshire, *The Innocent Eye* (1933), and two analytical volumes about the war, *In Retreat* (1925) and *Ambush* (1930), were later issued together as *Annals of Innocence and Experience* (1940).

Another delayed product of war experience was *In Parenthesis* (1937) by David Jones (1895–1974), a Welsh cockney and an artist of distinction who had enlisted in the Royal Welch Fusiliers and remained a private in the regiment in which Sassoon and Graves held commissions. Jones, who became a Roman Catholic in 1921, suffered from post-war neurasthenia, but he assimilated his war experiences by reconstituting them in this dramatic and largely prose poem of epic dimensions and spirit. They are framed within the context of the heroic Celtic and British past. Jones's Catholic sense of supernatural dimensions within which the totality of human history is contained is crucial to his method of interleaving past and present. Crucial too is the sacramentalist approach which holds microcosm within macrocosm and finds patterns of correspondence between the immediacies of the day and archetypal events of myth and history. His title 'In Parenthesis' is at once ironic and universally apt, chosen because 'the war itself was a parenthesis — how glad we thought we were to step outside its brackets at the end of '18 — and because our curious type of existence here is altogether in parenthesis' (Preface). This statement sums up the difference between Jones's final intellectual and emotional response to the war and that of war poets for whom it remained a monstrous abberration. The statement illuminates Jones's claim, 'I did not intend this as a "War Book" — it happens to be concerned with war. I should prefer it to be about a good kind of peace — but as Mandeville says, "Of Paradys ne can I not speken properly I was not there ...." ' Jones came to regard even the role of the private in the infantry as representative of the artist's duty to serve within the unit and not to adopt a 'staff mentality'. (See his *Epoch and Artist*, 1959.)

The inner assimilation of war service does not involve any idealisation of war or any cherishing of illusions. Jones is adamant· that the period of service covered by the poem (December 1915 to July 1916) represents a phase of fighting in which 'there was a certain attractive amateurishness, and elbow-room for idiosyncrasy that connected one with a less exacting past'. The mass slaughter of the Somme was to render the traditional moods and consolations of war meaningless. The action of the poem leads from pre-embarkation parade at home to France and the front, moving steadily towards the climax of battle in which the central figure, Private John Ball, is wounded.

> I have only tried to make a shape in words, using as data the complex of sights, sounds, fears, hopes, apprehensions, smells, things exterior and interior, the landscape and paraphernalia of that singular time and of those particular men.

Thus Jones defines his method. Amid the mass of descriptive detail the voice of the soldier is heard, astonishingly exact in its idiom and resonant with associations.

Jones's later work, *The Anathemata* (1952), is in immediate impact less accessible to the reader, for there is no recognisable continuity of narrative or sequence. The work is shaped only by thematic homogeneity which arises from the ingathering of fragments such as occur to the mind, Jones says, 'at any time and as often as not "in the time of the Mass" '. Thus Jones's subject is his 'own thing', as a cockney Welshman-turned-Catholic inheriting the tradition of his country. The mass provides a centre for reflections that sweep back to pre-history and move through Roman, Celtic, and Anglo-Saxon contexts. Christian symbols of wood and tree, vessel and church, and correspondences between type and archetype are used with Joycean dexterity. The first section starts from the consecration prayer in the mass. The poem ends with imagery of the Crucifixion. The intervening circular journey through history is made by the artist to be offered up in a spirit of obedience. 'Something has to be made by us before it can become for us his sign who made us. This point he settled in the upper room. No artefacture no Christian religion.' So Jones prefaces a work which has been compared in conception and execution with *Finnegans Wake*.

Of lesser poets from whom the war elicited notable work Edgell Rickword (1878–) stands out for a few distinctive verses of reflection such as 'Winter Warfare' and 'The Soldier Addresses His Body'. Totally unsentimental, Rickword's spare severity served him well later in satirical assaults on post-war decadence such as 'The Encounter', but his output has been small. (See *Collected Poems*, 1947.) Laurence Binyon (1869–1943), an expert on oriental art who worked at the British Museum, struck gold at least once in his lifelong practice of verse composition when he wrote the celebrated poem, 'For the Fallen', which was to become the most quoted of tributes to the dead.

> They shall not grow old, as we that are left grow old:
> Age shall not weary them, nor the years condemn.
> At the going down of the sun and in the morning
> We will remember them.

There is a moving 'Lament' too, not for the young men already dead, but for the young men of the world who 'have been called up to die / For the crime of their fathers', by F. S. Flint (1885–1960). Flint was active in the 'Imagist' movement. So too was T. E. Hulme (1883–1917), who was killed on the Western Front and who put the front-line scene into sharp focus in a few lines in 'Trenches: St Eloi'. Hulme, an anti-romantic, championed a revival of classical discipline and precision in literature and life in opposition to the emotional self-indulgence and idealistic progressivism recommended by the *Zeitgeist*. Herbert Read edited his literary and philosophical essays in *Speculations* (1924).

The Imagist movement in poetry derived impetus from Hulme's demand for accuracy of presentation and an end to verbiage. Ezra Pound was associated with the movement in its early days. Flint, who was well read in French symbolist poetry, contributed along with Richard Aldington (1892–1962) to the anthology *Des Imagistes* (1914), edited by Pound, and again to *Some Imagist Poets* (1915) for which Aldington wrote a Preface, defining the principles of Imagism. These are, briefly, to use the language of common speech, but exactly and not merely decoratively; to create new rhythms, and not to copy old rhythms which echo old moods; to be unrestrictive in choice of subject matter; to render particulars by means of images; to be hard and clear, not blurred or indefinite; to be concise. For Hulme the moon above the dock is 'a child's balloon' with its cord tangled in a ship's rigging, the sky is an 'old star-eaten blanket', and a lark crawls on a cloud 'like a flea on a white body'. For Aldington the 'white body of the evening' at sunset is 'slashed and gouged and seared' with scarlet and crimson.

IV Novelists and Chroniclers

Aldington was himself a war casualty in that, with the publication of *Images* (1915), he seemed to be on the brink of a promising career as a poet when the war claimed him. Thereafter, broken by shell-shock, he was slow to return to creative work. He seemed to sign himself off as a poet with *Collected Poems* (1928), but his war novel, *Death of a Hero* (1929), proved sensational. It is a bitter and breathlessly aggressive denunciation of the folly and wickedness of war. The outburst against cant provoked by the hero's death in battle lays the blame for bloodshed on a society dominated by fake religion, rigid morality, educational thuggery, and cultural philistinism. 'Hasten to adopt the slimy mask of British humbug and British fear of life, or expect to be smashed.' Aldington eventually turned from fiction to biography, portraying D. H. Lawrence in *Portrait of a Genius, But* ...(1950) and T. E. Lawrence in *Lawrence of Arabia* (1955).

This study of T. E. Lawrence (1888–1935) represents

perhaps the predictable reaction of an embittered soldier from the Western Front, where the war was all mud and blood, to the creation of a heroic legend around military exploits in a theatre of war more susceptible to being glamorised. T. E. Lawrence, the illegitimate son of an Anglo-Irish aristocrat, after doing intelligence work in Cairo, went into the desert to lead Arabs in guerilla activity against the Turks. How he turned 'Arab' in costume and manners, and carried out his daring mission, is told in his book, *The Seven Pillars of Wisdom* (1926). It is a vivid record of dashing exploits in the desert, aggrandised by a vein of philosophic rhetoric. A 'Lawrence of Arabia' legend grew up that gave Lawrence the status of a brilliant and courageous leader who made a mighty single-handed contribution to the Allies' victory and then retired into modest obscurity, nursing a tight-lipped disillusionment at the government's failure to keep faith with the Arabs in post-war diplomacy. When Lawrence was thrown from his motor-bike and killed in 1935, there were even whispers of secret service agents having fixed a wire across the road in his path. Such was the aura of mystery and deep involvement in international politics surrounding the man. That he hid as a ranker in the RAF made the legend plausible. On the day of his death he had just sent a telegram to his fellow-writer, Henry Williamson (1895–1977), who had conceived the idea of a meeting between Hitler and Lawrence as men of potentially common destiny for their respective countries.

Henry Williamson, like Aldington, never shook off the effects of his war experience in France. His book, *Patriot's Progress* (1930), traces the war career of a simple London clerk, John Bullock, who fights on the Somme and at Ypres. Arnold Bennett declared its descriptions unsurpassed 'in any other war-book within my knowledge'. Certainly it is a descriptive *tour de force* that reduces institutionalised warfare to nonsense without breathing a word to that effect. A disciple of Richard Jefferies, Williamson was most successful, however, in two animal stories, *Tarka the Otter* (1927) and *Salar the Salmon* (1935), richly detailed studies based on patient observation. But his major commitment was to two massive works of fiction, the tetralogy, *The Flax of Dream* (1936), which began with *The Beautiful Years* (1921), and the fifteen-novel sequence beginning with *The Dark Lantern* (1951) and ending with *The Gale of the World* (1969), which Williamson called *A Chronicle of Ancient Sunlight*. The respective heroes of these sagas (they are cousins) are harrassed idealists finding spiritual comfort only in nature. About a third of the larger *opus* is given over to the war. The whole suffers from repetitious projection of personal obsessions.

Personal documentation of the war, whether factual or fictional, is not solely preoccupied with the serviceman at the coal-face. Williamson looked back on the battlefield as 'a great livid wound stretching from the North Sea, or German Ocean, to the Alps, during four and a quarter years: a wound never ceasing to weep from wan dusk to gangrenous dawn...' But even when men were being lined up in their thousands for massacre before German machine guns on the Somme there was someone in an office with a map before him for whom the thing made sense. John Buchan (1875–1940), the Scotsman who rose to be Governor-General of Canada as Lord Tweedsmuir, introduced in his spy story, *The Thirty-nine Steps* (1915), the Scots hero, Richard Hannay, who figures again in *Greenmantle* (1916), *Mr Standfast* (1919), and *The Three Hostages* (1924). In the two central books of the series, where Major Hannay pops in and out of the Admiralty and War Office and dashes about the world on dangerous missions, the war emerges as an organised, directed business, 'a cosmic drama', in Buchan's words from his auto-biography, *Memory Hold-the-Door* (1940), with 'an apocalyptic splendour of design'.

The war produced a number of influential best-sellers such as, for instance, *Tell England* (1922) by Ernest Raymond (1888–1974), who served as a chaplain in the Gallipoli campaign and determined to acclaim the heroes of the Dardanelles. He did so by going back to the school-days of the young men caught up in the tragic venture and by deriving the maximum emotional thrust from contrast between the exploits of boyhood and the fate that overtakes them. At school the boys learn to stick it and take a licking. Thence to the Dardanelles, the crusade of the Cross against the Crescent, and the chaplain's exhortations, 'Do your duty, lads. Give 'em hell every time.' No overall judgment on the war mars the eulogy of courage. As a post-war tear-jerker *Tell England* was perhaps matched only by the play, *Journey's End* (1929), by R. C. Sherriff (1896–1975). The scene is a dug-out on the Western Front in 1918. A young soldier fresh from school comes to serve under Captain Stanhope from the same school, the object of his boyish hero-worship, but now shattered by battle and drink. The public-school background is again a source of ready-made sentiment. A now less-remembered novel, *Sonia* (1917), by Stephen McKenna (1888–1967), directly sets out to trace the careers of the sons of the governing classes who were thrust from public school into war service of one form or another. Although the central narrative is heavily sentimental, the novel contains percipient comment on politics and current social issues, and conveys a sense of the larger movement of history.

An ambitious attempt was made to record the broader changes of attitude and situation on the Western Front and to grasp the pattern of overall military movement in *The Spanish Farm Trilogy* (1927) by R. H. Mottram (1883–1971). Mottram had served as an interpreter. He focused on a farm twenty miles from the front in 1915. In the three volumes, *The Spanish Farm* (1924), *Sixty-four Ninety-four* (1925), and *The Crime at Vanderlynden's* (1926), Madeleine Vanderlynden doggedly holds on as the family farm becomes 'first a billet, then all but a battlefield', and as the volunteers of the early days are succeeded by the waves of conscripts flowing to and from the trenches. Though one of the officer heroes accepts that 'perhaps no exhilaration on earth will ever be again like that of crouching in a dug-out over hot black tea, gritty with sugar and stinging with rum', the admission gradually gains strength that, in 1917 and 1918, 'the real enemy had been not the Germans, but the war'. For all the obviousness of some of his fictional devices, Mottram achieves a lot in representation of detailed mood and response as fighting men learn 'the old, old lesson of the War — Never do anything, it is always too late', and begin to hope that perhaps 'our children may be able to imagine a way of settling disputes more intelligent than maintaining during years a population as large as that of London, on an area as large as that of Wales, for the sole purpose of wholesale slaughter by machinery'.

4
The modern movement

I Introduction

MOST of the revolutionary works of Modernism belong to the second and third decades of the century. Within twelve years of 1913 a sequence of remarkable publications had opened up paths of literary experimentation in an explosion of innovation: D. H. Lawrence's *Sons and Lovers* (1913) and *Women in Love* (1921), James Joyce's *Portrait of the Artist as a Young Man* (1916) and *Ulysses* (1922), T. S. Eliot's *Prufrock* (1917) and *The Waste Land* (1922), W. B. Yeats's *The Wild Swans at Coole* (1919) and *Michael Robartes and the Dancer* (1921), Ford Madox Ford's *The Good Soldier* (1915) and *Some Do Not* (1924), Wyndham Lewis's *Tarr* (1918) and Virginia Woolf's *Mrs Dalloway* (1925), Edward Thomas's *Collected Poems* (1918) and Edith Sitwell's *Facade* (1922). This innovatory output, accompanied as it was by the continuing simultaneous productivity of older writers such as Hardy, Conrad, Shaw, Bennett, and George Moore, as well as by the work of new and distinctive if less revolutionary writers such as Sassoon, Masefield, Strachey, Firbank, T. F. Powys, and Aldous Huxley, inaugurated an epoch of creativity unmatched in richness since Wordsworth, Coleridge, Byron, Shelley, Scott, and Jane Austen were at work a century earlier.

The twentieth-century outbreak of artistic innovation was not confined to literature. In painting, the revolt against representation and manual photography brought a new emphasis on design and texture, on modulations of masses and colours. At one extreme imitation and description were eliminated in favour of abstraction. At another extreme the surrealists juxtaposed incongruous forms and symbols, as Salvador Dali hung a melting watch from a tree in *The Persis-*

tence of Memory. Among English artists who turned to abstract painting Ben Nicholson made cunning use of geometrical shapes, while the two great sculptors, Henry Moore and Barbara Hepworth, managed both to keep sculpture in touch with nature by the way they handled their medium and to work on abstract lines. Conversely the British artist, Francis Bacon, achieved sensational and macabre effects by the surrealistic device of pushing figures out of shape.

The leading modern writers, Yeats, Eliot, Joyce, and D. H. Lawrence, together with associated figures such as Ford, Pound, and Wyndham Lewis, stand at the centre of a 'movement' in the sense that their overlapping achievements effected a literary revolution. Briefly, they represent in their work various ways of stamping upon literature the impress of contemporary life. The problem they all recognised is that the structures and idioms, the images and cadences, which literary tradition puts at the writer's disposal can be so handled that new experience is processed into a familiar literary stock-in-trade. The stuff of life is squeezed out as experience is packaged in literary merchandise. Or perhaps there is no stuff of life to begin with; but a writer is so bemused by the accredited contrivances of composition that he needs valid impulse neither from sense nor from feeling to set them in motion. Every great literary movement is the explosive result of some collision between sensitivity to the world and sensitivity to the literary tradition. Its effectiveness is not a matter of the relative importance to the practitioner of form and substance, medium and living experience. Form is as important to the writer who tries to cleanse it of traditionalisms as it is to the writer who makes them his happy hunting-ground. It is rather a matter of what Thomas Hardy, in his poem on the sinking of the *Titanic*, called 'the convergence of the twain'. Hardy's phrase for the collision of liner and iceberg, alien in themselves but destined for 'intimate welding' as 'twin halves of one august event', might be applied to that convergence of human experience and literary form which makes a great work of art an 'august event'. That writers as diverse in background as Yeats and Eliot, Joyce and Lawrence, and of course others such as Virginia Woolf, should have within a few years provided such evidence of the malleability of literature to the demands of sharply adjusted twentieth-century sensibilities constitutes the major literary phenomenon of the age.

II W. B. Yeats

In some respects the personal poetic development of the Irish poet, W. B. Yeats (1865–1939), represents in summary the poetic revolution of our time. Yeats began as a poet of the Irish Literary Renaissance which he served in journalism and public speaking, and this aspect of his work is treated in A. N. Jeffares's *Anglo-Irish Literature*. In London in the 1890s he belonged to the Rhymers' Club who met at the 'Cheshire Cheese'. Among his friends Lionel Johnson, Ernest Dowson, and Arthur Symons were representative of the *fin-de-siècle* decadence whose ethos he rejected, but they made him aware of the work of French symbolists, Verlaine and Mallarmé, at a crucial stage in his poetic growth. His father's post-Darwinian scepticism left him incapable of subscribing to Christian orthodoxy yet hungry for spiritual roots and religious synthesis. Hence he toyed throughout his life with theosophical and hermetic studies, with spiritualism and magic. He fell deeply in love with Maud Gonne, but she rejected his successive proposals of marriage. An Irish nationalist whose revolutionary zeal, unlike Yeats's nationalism, did not stop short of violence, Maud Gonne became for Yeats a symbol and a focus for personal dilemmas involving the relationship between public commitment to Irish identity and nationhood, and his deeply seated personal vocation as a poet. He was for long deeply involved with Lady Gregory in the formation of the Irish Literary Theatre and the running of the Abbey Theatre.

Yeats's early publications belong to his Celtic Twilight period. Irish legend forms the basis of the title poem in *The Wanderings of Oisin* (1889). In the verse drama, *The Countess Cathleen* (1892), Maud Gonne is idealistically projected as a compassionate aristocrat of 'old times' who, during a famine, sells her soul to the Devil in order to feed and save the peasants. The short play, *Cathleen ni Houlihan* (1902), is set in 1798 at the time of uprising. Cathleen ni Houlihan, first acted by Maud Gonne, comes as a symbol of Ireland to call a young villager on the eve of his wedding to sacrifice himself for her 'four beautiful green fields' stolen by a stranger. This was the influential play of which Yeats was to ask himself after the 1916 rising and executions:

> Did that play of mine send out
> Certain men the English shot?
>
> ('The Man and the Echo')

On Baile's Strand (included in *In the Seven Woods*, 1903) dramatises a tragic story from the Cuchulain cycle to which Yeats returned again in his short verse play, *Deirdre* (1907).

The drama of this period represents Yeats's creative contribution to the Abbey Theatre to which he gave so much time in administration and direction. The poetry of the same years is rich in Swinburnian rhythms, haunting cadences, and decorative imagery. The mood is often self-indulgently melancholy and inert. The sheer lyrical poignancy and verbal exuberance of yearning verse like 'The Lake Isle of Innisfree' or 'The White Birds' must not be undervalued, but Yeats was himself acutely aware of the need to achieve a more assertive and virile idiom, and he became sensitive to the demand for the syntax of common life so lacking from the polished phrases of the Rhymers. His theory, as we know from his letters, was ahead of his practice; but indefatigable self-education as a practitioner eventually effected a transformation.

The maturing of Yeats was at once a personal and a technical development. It can be traced through the successive collections, *In the Seven Woods* (1903), *The Green Helmet* (1910), *Responsibilities* (1914), and *The Wild Swans at Coole* (1919). The voice becomes steadier, the verbal embroidery is shaken off, and postures give place to honest analysis of the self and the world. Where symbolism is used, it does not decorate the real but transfigures it. A more dignified and detached *persona* emerges. He is capable in 'Friends' (*Responsibilities*) of frankly estimating his debt to the three women, Olivia Shakespeare, Lady Gregory, and Maud Gonne without either pretentiousness or understatement.

> And what of her that took
> All till my youth was gone
> With scarce a pitying look?
> How could I praise that one?

The range of mood and tone expands as Yeats puts ever more of his true self into his work. The development continues apace through the 1920s and 1930s in *Michael Robartes and the Dancer* (1921), *The Tower* (1928), *The Winding Stair* (1933), *A Full Moon in March* (1935), and *Last Poems* (1939). The executions after the 1916 rising provoked a tribute to the rebels in 'Easter 1916' which is at once deeply felt yet devoid of raised voice or florid gesture. 'The Second Coming' powerfully expresses the post-war sense of social disintegration sharpened by the Irish Troubles ('Things fall apart; the centre cannot hold'), and personal apprehension for the future is articulated in a magnificent image of a second incarnation:

> And what rough beast, its hour come round at last,
> Slouches towards Bethlehem to be born?

Yeats's diversity of tone and substance is unique. 'Prayer for My Daughter' is a moving personal meditation on his daughter's birth. 'Sailing to Byzantium' makes a complex, studied comparison between growing old in Ireland where —

> Caught in that sensual music all neglect
> Monuments of unchanging intellect

and the poet's 'holy city of Byzantium' whose art and artistry gather him into 'the artifice of eternity'. The devastating self-analysis of 'The Tower', loud with the irascibility of age, is as sure and unaffected in its touch as is the quietly appreciative rumination of 'Coole Park 1929'. The nostalgic flashbacks to lost great ones in 'Beautiful Lofty Things' —

> Maud Gonne at Howth station waiting a train,
> Pallas Athene in that straight back and arrogant head . . .

are as authentic as is the frank examination in 'The Circus

Animals' Desertion' of his own poetic development from impresario of performing animals to unaccommodated creature of illusionless old age.

> Now that my ladder's gone,
> I must lie down where all the ladders start,
> In the foul rag-and-bone shop of the heart.

III Ford Madox Ford and Ezra Pound

'I went to England in 1908 to "learn" from Yeats — and stayed to learn from Yeats *and* Ford.' Thus Ezra Pound paid tribute to perhaps the most underestimated of the great moderns, Ford Madox Ford (1873–1939), whose openness to innovation was no less stimulating than Yeats's. Ford was christened Ford Hermann Hueffer. He wrote as 'Hueffer' until as late as 1921 but changed his name to 'Ford' in 1919. Ford's importance derives not only from his creative work but from his critical and editorial work. The *English Review* which he founded in 1908 garnered contributions from some of the most distinguished writers of the day, the established (including Hardy, James, Conrad, and Wells) and the new (including Pound, D. H. Lawrence, Norman Douglas, and Wyndham Lewis). As editor Ford discovered D. H. Lawrence in 1909 when Jessie Chambers sent the journal some of his poems. Ford had collaborated with Conrad, each of them recognising that the traditional structuring of the novel in direct authorial narrative and contrived dramatic climaxes was exhausted. Ford saw the business of the novelist as to render, not to narrate. The novel that succeeds in representing life will be a sequence of selected impressions rather than an orderly and strictly chronological narration. Such impressions enable the author to be forgotten. The dynamic will arise, not from staged set-pieces representing moments of crisis, but from carefully juxtaposed actions or situations in themselves individually innocuous but sparking electrically by what their conjunction implies or reveals. Thus the reader loses the awareness that he is reading: he is immersed in a cunningly devised verisimilitude.

Ford's Tudor trilogy, *The Fifth Queen* (1905), *Privy Seal* (1907), and *The Fifth Queen Crowned* (1908), unfolds the story of Katherine Howard with vivid dramatic precision. As an exercise in recreating the antique past with sumptuous detail and yet focusing on the characters' every mood and movement with felt sympathy, it is remarkably effective. Yet looking back on it later, Ford defined the trilogy as 'nothing more than a *tour de force*, a fake more or less genuine in inspiration and workmanship, but none the less a fake'. What he meant becomes clear on reading *The Good Soldier* (1915), a contemporary study of tragic passion narrated by an American, John Dowell. The 'good soldier' is Dowell's friend, Captain Edward Ashburnham, an English gentleman. Dowell's wife, Florence, pretends to have a bad heart, and thus deceives him with other men, including Ashburnham. Both Florence and Edward eventually commit suicide. Ashburnham's young ward, whom he loves, goes mad. Leonora, his wife, survives to remarry. What gives the book its .power is the diversity of interpretation which it can accommodate. Dowell gradually emerges as an unreliable narrator — not because he is dishonest but because he is too emotionally involved, too much of 'a case' himself. Ford succeeds in his aim of entangling the reader in a complex network of situations where scattered clues tease and enlighten him in his search for understanding of the personalities confronting him.

When war came Ford, already forty, went into the army and saw service at the front. Back in England after the Armistice he found a changed world and started his tetralogy, *Parade's End*, in which he determined to 'register my own time in terms of my own time'. It covers the period from 1910 to the post-war world and moves from pre-war country-house week-ends and suffragette demonstrations to the trenches and the regions behind the lines. Christopher Tietjens, the hero, son of a Yorkshire landowner, a heavily built 'meal-sack' of a man, is tricked into marrying a worth-less woman, Sylvia, through excess of decency. His integrity and frankness, his refusal to compromise principles, land him in a mess. He becomes an easy target for false accusation, rumour, innuendo, and scandalmongering. He never defends himself ('he preferred it to be thought that he was the rip, not his wife the strumpet'). As a civil servant he pays for being too clever and honest; as an officer in the army he pays for being too considerate of his men. He joins up because he can't bear to be part of the 'brains' that play with lives. He is the idealist who makes everyone else uncomfortable and therefore must be stoned. He suffers a running campaign of denigration and torture from his wife and those in authority whose sympathy she enlists. He finds solace in a decent girl, Valentine Wannop, daughter of an old family friend, but will not take advantage of her love until the war has finished and put an end to the system of values such delicacy represents.

In the four volumes, *Some Do Not* (1924), *No More Parades* (1925), *A Man Could Stand Up* (1926), and *Last Post* (1928), Ford represents the passing of an age of which Tietjens is an ideal symbol, and its supersession by another whose values are alien to him. The war, which effects the change, is pictured with cool detachment and yet with fierce impressionistic vividness. Ford's placing of events bypasses chronological sequence. The narrative leaps forward and then gaps are filled in by flashbacks. Portrayal of the outer scene is interleaved with the inner life of agitation and reflection. At one and the same time, in the stress of battle, the mind may be focused on the immediate and yet also fixed on home. National and military affairs are mingled with private and personal matters. Ford is sensitive to the mud and the blood but also alert to the way a free-spoken critical general is being purposely deprived of men so that the enemy will break through in his sector and he can be packed off home where he can't be a nuisance. That is war, hideous and brutal, yet a ridiculous game too — 'seven to ten million men . . . all moving towards places towards which they desperately don't want to go'. The story reaches a full cadence when Tietjens and Valentine are united on Armistice Day at the end of *A Man Could Stand Up. Last Post* is an epilogue. It provides a post-war happy ending which Ford later came to think over-sentimental.

Ford was an impractical fellow in the mundane affairs of life and his relationships with women were notorious. His liaison with Violet Hunt, daughter of the painter A. W. Hunt, led to public scandal when Ford's legal wife took her to court for publicly posing as such herself. Violet Hunt's reminiscences, *The Flurried Years* (1926), paint a lively portrait of Ford in pre-war days, while a later mistress, the artist Stella Bowen, left a moving study of him at the time when he was working on *Parade's End* in her book, *Drawn from Life* (1940). Ford himself was an entertaining raconteur and his volumes of reminiscence, *Thus to Revisit* (1921), *Return to Yesterday* (1931) and *It was the Nightingale* (1934), are a mine of lively, if frankly unreliable, impressions of the literary world of his day. He wrote poetry too in his early years. His doctrine of Impressionism linked him naturally with the Imagists. Hence his influence upon Ezra Pound (1885–1972), the American poet from Idaho, a dominant figure in London in the Modern Movement between 1908 and 1921. He never concealed his admiration for Ford and on his death in 1939 he wrote appreciatively,

For the ten years before I got to England there would seem to have been no one but Ford who held that French clarity and simplicity in the writing of English verse and prose were of immense importance as in contrast to the use of a stilted traditional dialect, a 'language of verse' unused in the actual talk of the people, even of 'the best people', for the expression of reality and emotion . . .

Pound was in at the inception of Imagism and later described how he, Hilda Doolittle, and Richard Aldington agreed in 1912 upon the three principles:

1. Direct treatment of the 'thing' whether subjective or objective.
2. To use absolutely no word that does not contribute to the presentation.
3. As regarding rhythm: to compose in the sequence of the musical phrase, not in sequence of a metronome.

(See T. S. Eliot (ed.), *Literary Essays of Ezra Pound* (1954).)
   Pound, a flamboyant and aggressive personality, was an energetic propagandist, an indefatigable sponsor of new writers, and a vital if sometimes slapdash theorist on behalf of the *avant-garde*. T. S. Eliot dedicated *The Waste Land* to him as '*il miglior fabbro*', the better craftsman, and certainly Pound's technical equipment was immense: but there is some discrepancy between the impact of his personality on the literary scene of his day and the impact of his poetry itself. The poetry is the work of a literary scholar soaked in the

culture of the past. In *Homage to Sextus Propertius* (1919) Pound adopts the *persona* of a Roman elegiac poet of the first century B.C. who had connections with the imperial house. He suffered an anguished love affair with a Roman courtesan and sought consolation in art. Propertius is a forceful writer with a sharp visual imagination and a sense of the legendary past, whose highly individual style registers abrupt transitions of thought and mood. Pound's free rendering of this poet has been praised by classicists for its sensitivity to Propertius's manner. In *Hugh Selwyn Mauberley* (1920) Pound adopts the *persona* of an imaginary late nineteenth-century English poet. In each of these impersonations Pound chose a figure surrounded by the rich bric-à-brac of a decadent culture, and the influence of Browning's dramatic monologues is apparent. So it is too in Pound's life's work, the *Cantos*, published over many years. They bring the stuff of past centuries within the compass of a twentieth-century imagination, assembling characters and perceptions from widely scattered periods of history, Classical, Renaissance, Oriental, and European. Poised pastiche and vernacular colloquialisms are alike alive with energy and wit. But the predilection for what is fully accessible only to cultivated minds, which is evidenced again in his translations and adaptations of Chinese writings and of the Provençal songs of the troubadours, seems to distance Pound's practice from those principles of 'clarity and simplicity' which he praised in Ford. It is in the early poetry of T. S. Eliot (1888–1965) that the theory represented in Aldington's original Imagist manifesto seems to bear fruit.

IV T. S. Eliot

Eliot was born in St Louis, Missouri, son of a well-to-do Unitarian businessman whose seventeenth-century ancestor had emigrated to New England, where the family still had a holiday home. It was an area which Eliot learned to know better still when he became a student at Harvard in 1906. Like the Mississippi at St Louis, the New England scenery and especially its coastline, which Eliot knew as an accomplished yachtsman, left its marks on the imagery of his poetry. After further studies at the Sorbonne, for a second time in Boston, and in Oxford, he settled in London to be involved with vital and innovatory literary personalities such as Pound, Wyndham Lewis, and Ford. His parents had looked for him to embark upon a distinguished academic career, and his choice of London and seeming obscurity dismayed them. His sudden marriage at a Registry Office in 1915 to Vivienne Haigh-Wood — a partnership that was doomed to end in separation — deepened the rift. He worked first as a schoolmaster, having the young John Betjeman among his pupils at Highgate School, and then made a career in the Foreign Branch of Lloyds Bank, before eventually becoming a director of the publishing house, Faber and Faber.

Meanwhile Eliot's literary connections had rapidly increased. He knew Joyce, he visited Garsington, he was in touch with Bloomsbury. He edited *Criterion*, a literary quarterly, from 1922, and he was a regular reviewer for the *Times Literary Supplement*. Having joined the Church of England in 1927 and adopted British citizenship in 1928, he proclaimed himself a 'classicist in literature, royalist in politics, and Anglo-Catholic in religion'. In literary terms perhaps Pound was the most influential personal contact, but study of the French symbolists from Baudelaire to Valéry, of Laforgue, Dante, the Elizabethan and Jacobean dramatists, the seventeenth-century Metaphysical poets, and the philosophy of F. H. Bradley took its place in moulding the mature man alongside Aristotle, Hindu and Buddhist writers, St Augustine, St John of the Cross, the King James Bible, and a vast store of nineteenth-century poetry Eliot carried in his head. Threaded into his work through verbal reminiscences from these multifarious sources are the contemporary accents and idioms, reproduced with uncanny fidelity, of the society drawing-room or the London street, the opera-house foyer or the public bar.

Prufrock and Other Observations (1917), *Poems* (1920), and *The Waste Land* (1922) together represent a momentous literary breakthrough. There is no question of turning the back on the past or on even the most obvious of stanzaic patterns, but neither in tone nor in sensibility is there any trace of the Georgian.

Webster was much possessed by death
And saw the skull beneath the skin;
And breastless creatures under ground
Leaned backward with a lipless grin.

(Whispers of Immortality')

In 'The Love Song of J. Alfred Prufrock' a living voice is at our ear but narrative elaboration is eschewed. The enigma of who and where and why and how, superimposed upon the ambiguities of a character who has measured out his life 'with coffee spoons' and is lost in his own inert failure to come to grips, focuses a universal burden of contemporary insecurity and inadequacy upon the individual's lack of footing and purpose. The rejection of decisiveness and heroism initiates a theme deep in Eliot's thinking. The poem voices a pre-conversion mentality. Prufrock is 'Rock-proof'.

And I have seen the eternal Footman hold my coat, and snicker,
And in short, I was afraid.

Yeats, like others, early complained that Eliot's poetry was 'grey, cold, dry'. Yet Eliot's gift for ironic juxtaposition sauces his drabbest images with piquancy. The dingy London scenery of 'Preludes' — the broken chimney-pots and the steaming cab-horse, the hair in paper-curlers and the yellow-soled feet clasped in soiled hands — evokes the cry:

I am moved by fancies that are curled
Around these images, and cling:
The notion of some infinitely gentle
Infinitely suffering thing.

The word 'curled' hits the ear like a gong because it echoes the earlier line, 'You curled the papers from your hair'. Again the prostitute of 'Rhapsody on a Windy Night' has the border of her dress 'torn and stained with sand' and seems to be related to the girl in The Waste Land with broken finger nails on Margate sands, but she is given potential Beatrician status by the Dantean echoes and the lamp on the stair. It is this fitfully glimpsed radiance, the momentary echo of the song of nightingales or mermaids, the sunlight woven in a girl's hair, or the imminent approach in the juvescence of the year of 'Christ the tiger' that dislocates any simplistic response of disillusionment to disillusionment. Eliot is superficially the most undemanding of poets in his personal self-imposition upon the reader, and yet, such is the power of impersonality harnessed and ridden astride, that he never leaves the reader alone.

The Waste Land brings into play not only some thirty years' accumulation of pondered sensation and emotion, and the technique of managing in concert the rhythms of conversation and of highly formalised versification, but also a now fully developed capacity to compress moments of the historic past into verbal clusters of rich connotative substance by direct quotation, echo, or allusion. These devices came to Eliot's hands at a time of convalescence from a breakdown. It was a time at which the sensitive poet saw around him the ruins of post-war Europe. The attempt to render some poetic account of a fragmented culture and an artistic inheritance of shattered débris fused with the perfecting of a style exactly appropriate to the need. The movements of the poem may be related to the Grail legend and the story of the Fisher King who figures in fertility myths. But these thematic strands are only two among many recurring threads and Eliot, who supplied some Notes for the poem, later came to regret that he had 'sent so many enquirers off on a wild goose chase after Tarot cards and the Holy Grail'.

The poem defies reading as a narrative sequence. The grave and the trivial, the homely and the momentous, the ornate and the sordid, succeed each other in images which string a moment of blind ecstasy in love alongside the chatter of a clairvoyante reading her cards, the procession of war dead flowing over London Bridge alongside a Websterian memory of the Hound of heaven digging up corpses. More sustained passages present the seduction of a London typist by a house-agent's clerk so numbly that love, joy, and meaning are all flattened out under drab, unfeeling habituation, and record vulgar gossip between working women in a London pub about demobilised husbands and aborting pills. In such episodes a definable locale and a decipherable situation emerge. But for the most part Eliot is content to let the gathered remnants, the hoarded souvenirs, the swept-up rubbish of a broken civilisation with its unslaked spiritual thirst bear unglossed witness to the modern condition.

Eliot's baptism in the Church of England in 1927 marked the turning-point which in poetic terms produced *Ash Wednesday* (1930), a poem of prayer and penitence. It is a stepping-stone between the studies of disintegration and re-integration made in *The Waste Land* and *Four Quartets* respectively. Though the poem makes much of the penitent's need to lay no claim upon the distractions of the sensuous and suggests a spiritual need for ascetic self-denial, yet the image of broken humanity restored is implicit in crucial echoes of *Ezekiel*. 'Shall these bones live?' and 'Prophesy to the wind' together point to the reconstitution of the dismembered body and thus prepare the ground for replacing the scattered Sybilline leaves of *The Waste Land* with the infolded, living rose-leaves of *Four Quartets*.

Four Quartets is a work of epic scope in enquiry and celebration. The four poems, 'Burnt Norton' (1936), 'East Coker' (1940), 'The Dry Salvages' (1941), and 'Little Gidding' (1942), make a meditative study of the relationship of time to eternity as presented to man by those moments and experiences in which he finds time transcended. But Eliot brings to this philosophical quest the gathered experience of a lifetime caught in image after image of such packed symbolic substance and such subtle connotative reach that the whole verbal structure is a fabric ringing with echoes and harmonics. These echoes and harmonics have thematic relationships that bind the work together with the kind of network of correspondences which Joyce had exploited in *Ulysses*. The technical basis of Eliot's method is musical. The philosophical basis is a realisation of experience in sacramental and incarnational terms — a recognition of life as interpretable by the garnering of high moments of transcendence and transfiguration without which our 'waste sad time' here is 'ridiculous'. The setting of the successive quartets in locations significant in the poet's personal pilgrimage and carrying also wider symbolic reference enables him to blend the personal with the historic and the cosmic. The Christian assessment of the human situation and human destiny is deeply ingrained in the total articulation, as the sustained image of the earth as a hospital illustrates.

> The wounded surgeon plies the steel
> That questions the distempered part;
> Beneath the bleeding hands we feel
> The sharp compassion of the healer's art
> Resolving the enigma of the fever chart.

Eliot played his part in the revival of poetic drama, first by supplying choruses for a religious pageant, *The Rock* (1934), and then by writing *Murder in the Cathedral* (1935) for the Canterbury Festival. The martyrdom of St Thomas à Becket provided Eliot with the opportunity to bring together the form of classical tragedy utilised by Milton in *Samson Agonistes* and the allegorical machinery of the Morality play. The use of Tempters from the old psychomachic drama allowed Eliot to externalise the spiritual conflict in Thomas between the claims of God and of Caesar, the call to martyrdom and the attractions of worldly pleasure and power. At the same time a classical Chorus of Women of Canterbury elaborates the struggle in terms of universal human unwillingness to be involved when the divine challenge threatens painful upheaval. They are a chattering band of female Prufrocks. Eliot's patterned treatment of the theme of dying in order to live achieves its dramatic thrust through the liturgical comprehensiveness that confers on the action the status of myth and rite.

In later plays Eliot divested his scenario of all such built-in guarantees of solemnity and profundity. Eschewing overtly religious subjects and backgrounds, he endeavoured to float plausible plots from contemporary life, at once topically and convincingly peopled, and fraught with a cargo of symbolic correspondences below the water-line. In the successive plays, *The Family Reunion* (1939), *The Cocktail Party* (1949), *The Confidential Clerk* (1953), and *The Elder Statesman* (1959), the pressure of symbolic freight is gradually reduced without being thrown overboard, and the conversation on deck is correspondingly relaxed from conscious poetic constraints.

Eliot also assumed a mantle of commanding authority as a critic. He edited the *Criterion* from 1922 to 1939. In a series of critical books, beginning with *The Sacred Wood* (1920) and including *The Use of Poetry and the Use of Criticism* (1933), *Elizabethan Essays* (1934), and *Notes towards the Definition of Culture* (1948), he emerged as an oracular arbiter, precise and lucid in his judgments, with a rigorous scale of values, a deep feeling for tradition, and a hearty dislike for writing that is vague, indisciplined, remote from living language, or self-indulgently subjective.

V James Joyce

Eliot was quick to recognise the quality of James Joyce (1882–1941). 'Mr Pound, Mr Joyce, and Mr Lewis write living English,' he wrote in the magazine, *The Egoist*, in 1908. Joyce, a self-exiled Irishman, spent his mature life on the continent while focusing mentally in his work on the city of his birth and upbringing, Dublin. He was the son of a strange, shiftless fellow who had inherited property, had been pensioned off at the age of forty-two from his post as Collector of Rates in Dublin, and suffered a steady social decline. Extravagant, talented, a fine singer with a voluble and thirsty tongue, he led his suffering wife and family from house to house into increasing squalor as money ran out and landlords went unpaid. The young James Joyce's schooling at Clongowes Wood College, County Kildare, and Belvedere College, run by the Jesuits, gave him a sound education, in languages especially; he won several academic prizes, and he went on to University College, Dublin, in 1898 to take his degree in modern languages four years later. Joyce's early Catholic piety seemed to destine him for the priesthood, but he rejected first the priestly vocation, then the Church itself, choosing for himself rather the calling of the dedicated artist. He early came under the influence of Ibsen and this played its part in separating him from the ideals of those who supported the new national theatre. After taking his degree he went to Paris, but was recalled in 1903 by the impending death of his mother. When he returned to Paris the following year it was to shake the dust of his native land from his feet, and he took with him Nora Barnacle, a girl from Galway with whom he spent the rest of his life and whom he married, for the sake of their two children, in 1931.

The Joyces lived for ten years mostly in Trieste where Joyce earned his living by teaching English. They moved to Zurich, Switzerland, during the war, returned to Trieste for a time afterwards, then settled in Paris until the Second World

War dislodged them. Joyce's work and his family life were his two crucial priorities, and he suffered personally both from cataracts which necessitated painful operations on his eyes and from the developing schizophrenia of his daughter, Lucia. Among the many admirers and disciples who gathered round Joyce as his publications made the quality of his work known was the young Samuel Beckett who shared in some respects his alienation from his homeland. For Joyce could not embrace the tenets of the Irish literary movement nor enter with conviction into the political struggle for independence. He was at once at loggerheads with the Irish Catholic community and deeply immersed in the Thomist rationale, the symbolism and sacramentalism of the faith he rejected. He was at once at loggerheads with contemporary cultural and nationalistic Irish movements and deeply immersed in the stuff of Irish life — its capital, its people, their talk, their humour, their melancholy, their sentimentality, their irony, their bitterness. He was too individualistic to identify with their cause and too European to be content with their intellectual environment. Perhaps he loved his home city too sentimentally to be able to risk sharing the paralysis of action such sentimentality could impose.

Joyce's book of short stories, *Dubliners* (1914), pictures a variety of Dublin inhabitants, first children, then in successive stories older people, trapped by the pervasive mental frustration of the Irish capital. 'I call the series *Dubliners*,' he wrote to C. P. Curran when he started working on the stories, 'to betray the soul of that hemiplegia or paralysis which many consider a city.' In the story 'Eveline', a Dublin girl, weary of her tedious job and her cruel father, has the chance to escape to a new life with a sailor who has made good in Buenos Ayres and wants to marry her. The dreams for the future he opens up represent a break with all that has fettered and repressed her. At the last moment she clings to the iron railing at the docks, mentally and morally incapable of following her suitor as he embarks. The reversal of hopes, dreams, aspirations, and ideals is presented in several instances of such sudden awakening and disenchantment. The Dublin Joyce condemned and forsook in 1904 as paralysed was the stirring Dublin of the new Irish Theatre, of Yeats and Moore, of Russell and the Gaelic League, the Dublin from whose political and cultural ferment the independent Irish state was to be born. But Joyce was no doubt conscious of the epic writer's need to distance himself from his subject. His work unites intimate projection of self with distanced judgment upon self, and it unites intimate projection of Dublin with distanced judgment upon it. The artist offers up his city as well as himself that the reader may enter upon an epiphany.

A Portrait of the Artist as a Young Man (1916) lays childhood, youth, and early manhood on the altar. Stephen Dedalus's upbringing and schooling parallel Joyce's own. This is one of the century's most penetrating records of growing up. It presents a sensitive youth responding both to the promise held out by the education and the tradition he is brought up in and to the reality of an environment which is at odds with its ideals and its ethos. Through the torment and inner conflict induced by the discovery of incongruity and hypocrisy he comes to self-knowledge and self-determination. Unforgettable episodes include the child's earliest memories, the boy's first visit to a prostitute, and the subsequent agony of guilt endured in a retreat. When Stephen, as a university student, finally decides to break out, his is a rebellion with a difference:

I will not serve that in which I no longer believe, whether it call itself my home, my fatherland, or my church: and I will try to express myself in some mode of life or art as freely as I can and as wholly as I can, using for my defence the only arms I allow myself to use — silence, exile, and cunning.

There is an element of disciplined self-dedication in Stephen's outburst, and that note marks the rest of Joyce's career. Stylistic acrobatics in the *Portrait* render changes of vocabulary, idiom, and prose structure appropriate to the various stages of the hero's development from infancy to studenthood. Even in the excesses of spiritual self-castigation style matches substance. This proved to be a preliminary canter over the field of infinite stylistic adaptability. In Joyce's seven years of labour on *Ulysses*, from 1914 to 1921, he experimented with a vast range of stylistic devices including pastiche and parody from the worlds of literature, scholarship, journalism, and commerce. He broke through the fetters of syntax in representing the flow of inner thought and feeling, and invented a system of annotational continuity that strings together unstructured impressions, mental jottings, ejaculations, evanescent half-thoughts, and the fleeting inarticulacies of cerebral and gut reaction that trail off into reverie or reminiscence. He experimented with prose that approximates to music in the manipulation of phrase, word, and syllable to match the techniques of musical development by figure and motif, in the mimicry of rhythmic patterns, tonal contrasts, and the instrumental *timbres* of strings, wind, and percussion. He drew his form of prose presentation now from standard narrative techniques, now from drama, now from journalism, now from encyclopaedias, and now from the verbal litter of hoarding and shop-window, of advertisement and catalogue, of theatre programme and textbook, of ballad and sentimental song.

Joyce's search was for the comprehensiveness and universality of the classical masterpiece. His subject was the Dublin of his young manhood, its life cut off in cross-section and put under the microscope on 16th June 1904. For the basic structure of the book he turned to Homer's *Odyssey*. The lost hero of classical antiquity, separated from wife and home, searched for by his faithful son, tossed about from adventure to adventure in the ancient world of monsters and giants, whirlpools and drugs, temptresses and enchantresses, becomes Leopold Bloom, a Dubliner, a Jew, displaced, rootless, walking the Dublin streets about his daily business as advertising agent, tempted by its barmaids, lured by its shop-windows, rejected by its sentimental nationalists, threatened by its aggressive nationalists, and bearing in his mind all day the image of his Penelope at home, Molly, emotionally torn from him by her adultery with an impresario, 'Blazes' Boylan. And his searching son? That is Stephen Dedalus of the *Portrait*. He went to France but was recalled by a telegram announcing his mother's imminent death. And now, still rejecting the fatherhood of God, of homeland, and of the ruinous wastrel, his father Simon Dedalus, he seeks for some compensatory 'fatherhood' as a spiritual anchorage. Bloom, the Jew to whom a son is so important as potential messiah, lost his own son by death in babyhood. The needs and hungers of three Dubliners are therefore ripe for fulfilment and satisfaction; for Molly, though she is sexually dependent just now on her lover, loves her husband and has been driven to infidelity by his fastidiousness, forbearance, and unassertiveness.

T. S. Eliot described Joyce's running parallel between contemporaneity and antiquity as 'simply a way of controlling, of ordering, of giving a shape and a significance to the immense panorama of futility and anarchy which is contemporary history'. Yet the Homeric parallel is but an artificial and external framework, and far more important in giving shape and significance to the vision of Dublin life is the elaborate system of parallels, symbols, and correspondences by which further historic and cosmic dimensions are suggested, and by which the social, cultural, and spiritual problems of twentieth-century man are focused on the main characters of the book.

Joyce's refusal to treat *Ulysses* as the consummation of his artistic pilgrimage dismayed even fervent admirers. He had gone as far in verbal experimentation as most readers, even cultured readers, would be prepared to follow. Nevertheless he devoted seventeen years, from 1922 to 1939, to *Finnegans Wake* (1939), whose verbal quality may be judged by the fact that 'Finnegan' combines 'finis' as end with 'again' as recurrence, and 'Wake' combines the Irish sense of funeral celebration with the more general sense of awakening and resurrection. The circularity and inclusiveness thus represented in the title are characteristic of the book. Joyce developed the technique of connotative multiplicity to a stage at which only those versed in several languages, well-read in literature, and even acquainted with the personal biography of the writer could fully understand the text. But Joyce would have argued that such full understanding was not the only reward for receptive attention to a text which, when read aloud, is musically satisfying and continuously suggestive by force of that proportion of the multitudinous parallels that are taken in at each reading. The parallels, expressed in multiple puns and arduously contrived connotative densities, confer upon a Dublin publican's family and customers an ever-expanding series of identities and significances in the attempt to merge myth, history, and topical portraiture in a comprehensive representation of human life. The cyclic theory of history found in the eighteenth-century Italian philosopher, Vico, plays a part in the basic structure. The shifting identities and irrationalities of the dream-world provide a justification for the method.

VI D. H. Lawrence and Wyndham Lewis

In literary status and achievement Joyce is often matched with D. H. Lawrence (1885–1930), but the matching is that of opposites. For all his innovations Joyce, like Eliot, had firm allegiance to the cultural tradition of the West, while Lawrence, who was not a stylistic experimenter like Joyce or Eliot, rejected the past and sought his justification and inspiration in a self de-cluttered of historic frameworks, social or moral, and the artifices and inhibitions they imposed. The imaginative writer who ransacks the resources of words and of literary structure in the effort to produce a masterpiece is differently motivated from the writer who fastens on the human heart in order to lay its claims before the reader with sharp fidelity. The two priorities represent a duality with a long history in English fiction from the days of Fielding and Richardson.

Joyce fled Dublin with Nora Barnacle in 1904, and Lawrence fled Nottingham with his professor's wife, German-born Frieda Weekley, in 1912. 'Exile was to become the dominant note of Lawrence's life from this point,' writes John Goode, and goes on to describe *Sons and Lovers* as 'the novel that was to present the inevitability and representativeness of that exile'. (See B. Bergonzi (ed.), *The Twentieth Century* (1970), volume 7 of the *Sphere History of Literature in the English Language*.) If Lawrence's novel of growing up is then, like Joyce's, an *apologia pro suo exsilio*, it expresses no comparable predilection for silence or cunning. Joyce projects himself as 'Stephen', the first martyr, and Lawrence's *alter ego* is 'Paul', the apostle to the gentiles who made himself heard. Paul Morel's home situation parallels Lawrence's. His father is a Midlands miner, his mother a middle-class woman who has married beneath her out of passion and lives to reject the plebeian roughness and illiteracy of her collier spouse. She cherishes her four children in emotional separation from him. After his elder brother's death, Paul receives the full force of his mother's special affection, so possessive and demanding that it mars his chances of natural fulfilment in love for Miriam Leivers. In Miriam is portrayed Jessie Chambers who sent Lawrence's poems to Ford and sparked off the recognition of his talent.

As an autobiographical novel deeply revelatory of Lawrence's personal predicament the book provides a logical entry into the Lawrentian canon, yet it compels in portrayal not only of a working-class boy's adolescence but also of the Midlands environment, urban and rural, the two closely mingled in this mining area. Against this vivid background Paul's search for release from a family life where relationships are askew is tracked with subtlety. Indeed Lawrence's home brought him face to face with social tensions in microcosm. The middle class had culture and understanding but it was divorced from contact with the earthiness of natural man. The uneducated workers had vitality and warm mutual contact that the middle class lacked. Lawrence's wider environment reinforced and elaborated his sense of fractured human kinships. The mining villages were drab and shabby, the pit-heads and slag-heaps were dirty and unsightly, yet they were deposited, like the marks of a disease, in a rich countryside where the farming life of the centuries persisted. Lawrence's education, first at the hands of an evangelically-minded nonconformist mother, then at local elementary school and at Nottingham University College, where he took a teacher-training course, brought him knowledge of books, painting, and ideas, but it was culture funnelled through the narrow and parsimonious agencies of minimal state provision. It is not difficult to understand how an assertive, sensitive, and deeply moral intelligence should turn, in the role of imaginative writer, to analysis of 'mighty opposites' by which personal and communal life were jarred. There was urban world and rural world, industrial world and farming world, the world of culture and the world of animal vitality. Moreover, in mining areas the masculine way of life was starkly differentiated from the feminine way. The two did not fuse even in off-time in a household like the Lawrences' where the matriarchal home was uncongenial to the husband and the pub offered a continuance of the day's matiness and banter.

Such dichotomies supplied opposing poles by which Lawrence analysed his century's condition. He was motivated by passionate rejection of what confronted him and prophetic fervour to urge renewal of human vitality through man's physical rootedness in the natural order. Lawrence brought to this task nothing of the interest in technique that had possessed Ford and Conrad or of the verbal legerdemain that preoccupied Joyce. It was in keeping with his message that he should not have sought to impose contrived structure on to his recreation of the natural and human world. Lawrence's artistic power lies rather in the exactitude with which he embodies his awareness of cramping servitudes and urgent demands for release in the articulation and cross-play of his characters.

Sons and Lovers (1913) had been preceded by *The White Peacock* (1911) and *The Trespasser* (1912). It was followed by a drama, *The Widowing of Mrs Holroyd* (1914), a book of stories, *The Prussian Officer* (1914), and *The Rainbow* (1915), which was to have a sequel, *Women in Love* (1921). These two novels study succeeding generations of a Nottinghamshire family, the Brangwens. The rainbow is a symbol of the rounded perfection of relationship fulfilled; it is an image of the new world, whose glowing natural curve is to supersede the dead architecture of the old cathedral arch. In *Women in Love* the two sisters, Ursula and Gudrun Brangwen, are matched respectively with a young school-inspector who has a Lawrentian hatred of the tyranny of the machine and of cold intellect, and with a rich, handsome mine-owner's son who is more fitted to running a business efficiently than to opening himself to another in love. Subtle explorations are made of the collision between the way of instinctual rootedness in the rhythms of nature and the ways of social consciousness, of urbanism, and of industrialism. Lawrence's protest was against industrial progress for its cut-throat competitiveness and its encouragement to war, against mechanical progress for its standardisation of the ready-made and its diminution of individual creativeness, and against the intellectualism that dries up the springs of human vitality. He insists that the quality of man's life has to do with his relationship to his physical environment. He values the sense of mystery and laments its elimination by mechanisation. Yet he is no sentimentalist about human relationships. His notion of an ideal sexual partnership is one in which unblunted individualities clash fruitfully.

Frieda Lawrence's nationality and Lawrence's personal opposition to the war brought suspicion upon them when the war confined them to England and to a Cornish cottage. The frustrations then endured and the tensions of married life surfaced in the autobiographical content of *Kangaroo* (1923), a novel set in Australia which examines the inadequacy of fascism as a means of regenerating society and contains unsurpassed descriptions of the bush. In *The Plumed Serpent* (1926) the setting is Mexico where a new religious cult involves a mindless passivity in submission to the leader. The violence, the sexuality, and the mass hysteria reflect a passionate dissatisfaction in Lawrence himself as he pursues his doomed quest for natural affiliations that will free man's instinctual nature from the constrictions of self-consciousness. Lawrence's final parable, *Lady Chatterley's Lover* (1928), created a sensation and unexpurgated publication was banned until 1959. Sir Clifford Chatterley, paralysed below the waist by a war wound, is by his impotence a symbol of the moribund power that has ruled the country and defiled the landscape. His gamekeeper, Mellors, a classless Lawrentian freeman, answers the needs of Chatterley's frustrated wife, Constance. Lawrence underlines the collision of *mores* by giving Mellors a frank four-letter-word vocabulary for sexual organs and functions.

Lawrence's output includes novellas and short stories, such as 'England, my England' (1924), 'St Mawr' (1925), 'The Woman Who Rode Away' (1928), and 'The Virgin and the Gipsy' (1930), travel books such as *Sea and Sardinia* (1921) and *Mornings in Mexico* (1927), and works of direct polemic such as *Fantasia of the Unconscious* (1922). His numerous collections of poems began with *Love Poems and Others* (1913) and ended with the posthumous *Last Poems* (1932). Lawrence used poetry for autobiographical commentary, for recapitulating aspects of emotional experience explored in the novels, and for responding to the natural world. He moulds language malleably to his will in a free verse of remarkable flexibility. While recognising the kind of poetry in which completeness and perfection are embodied in exquisite form, he pleaded in his Introduction to *New Poems* (1918) for poetry of the immediate present which has neither static perfection nor finality but which is 'direct utterance from the instant, whole man. It is the soul and the mind and the body surging at once, nothing left out. . . . In free verse we look for the insurgent naked throb of the instant moment.'

Like Lawrence, Wyndham Lewis (1884–1957) was one of the great propagandists of modernism, and like Lawrence he lamented mechanical advance, but chiefly because it had been accompanied by a 'backsliding of the intellect throughout the civilised world'. It was to this intellectual collapse that he attributed the impoverishment of artistic expression. Ezra Pound and he invented the word 'Vorticism' to describe a movement that was a by-product of Imagism. Pound defined the development thus in the *Fortnightly Review* in 1914: 'The image is not an idea. It is a radiant node or cluster; it is what I can, and must perforce, call a VORTEX, from which, and into which, ideas are continually rushing.' Lewis edited the periodical, *Blast*, from 1914 to 1915. He was a painter of distinction known for portraits of Eliot, Pound, Edith Sitwell, and Joyce, and for celebrated cubist landscapes.

I am a novelist, painter, sculptor, philosopher, draughtsman, critic, politician, journalist, pamphleteer, all rolled into one, like one of those portmanteau-men of the Italian Renaissance.

So Lewis presented his credentials in introducing his lively autobiographical book, *Blasting and Bombadiering* (1937), which sheds light on his involvement with Eliot, Joyce, Pound, Ford, Hulme, and T. E. Lawrence, and upon his dislike for D. H. Lawrence. Lewis's emphasis upon intellect and objectivity made sympathy for Lawrence impossible. For Lewis the new movement was an attempt to get away from romantic art into classical art, from political propaganda into 'the detachment of true literature'.

Lewis expressed his views in philosophical and critical works like *Time and Western Man* (1927), *Men Without Art* (1934), and *The Writer and the Absolute* (1952), and returned again to autobiography in *Rude Assignment* (1950).

His public *persona* was that of an angry, aggressive prophet, loftily impatient with the artistic nonsense that bemused the masses and enriched its purveyors. He was burdened with an intelligence equally sensitive to the shallowness of current fashions and of discredited past conventions. His first novel, *Tarr* (1918), portrayed the bohemian life of pre-war Paris with devastating frankness and with a deft stylistic flamboyance. Lewis can be incisive and epigrammatic. His prose sometimes has a staccato explosiveness, and the reader is carried along on a current of restless energy. But the briskness soon loses its freshness. Awareness of the author rubbing his hands in self-congratulation intrudes upon the reader's responses. The lack of human sympathy gives Lewis's novels a wearying aridity. The managerial cleverness with which human beings are manipulated and mocked is not the badge of magnanimity or sensibility.

Lewis's abrasiveness, the cutting satirical edge, and the detachment alike from the ethos of convention, of Bloomsbury, of Lawrentian primitiveness, and of Forsterian liberalism, was not calculated to win friends. In *Apes of God* (1930) he directed his fire in comic irony on the arty circles of the 1920s. But by the turn of the decade he had already published *Childermass* (1928), the first volume of an intended tetralogy, *The Human Age*, of which two more volumes appeared long afterwards in 1955 — *Monstre Gai* and *Malign Fiesta*. The trilogy is set in a fantastic region beyond the grave. Two pilgrims from earth, Pullman and Satters, are present at an absurd tribunal outside a city, where a grotesque examiner and his rebellious examinees confront each other with nightmare dialectic. The men get inside the city in *Monstre Gai* to discover that it is under attack from Hell, whither they flee in *Malign Fiesta*. Moral, political, and philosophical themes adumbrated have their bearing on our twentieth-century world. But for all Lewis's sense of the menace of rottenness and the process of human corruption, the lack of clear moral affirmatives, defined or implicit, to counterpoise the satire, detracts from overall clarity and cohesiveness.

5

The post-war scene
The 1920s and 1930s

I Introduction

RHYS Davies, a young writer in London in the twenties, later described the exhilaration of the time in his autobiography, *Print of a Hare's Foot* (1969).

The Twenties . . . corruscated with intimations of complete personal liberty. The animated metropolis thrived in a sociable attempt at demolition of class attitudes, the Labour Party was intellectually respectable, and Freud a newly canonised redeemer. It was a time to be young in; and also industrious. God had lost his formal terrors, and the Communists of the Thirties were in bud. Bounty, especially from the enfranchised women, was rife. Necessities were dirt cheap, and death at a halt.

The relief was too hectic, the sense of liberation too feverish to last. Retrospectively the ways in which the young of the inter-war years grasped at the dawning of a new age have acquired an air of unreality. Even positive, sober achievements like the formation of the League of Nations in 1920 stand in subsequent memory wrapped about with an air of doom. How much more vividly does a sense of fatality hang over recollection of the antics of the Bright Young Things whom the jazz craze and the party craze swept into knocking their knees and jerking their bottoms in the Charleston in a vain attempt to escape the voguish 'boredom'. In the 1920s not even the remote past could be investigated without invoking Nemesis. When the Earl of Carnarvon's Egyptological researches culminated in the discovery of Tutenkhamen's tomb in 1922 it was popularly assumed that the curse of the Pharaohs would strike him down, and shortly afterwards he died in Cairo.

English literature has its own record of the frivolities and follies of the twenties. And it reveals much about the sombre experience of seeing post-war hope turned into hopelessness as governments failed to grapple effectively with slump and unemployment. The General Strike of 1926 was brought to an end without grave civil strife, and the following year the Conservative government's Trades Disputes Act (to be repealed twenty years later by Attlee's Labour administration) made general strikes illegal. But after the collapse of the New York Stock Exchange in 1929, the increasing number of workless men 'on the dole', the miserable privations of a life of bare subsistence in the depressed industrial areas, and the mass hunger marches from the North to London which they provoked made the feeble ameliorative measures to which government had recourse seem pathetically inadequate. Labour administrations were briefly in office in 1924 and from 1929 to 1931, when a coalition called the 'National Government' was formed with the Labour Prime Minister, Ramsay Macdonald, running in harness with the Conservative Leader, Stanley Baldwin. By 1935 Baldwin was himself in the saddle as Prime Minister. The coalition had split the Labour Party and given it an ineffaceable distrust of coalitions in peace-time. It was this Conservative-dominated National Government which increased its majority in 1935 and left the Tory Party burdened for decades with the blame for the failure to alleviate the distress of a generation for whom Lloyd George had promised 'homes fit for heroes' on their return from the battlefield.

The inter-war period was an age of rapid technological progress. The 1920s and 1930s supplied to the fortunate few several of the aids to good living which the 1950s extended to the many: cars, telephones, and electric appliances in the home. The magnificent airship R 101, bound for India laden with notabilities on its maiden voyage, came to grief on a French hillside in 1930, but Amy Johnson flew solo to South Africa in six days in 1932 and Major Seagrave touched 231 miles per hour in his record-breaking car, the 'Golden Arrow', in 1929. John Logie Baird gave a television demonstration in 1926 and a transatlantic radio-telephone was established in 1927. The British Broadcasting Company became the British Broadcasting Corporation under Royal Charter in 1927, and its services rapidly increased so that by the time the mid-1930s came major public events were being brought into the home all over the country. There was no lack of public drama to transmit. No sooner had George V died in 1936 and Edward VIII succeeded him than the new king's desire to marry a twice-divorced American, Wallis Simpson, produced a major national crisis with repercussions even in the Dominions, to which the 1931 Statute of Westminster had granted independence. When the king abdicated the whole nation listened to his farewell broadcast.

Reading habits in the inter-war period were affected by the development of secondary education, the redbrick universities, and adult education. The Workers' Educational Association (WEA) grew rapidly under the leadership of such men as R. H. Tawney, author of the formative study, *Religion and the Rise of Capitalism* (1926), who was its President from 1928 to 1944. Books for the growing intelligentsia made new thinking available to a wide audience in a number of fields. A. N. Whitehead, the mathematician, published *Science and the Modern World* (1926), Sir Arthur Eddington, the astronomer and physicist, published *The Nature of the Physical World* (1928), and Sir James Jeans, the mathematician and astronomer, published *The Universe Around Us* (1929) and *The Mysterious Universe* (1930). These popular books, like those of J. B. S. Haldane, the biologist, and Sir Julian Huxley, the zoologist, represent the soberer aspect of the inter-war mental climate. At the more rigidly technical level the books of scholars affect the public mind more slowly. J. M. Keynes, a member of the Bloomsbury Group, had published *The Economic Consequences of the Peace* in 1919, but the 'Keynesian era' of economic thinking which he inaugurated did not become a practicality until the 1940s. Keynes's radical ideas challenged traditional economic theory by adding to the limited monetary aspect of the subject an analysis of all factors affecting demand for goods and services.

In literature the 1920s, the decade of *Ulysses* and *The Waste Land*, of *Parade's End* and *Women in Love*, were plainly alive with creativity. But the 'difficulty' the common reader encountered in the works of writers such as Joyce and Eliot became a source of controversy just as the parallel experimentation in the increasingly fashionable work of artists such as Picasso did. Schisms were opened up in public reaction to art, music, and literature between the *cognoscenti* who understood and appreciated the 'new' and the public who were content to have the well-worn formulae repeated. This controversy induced new habits of classification. Writers were experimental or traditional, highbrow or middlebrow (for the 'lowbrows' didn't count). The middlebrows were allowed to get on with their job of entertaining the public, but the highbrows had to administer shocks by what they had to say or by the way they said it. They wrote for 'clever' readers — as, for instance, Bennett and Wells did not.

II Sophistication and Satire

Virginia Woolf and Aldous Huxley are cases in point. Virginia Woolf (1882–1941) demanded a fastidious literary sensibility, and Aldous Huxley (1894–1963) demanded some intellectual interests. Huxley's work cannot be discussed without reference to his view of life, Virginia Woolf's without reference to her view of the novel. Virginia Woolf's rebellion against Victorianism was not that of working-class-bred writers like Wells. The Bloomsbury Group, of which she was a key member, were more interested in sexual freedom for themselves than in economic freedom for others. Virginia Woolf's driving force as a novelist lay in her rejection of realism. 'We want to be rid of realism, to penetrate without its help into the regions beneath it,' she wrote in a review of Dorothy Richardson's *The Tunnel* in 1919. She cared little for the industry of novelists like Bennett who fabricated a model of life by heaping up facts. They were obsessed with inessentials and the effort to achieve 'infantile realisms'. The plotted novel of action with its artificial story-line, its logically ordered causes and effects, its staged characters, and its materialistic respect for externality, was superficial and no fit vehicle for getting to the centre of the mind's experience.

Virginia Woolf's earliest novels, *The Voyage Out* (1915) and *Night and Day* (1919), are not innovatory, but in her great novels of the 1920s and early 1930s she breaks away from external narration interspersed with dialogue to plunge the reader into the internal life of her characters. And those characters are not presented to the reader from the outside to be eyed and docketed. Instead the reader rides on the current of their thoughts and feelings, to experience the world and its inhabitants only as they encroach upon the characters' consciousness. The time-scheme of *Mrs Dalloway* (1925) is twenty-four hours in the life of a middle-aged woman, the wife of an MP, who prepares and gives a party at a time when an old friend whom she might have married has just come back from India. It is a natural occasion for mental recall of the past, and some variety of thought-texture is achieved by counterpointing Clarissa Dalloway's mental day with that of a shell-shocked suicide. *To the Lighthouse* (1927) fastens on two days separated by a ten-year gap. The first is a pre-war summer evening on which the Ramsay family, at their holiday home in Skye, plan a possible visit to a· lighthouse for the next morning. As night falls the weather makes it increasingly unlikely that the visit will come off. The hopes and disappointments of the children, and the sensitivity or insensitivity with which their parents treat them, are explored with subtlety. When time and the war have done their worst to the family, two of the children actually make this now highly symbolic trip in the last section of the book. In *The Waves* (1931) Virginia Woolf's journey into the inner lives of her characters is made without any concession to notions of plot or imposed design. Six characters, three male and three female, who know each other as children, then go their separate ways and gather only at reunions later in life, are with the reader, not as speaking actors but as reflecting consciousnesses. The medium of their contact with the reader is neither realistic conversation nor any attempted approximation to the flow of articulate thought and sensation, but stylised interchange of reflection – a kind of poetic by-product of external life.

Orlando (1928), a fantasy, traces the career of its hero/ heroine (he changes sex) through four centuries, and the imaginative dexterity is undeniable, but the personal impulse behind the book – to celebrate Virginia Woolf's love for Victoria Sackville-West – obtrudes its lesbian implications. *Orlando* stands apart from the main canon, culminating in *The Waves* and including the later novels, *The Years* (1937) and *Between the Acts* (1942), where Virginia Woolf's focus upon what she held to be the real stuff of life, located as it is in the secret places of the heart, enabled her to get rid of 'the old deliberate business: the chapters that lead up and the chapters that lead down; the characters who are always characteristic; the scenes that are passionate and the scenes that are humorous; the elaborate construction of reality' and to expose the denuded, unsheltered consciousness, unbegun and unfinished. So doing, she broke out of the masculine sphere of organising and codifying by the light of reason and brought feminine sensibility to bear on our moment-by-moment immersion in what reaches us through sense and emotion, imagination and memory.

Virginia Woolf's critical work, available in such volumes as *The Common Reader* (2 vols, 1925 & 1932), *Contemporary Writers* (1965), and *Books and Portraits* (1977), contains lively and discerning reviews of other writers, but her boldness in transforming the form and substance of the novel did not bring all *avant-garde* opinion to her side. Ezra Pound scorned her work. Even Edwin Muir complained in *The Present Age* (1939) that 'she writes about the ordinary passions of men and women as if she had been told about them by someone who regarded them as interesting but unreasonable . . .'

By an odd coincidence *Orlando* was published in the same year as *The Well of Loneliness* (1928) by Radclyffe Hall (1886–1943), one of the most talked-about books of the age. Radclyffe Hall's story of a woman afflicted by lesbian proclivities voiced earnest protest against social attitudes that made no allowance for sexual inversion. The book created a public sensation and was banned. It is highly sentimental and melodramatic. 'I would rather see you dead at my feet than standing before me with this thing upon you,' the heroine is told by her mother. But Radclyffe Hall and her companion, Una Lady Troubridge (who at one stage dabbled with Yeats in spiritism), challenged society head-on by the aggressive openness of their behaviour. No such publicity attended the liaison between Virginia Woolf and Vita Sackville-West (1892–1962), who was brought up at the magnificent ancestral home of the Sackvilles at Knole in Kent and married the diplomat, Harold Nicolson, himself a writer and journalist. Vita Sackville-West, a keen horticulturalist, wrote a pastoral poem about rural life in the manner of Virgil. *The Land* (1926) is a knowledgeable, observant, and unsentimental poem refined by deliberate craftsmanshp, but Vita Sackville-West became known to the public chiefly through her novel, *The Edwardians* (1930), which portrays life in an aristocratic mansion in the early years of the century with sharp definition of accepted *mores*. The book is enlightening on such matters as the relative cost of a staff wage-rise all round and of a single ball, and the Duchess's response when young Viola wants to go off and live on her own in London. 'Up to a certain point, people can sympathise with lovers — only, of course, they can never be received — but for a woman to go off with herself is unheard of . . . .'

Virginia Woolf reviewed the first volume of short stories by Aldous Huxley (1894–1963) in 1920 (*Limbo*) and complained that he was too well-read to be interesting. Huxley's erudition was wide-ranging. The grandson of the eminent biologist, T. H. Huxley, educated at Eton and Oxford, he early established himself as a cynical and witty commentator on his times. His registration of post-war society seems to mock an exhausted culture whose religion and morality are spent, whose ideals have evaporated, and whose notions of romantic love have faded into animal promiscuity. Yet the wit, the comic inventiveness, the scintillating dialogue, and the devastatingly ironic human portraiture give a brilliance and zest to the early fiction which often submerges disillusionment in laughter and exhilaration. These qualities endeared Huxley to the educated young of the post-war generation. The volumes of short stories, *Limbo, Mortal Coils* (1922), and *Little Mexican* (1924), perhaps because the form does not lend itself to polemical exploitation, contain some of Huxley's gayest work. The early novels, *Crome Yellow* (1921), *Antic Hay* (1923), *Those Barren Leaves* (1925), and *Point Counter Point* (1928), develop the technique of the conversation-piece which Huxley acquired from Thomas Love Peacock. Society house-parties and town-parties supplied Huxley with material, as did bohemian and intellectual coteries of the day. In *Crome Yellow* and *Those Barren Leaves* there are recognisable studies of Bertrand Russell, Ottoline Morell, and Norman Douglas.

Critics have detected the influence of André Gide on the structure of *Point Counter Point*, whose hero, Philip Quarles, is writing a novel, like Edouard in Gide's *Les faux-monnayeurs* (1926). The counterpoint weaves together the pursuits, largely sexual, of a number of couples with diverse attitudes and notions, and builds up a multiple thematic pattern with distinct contrasts of tone and mood on a principle analogous to symphonic development. The novelist-within-the-novel superimposes an additional counter-subject. Philip Quarles, like Huxley himself, experiments with 'the musicalization of fiction' but, for all his technical expertise, he is aware of deficiencies in himself of emotional sympathy which the born novelist would have. His opposite number, Mark Rampion, portrays D. H. Lawrence. 'Your Rampion is the most boring character in the book — a gas-bag,' Lawrence declared, while Huxley insisted that 'Rampion is just some of Lawrence's notions on legs'. The book also contains portraits of Middleton Murry as Denis Burlap, Augustus John as John Bidlake, Nancy Cunard as Lucy Tantamount, and Oswald Mosley as Everard Whebley.

Rampion is portrayed with admiration. Huxley was aware of the temperamental deficiencies he himself suffered as a prisoner of the intellect. He was too wise and essentially moral to be satisfied with a continuing literary career as a castigator of human silliness. Since he lacked the heart of the novelist, his positive response to the decadence of the day became that of the preacher. His *Brave New World* (1932) uncovered deep worry over the drift of modern civilisation. It is an 'anti-Utopia', a fantasy picturing life at a future date when current trends have produced their logical consequences. The date is 632 AF (After Ford) and science has mastered civilisation and trampled on real freedom. Genetic, psychological, and social engineering conditions human beings from the time of their incubation in the test-tube. Human needs and desires are manipulated for appropriate economic and social ends. Creativity and independence have been obliterated; the family has been abolished and privacy rooted out; emotion is indecorous, fidelity and passion are obscene; sex is fun and promiscuity compulsory. Hygiene is supreme. ('Streptocock-Gee to Banbury T to see a fine bathroom and W.C.') Diversity and individuality have been steam-rollered and sloganised into universal togetherness and standardised well-being. When a 'savage' is introduced from a reservation where pre-civilised specimens of our own type survive, he kills himself in despair.

After *Brave New World* Huxley increasingly used fiction for didactic purposes. *Eyeless in Gaza* (1936) advertises the doctrine of non-attachment propagated more directly in the polemical pacifist study, *Ends and Means* (1937). *After Many a Summer* (1939) and *Time Must Have A Stop* (1945) carry obtrusive philosophical freight. Neither these, nor the later light-weight novels, *Ape and Essence* (1949) and *The Genius and the Goddess* (1955), match up to the work of the young satirical Huxley. Speculative passion drove him to the study of mysticism and of less licit modes of transcendence, and non-fiction carries the main impress of his later role as sage and mystic, oracular moral legislator self-wrapped in the mantle of magus and seer. *The Doors of Perception* (1954) and *Heaven and Hell* (1956) set hallucinatory states induced by mescalin and lysergic acid alongside the beatific vision of disciplined mystics. The reduction of the mystical state to a matter of glandular chemistry equates with a continuing obsessional disgust in Huxley's fiction at the basic animal crudity of sexuality.

The young Huxley was included by Edith Sitwell among the poets in her serialised anthology, *Wheels* (1916–21), which assaulted the smug respectabilities of the social establishment and the decorous, faded sentimentality of literary 'Georgianism'. Though there is much that is tenuous and shallow in the series, it launched the Sitwells on their notorious career as literary iconoclasts taking on all comers. The Sitwell trio, Edith (1887–1964), Osbert (1892–1969), and Sacheverell (1897–), belong beside Huxley among the Clevers of the twenties. Their rejection of Georgianism was essentially a rejection of simplicity and homeliness by intelligence and urbanity, but the aesthetic aggressiveness of flashy aristocrats was calculated to gall not only the philistines. *Facade* (1922) struck the social scene like a bombshell. Edith's experiments in exaggerated rhythmic, onomatopoeic, and metaphorical effects were declaimed through a megaphone to the accompaniment of an appropriately jaunty orchestral background by the young Lancashire composer, William Walton. Parody and pastiche, metrical gymnastics, absurd noise-effects, and

metaphorical frolics ('The light is braying like an ass . . .')
made a heady diet when washed down with Walton's vintage
instrumental appetisers. But *Facade* was succeeded by *The
Sleeping Beauty* (1924), a romantic evocation of the world of
childhood — a childhood spent by the Sitwells in the family
mansion, Renishaw, and a villa in Scarborough. Edith's verse
alchemises nostalgic memories of places and persons into the
remote stuff of fairy tale, and it is festooned with luscious
and jewelled imagery, sometimes uncannily vivid:

> And underneath the cotton-nightcap trees
> Wanders a little cold pig-snouted breeze.

Edith Sitwell entered a third phase with *Gold Coast Customs*
(1929), which has been called 'her *Waste Land*', for it speaks,
she said, of a world 'that has broken down, but where a feverish, intertwining, seething movement, a vain seeking for excitement, still exists . . .'. The poem sets savage Ashantee orgies
and bloodshed, marking the death of a rich man and known
as 'Customs', alongside the society parties and the contrasting
squalor of the slums at home. Jungle rhythms and ghoulish
images give a throbbing, eerie intensity to the work. In her
fourth and last poetic phase, Edith Sitwell, now a Roman
Catholic, became a prophetic commentator on the human
scene during and after the Second World War. As such, she
drew upon the more public symbolism of traditional Christian
literature. Her 'Still falls the Rain' (from *Street Songs*, 1942),
born of air raids in 1940, parallels the incendiary downpour
with the saving rain of blood from the Cross. *Green Song*
(1944), *The Song of the Cold* (1945), and *The Canticle of
the Rose* (1947) also belong to this phase. It is a long literary
journey from *Facade* to the dignified oracular odes of Edith
Sitwell's last years. Yet, unlike Huxley's pilgrimage from satire
to vaticination, it is also a craftsman's progress in disciplined
mastery of a single art.

Edith Sitwell, a tall woman with an immense nose, liked to
appear in elaborate mediaeval or Tudor costume, heavily
decked with jewelry. The public gestures of the Sitwells
expressed scorn of the prosaic and the vulgar. Osbert proclaimed his opposition to philistinism, Public Opinion, and
'the rationing of brains'. In volumes of verse such as *England
Reclaimed* (1927) and *Wrack at Tidesend* (1952) he drew

witty satirical portraits in a lucid, fluent idiom, with the air of an amusing raconteur. But metrical structure is haphazard, conciseness is undervalued, and aphoristic acerbity is too rare. Though Osbert Sitwell had an early success with a novel about the social scene in pre-1914 Scarborough, *Before the Bombardment* (1933), his major prose work is his five-volume autobiography, *Left Hand! Right Hand!* (1944), *The Scarlet Tree* (1946), *Great Morning* (1947), *Laughter in the Next Room* (1948), and *Noble Essences* (1950). Details of the Sitwells' family life and the upbringing of the literary trio are fascinating, but too often the crowded pages of eloquent reminiscence and portraiture fail to distinguish between evocations that can be publicly savoured and those that retain only a private tang.

Sacheverell Sitwell has an immense list of publications that includes travel books and books on architecture and the arts, of which *Southern Baroque Art* (1924) is especially highly regarded. His work of autobiographical fiction, *All Summer in a Day* (1926), and the miscellany, *Splendours and Miseries* (1943), show the breadth of his interests. Fifteen published volumes of poetry were drawn upon for *Selected Poems* (1945). Reviewing his earliest efforts as poet, T. S. Eliot wittily adapted Matthew Arnold's criticism of Shelley. 'He tends in his weaker moments to fly off like a beautiful but ineffectual aeroplane, beating its propellor vainly in a tree.' Somehow the note of ineffectuality has lingered about his poetry. In his more serious work he tends to inhabit a world of rarefied aesthetic lyricism, and his vein of august grandiloquence suggests mummification.

The young Clevers of the twenties tended to sober with age. Rose Macaulay (1881–1958) is a case in point. To read Frank Swinnerton's account of her in *The Georgian Literary Scene* (1935) is to be confronted by a writer given over to post-war derision that washed its hands of serious concern for a race of cranks and sentimentalists, a woman impatient of human idiocy who has sympathy only for those who stand aloof from the prevailing folly and laugh. Rose Macaulay found her brilliant satirical vein in *Potterism* (1920). Mr Potter is a press magnate and his wife is a hack novelist. They represent conventional humbug, hypocrisy, selfishness, and tastelessness. They are cocooned in sentimentality and commercialised unreality. Their children and others of their generation make some attempt to reject and counter the hollow sham of their smugness, but idealism is no match for the monstrous tyranny of 'Potterism' and they have to capitulate. *Told by an Idiot* (1923) reworked the satirical vein on the religious tergiversations and successive ideological fads of a Victorian parson. Rose Macaulay's zest in making hay with unexampled human silliness provided a salty diet for the public. But Swinnerton's unease with Rose Macaulay's work was perhaps that of a sensitive artistic instinct. For there is an awkward incongruity between some of her accounts of human need and distress and her jaunty authorial voice. More earnest interests in her fiction, such as those of love and the generation gap, sometimes sit uncomfortably alongside the flippant exaggerations and the ironic cartoonery. The last novel, *The Towers of Trebizond* (1956), like some of its predecessors, is at least two books in one. There is light-hearted mockery of everyone's oddities from the voice of a gossipy woman in full spate: and there is also what Rose Macaulay herself called 'the struggle of good and evil in the human soul'.

The early success of the satirical novelist may prove to be a flash in the pan. David Garnett (1892–1981), the son of the influential critic, Edward Garnett, had youthful access to the Bloomsbury clique and related literary circles, and was to write three volumes of autobiographical reminiscence, *The Golden Echo* (1954), *Flowers of the Forest* (1956), and *The Familiar Faces* (1962). His first novel, *Lady into Fox* (1922), won high acclaim. In coyly prim prose it tells how Mr Tebrick remains loving and faithful to his wife when she is transformed into a fox. This fable in mockery of fidelity in marriage was followed by *A Man in the Zoo* (1924), the story of a man who makes a zoo more fully representative by exhibiting himself in a cage as a specimen of his kind. These quiet, inventive exercises seemed to hint at a potential distinction which Garnett's later novels scarcely realised. There was comparable early promise in the early work of William Gerhardie (1895–1977). Born of British parents in St Petersburg and brought up there, he was sent with the British Military Mission to Siberia in 1918. A lively account of his Russian experiences and of his subsequent entry upon the English literary scene is given in his autobiographical book, *Memoirs of a Polyglot*

(1931). His first novel, *Futility* (1922), tells the story of a young Englishman's unrequited love for a Russian girl against the background of the Russian revolution. The girl's father owns gold mines whose profits never materialise, but he is surrounded by squabbling parasitical hopefuls, and Gerhardie's mockery of Russian character is high farce. Inertia and failure to face reality are comic and tragic. Gerhardie turned his fire on English public figures in *Jazz and Jasper* (1928) (now re-titled *Doom*). Influential writers made the highest claims for Gerhardie, Lord Beaverbrook put his publicity machine behind him, he became a social lion, yet public acclaim was only very briefly and modestly translated into sales. *Pending Heaven* (1930) and *Of Mortal Love* (1936) received little attention. Gerhardie suspected that his early reputation for ironic sophistication and cynicism became a millstone round his neck. 'England had ceased to read his books once he had begun to write about Englishmen,' Michael Holroyd has written.

But there is no evidence that English people do not like to see themselves as victims of sophisticated mockery. Noel Coward (1899–1973) had great theatrical successes in the 1920s by portraying the frivolity, permissiveness, and neurosis of well-to-do post-war society. In *The Young Idea* (1923) a bright young brother and sister bring their long-divorced parents together again by a series of cheerfully deceptive machinations. The middle-aged heroine of *The Vortex* (1924) feeds the illusion that she is still young on affairs with her juniors. *Private Lives* (1930) pitches two former partners, now remarried divorcees, into adjacent honeymoon hotel rooms. Comparisons have been made between Coward and Wilde, and indeed the conversational ploys of the smart set are deftly manipulated by Coward. Dialogue simmers with fashionably brittle flippancies, but re-minted vapidities tend to be vapid and the wit is thinly spread.

Coward's successes in the London theatre of the 1920s were matched by those of a writer twenty-five years his senior, Somerset Maugham (1874–1965), widely known as a novelist. His *Of Human Bondage* (1915) was a resentful specimen of the protest novel in the tradition of *The Way of All Flesh*. The hero has a physical disability, lameness, to deal with (Maugham had a stammer) as well as the standard inhibiting agonies produced by parson—guardian, boarding-school, and the 'degrading bondage' of Christianity. Maugham had also written a fictional life of Gauguin, *The Moon and Sixpence* (1919), but his more celebrated novel, *Cakes and Ale* (1930), with its satirical portrait of Hugh Walpole, was still to come when he returned to the London theatre to repeat his pre-war successes with new plays such as *The Circle* (1921), *Our Betters* (1923), and *The Constant Wife* (1927). Their dialogue rings hollowly now. Flippant slickness masquerades as wit, scathing disparagement as satire. The supercilious cynicism is obsessive.

III Moral and Social Concern

There was little from new writers on the London stage of the 1920s to match the late efforts of surviving pre-war dramatists such as Shaw and Galsworthy. Sherriff's *Journey's End* was produced in 1928, and in the same year John van Druten's *Young Woodley*, banned from performance since 1925, reached the boards, and emerged as a touchingly unsensational story of a sixth-form boy's sexual awakening at a public school. Woodley ('My mother died when I was a baby') falls in love with the beautiful young wife of his crotchety housemaster. Everybody talked about the play when they weren't talking about *The Well of Loneliness*, but its framework of dated inhibitions guaranteed ephemerality. ('I feel dirty all over,' says Woodley, having picked up a shop-girl on the rebound.) There was topical controversy too about *A Bill of Divorcement* (1921) by Clemence Dane (pseudonym of Winifred Ashton, ?—1965). Set ten years in the future, the play presupposes that the then controversial Act allowing divorce of an insane partner has become law, and it explores the personal dilemma of a woman with a husband who escapes from an asylum after a fifteen-year confinement.

This is the lesser stuff of literature, on which too often the literary historian of the present century must turn his eye in the effort to give drama parallel attention with the novel and poetry. But in Dublin something new was afoot in the theatre of the 1920s. Lady Gregory discovered a second-generation dramatist for the Abbey Theatre in Sean O'Casey (1880—1964). O'Casey was a product of the Dublin slums and his first play to be performed, *The Shadow of a Gunman* (1923), is set in a city tenement during the Troubles. The heroine is shot by the Black and Tans for concealing a bag of IRA bombs. First-hand experience of the Troubles, the ordinary men and women involved, their passions, their sufferings, and their humour, provided the material for O'Casey's finest plays. His mastery of dialogue and his capacity to tackle the issues magnanimously gave quality to his work. *Juno and the Paycock* (1924) is again set in a Dublin tenement. The year is 1922 and the diehard republicans are in rebellion against the newly established Irish Free State with its constitutional dependence upon the British crown. Captain Boyle is the paycock ('peacock'), a vain, flamboyant, lazy Dubliner who struts from bar to bar while his burdened, struggling wife, Juno, pays the price of his thriftlessness at home. Her son John lost an arm in the 1916 rising and now, having lost his nerve too, is unemployed, while her daughter is on strike. Juno is at the receiving end while the rest of the family are indulging their lofty principles or their lack of them, in either case to identical cost in maternal suffering. The play is rich in humour, yet Juno's compassion and fortitude give her the dignity of a great tragic heroine.

O'Casey's next play, *The Plough and the Stars* (1926), goes back to trace the effects on a Dublin family of the preparation for the 1916 rising. Irish manhood is represented by a hero compounded of political fanaticism, rebellious fervour, and incurable vanity, while Irish womanhood pays the price in bereavement. In displaying the hypnotic potency of barbaric revolutionary rhetoric O'Casey utilised passages from the oratory of the rebel leader, Padraic Pearse. O'Casey's forcefulness in showing how such verbalism can anaesthetise the fibres of humanity in men blinded by spurious self-importance gives the play a rare dramatic thrust. The treatment transcends topicalities and partialities to a degree remarkable in a writer so personally close to his subject.

O'Casey, a communist who could not align himself with any Irish movement, political or literary, came to England and settled in Devon. When his play, *The Silver Tassie* (1928), was rejected by the Abbey management on Yeats's advice, O'Casey's alienation from his homeland became permanent. The play is a powerful representation of the effect of the

First World War in wrecking a strong young man physically, emotionally, and morally. Of later plays perhaps only *Red Roses for Me* (1942), built on memories of the Great Lock-out in Dublin in 1913, recaptures the emotional power of the vintage 1920s O'Casey. It has been argued that O'Casey's exile severed him from his source of inspiration and that he tried to do too much out of his own head in isolation from the realities he sought to explore. Certainly the later plays, such as *Cock-a-doodle Dandy* (1949), *The Bishop's Bonfire* (1955), and *The Drums of Father Ned* (1959), focus upon an Ireland conceived cerebrally, portrayed fantastically, and analysed with obtrusive polemical intent. O'Casey was no spent force, however, for he delivered himself between 1939 and 1954 of a lively six-volume autobiography of which the first four books are concerned with his Irish upbringing and the days of the Troubles: *I Knock at the Door* (1939), *Pictures in the Hallway* (1942), *Drums under the Window* (1945), and *Inishfallen, Fare thee well* (1949).

In terms of literary productiveness the Irish Troubles are perhaps second only to the First World War in twentieth-century literature in these islands. These events seem to provide, not just the living experience which is the raw material of literature, but experience so intensified that its embodiment in imaginative literature perhaps asks less of the writer's personal resources than is normally asked. Thus Liam O'Flaherty (1896–) from the Aran islands, who served in the First World War, then turned militant communist for a time and was involved with the republicans in the Irish civil war, impressed the public most with his third novel, *The Informer* (1925). Its hero, Gypo Nolan, is a Dublin policeman-turned-revolutionary who is expelled from his 'cell' and then betrays a comrade to the police for money. The comrade is trapped and killed. The retribution that follows is traced with blood-curdling rhetoric and is compounded of every sinister and brutal ingredient in the underground terrorism manual. Yet for all the book's crudity of conception and vulgarity of presentation, the reader's awareness of its frightening authenticity sweeps him along on the current of O'Flaherty's emotionalism. O'Flaherty was acclaimed by AE and Yeats. And indeed there is another side to his work. As well as novels of the Irish past such as *Famine* (1937), novels of war and violence, such as *The Assassin* (1928), and novels about post-revolutionary Ireland such as *The Puritan* (1931), he has published short stories whose simplicity and directness in dealing with peasants and with animals are in marked contrast with his more strident and sensational fiction.

An English writer who never sought the headlines but who quietly cultivated a rare craftsmanship as a short-story writer was A. E. Coppard (1878–1957). His collections have great versatility of theme and treatment. They include *Adam & Eve & Pinch Me* (1921), *Glorinda Walks in Heaven* (1922), *The Black Dog* (1923), and *The Field of Mustard* (1926). There are moving tales of human suffering, fantasies gossamer-like in texture, epiphanies that suddenly illuminate the prosaic, and ventures into the paranormal that end in a question-mark. Coppard's best tales are gems of compression, the product of exquisite workmanship.

The writer who invests in the elemental simplicities of rural life and allows the great public upheavals and the fashionable literary movements of the day to pass him by always runs the risk of neglect. T. F. Powys (1875–1953) buried himself in rural Dorset to live in seclusion and privation on a small allowance from his father and to write. For many years publishers rejected his work and when *The Left Leg* (1923) was at last published Powys was nearly fifty and he had a pile of manuscripts in his cupboard. Thus *Black Bryony* (1923), *Mark Only* (1924), and *Mr Tasker's Gods* (1924) quickly followed, and a novelist of unmistakable forcefulness and integrity emerged. He has been compared to Bunyan for the quality of his prose — his crisp, abrupt style that eschews rhetorical elegance and shapely cadence but has a sinewy, take-it-or-leave-it thrust in keeping with a down-to-earth portrayal of rural life which counters notions of idyllic rusticity.

Powys's vision of rural life in its comic and savage aspects, and his human portraiture with its extremes of self-effacing compassion and ruthless brutality, are rooted in a moral dualism that has led critics to speak of his novels as 'modern moralities'. Powys found the work of the eighteenth-century poet, George Crabbe, especially congenial and, like Crabbe, he unearths the seamier side of village life with its wastrels and ravishers, its drunks and tyrants. Mr Tasker, in *Mr Tasker's Gods* (1924), gets rid of his unwanted old tramp of a father by maddening his savage dog with the scent of his father's hat. The dog gets its teeth into the old man's throat when he visits his son, and the pigs, who have been fed on dead horse, polish off the corpse. In the same book there figures a saintly if ineffective drop-out in the Vicar's son, Henry Turnbull.

The danger of Powys's selective didacticism is that he may purchase moral sharpness at the cost of overstatement. A further danger is that allegory may produce contrivances so mechanical that the artifice seems unworthy of the implicit moral gravity. Some of the stories in *Fables* (1929), later re-issued as *No Painted Plumage* (1934), illustrate the danger. John Purdy, the family failure, chats with the waves before walking into them in 'John Purdy and the Waves'. In 'The Spittoon and the Slate' the two objects converse. The world's go-getters are under judgment in the former story and the despoliation of virgin beauty in the latter — where the local procuress for the squire, a familiar village functionary in Powys, supplies him in his cups with the innkeeper's fifteen-year-old daughter. Talking furniture and utensils can irritate, but a residue of genuine moral fervour lingers nevertheless on the reader's palate.

When properly disciplined, the allegorical method produced a fine novel in *Mr Weston's Good Wine* (1927). The village of Folly Down receives a divine visitation on a November evening. God has already appeared in Powys's *The Left Leg* as a travelling tinker called 'Old Jar'. Here he reappears as a travelling wine merchant, Mr Weston, offering two brands of merchandise, the Light Wine which is Love and whose price is the return of Love, and the Dark Wine which is Death and whose price is life itself. And the two are not two wines but one. Mr Weston longs to drink his own dark wine of death but cannot. He comes in a Ford delivery van accompanied by his (angelic) assistant, Michael. At his arrival time stands still and the human sheep and goats of the village come under judgment. The power of the symbolism, superimposed on a portrayal of village life in the raw, lies in its neatness, its subtlety, and in the pervasive ironic humour. Powys's last novel, *Unclay* (1931), in which characters from his early fiction reappear, is less successful artistically, yet significant in the unfolding of Powys's probing pilgrimage through some of the quirkier byways both of bitterness and of reconciliation.

T. F. Powys's two brothers, J. C. Powys (1872–1963) and Llewelyn Powys (1884–1939), were also writers. There has been a tendency to treat the brothers as a nest of geniuses, a trio of homespun Sitwells or trousered Brontës, but the three of them went their separate ways. Llewelyn Powys was more successful in books of travel sketches and essays than in his novels. J. C. Powys had a career as a free-lance lecturer on literature and several philosophical and other publications behind him when he turned serious novelist in his late fifties. 'Nature from the start had made me an actor,' he wrote in his *Autobiography* (1934). His oratorical fluency and fervour on the platform spilt over into his fiction. Where T. F. was the most economic of stylists, J. C. was the most profligate. The four Wessex novels, *Wolf Solent* (1929), *A Glastonbury Romance* (1932), *Weymouth Sands* (1934), and *Maiden Castle* (1936), are massive, powerful, but erratic books whose quality lies in fitful bursts of effervescence rather than in homogeneity of substance and conception. Vital characters tumble about the pages. Thematic development of symbolic contrasts, such as those between nature and intellect, is intermittently convincing. Sexual polarities are explored in places with teasing intensity, and human relationships are analysed with insight. But ventures into such subjects as the Grail Quest, the cults of pagan gods, and the power of the underworld, sit unevenly in their contexts. Nevertheless J. C. Powys is a writer with mastery in representing tense moments that have 'the power of generating palpable force', so that at many points the sheer thrust and sweep of his inventive vision compels and entrances.

The Powyses came of Welsh stock much diluted by English and continental connections. The *hwyll* is J. C.'s birthright. Something of the same compulsive zest is found in the work of the Surrey-born novelist, also of Welsh stock, Richard Hughes (1900–76), whose *A High Wind in Jamaica* (1929) pitchforks a family of five, the children of Jamaican settlers, into high adventure in the hands of pirates when they are voyaging to school in England. Youthful high spirits and youthful pragmatism, youthful naivety and youthful guile, stirred to action by adult criminality, culminate in brutality and farce conjoined. Certain facets of the child mind – the imbalance, the gift for fantasising, and the self-centredness –

are projected in isolation from the normal dependence on parental discipline and domesticity. Hughes, a virile stylist, had another success with a Conradian yarn of the sea, *In Hazard* (1938). He then directed his energies to a vast trilogy, *The Human Predicament*, intended to trace the development of European events that brought about the Second World War. Two volumes had been published when Hughes died, *The Fox in the Attic* (1961) and *The Wooden Shepherdess* (1972). They sweep from country to country, tracking down the movement of social and political action from 1923 to 1934. Events such as the Hitler Putsch of 1923, the Night of the Long Knives in 1934, the Slump, the General Strike of 1926, and the American Stock Market crash of 1929 are dramatically recorded. The documentation is often illuminating, as, for instance, in the presentation of middle-class 'skylarking' — playing at being engine-drivers and bobbies — during the General Strike, but the work lacks human centre and the reader is swamped under literary technique.

Celtic fluency is more winningly displayed in the novels of Lewis Grassic Gibbon (pseudonym of James Leslie Mitchell) (1901–35). Born and brought up in rural Aberdeenshire and Kincardineshire, he wrote a trilogy of novels set in his native countryside, *Sunset Song* (1932), *Cloud Howe* (1933), and *Grey Granite* (1934). They tell the life story of Chris Guthrie, the daughter of a crofter. The picture of rural life before the First World War is vivid. Chris is married in time to have her first husband, Ewan, snatched away by the war, coarsened by army life, and executed as a deserter. Later Gibbon pictures the post-war depression, shifting his view to take in town life in the 1930s. Gibbon's notable achievement was to invent a prose style that utilised the 'speak' of the region. Local mannerisms, rhythm, and cadence are exploited in a lilting idiom that seems to authenticise the exploration of peasant thought and feeling without gimmickry or patronisation. Gibbon sometimes overdoes the rhetoric of emotion, and narrative control is inadequately exercised in the later volumes, but the human chronicle is animated and it is rooted in the Scottish earth.

A different school of Scottish regionalism was represented by George Blake (1893–1961) from Greenock, who had served in the war and been wounded in Gallipoli. Blake resented the 'kailyard' writers' idealisation of rural Scotland and focused as a novelist on industrial Clydeside. *The Ship-builders* (1935) studies masters and men during the inter-war slump by the device of centring on a shipyard boss and a humble riveter who served together as officer and batman during the war. The social picture sets the record straight over inequalities such as the relative cost of the workers' necessities and the bosses' pleasures ('the riot of meaningless spending in a world slowly starving'). An ex-serviceman worker dies from gas-poisoning and his friend gets the sack for attending his funeral. The destitution around the deserted shipyards is feelingly depicted, and the shifts to which privation drove the unemployed:

He saw men selling apples from barrows, men oscillating between mendicancy and commerce with boxes of Russian matches on the pavements' edges, men selling briquettes from hired floats, and men imitating Charlie Chaplin to the music of piano-accordions.

Later novels include *The Westering Sun* (1946) and *The Five Arches* (1947). *The Piper's Tune* (1950) is set in Clydeside during and after the Second World War. Blake's strength is as a percipient and detailed documentor: his weakness is that he sacrifices intensity and dissipates cohesion with an overload of annotation.

While George Blake focused on Pagan's Clydeside shipyard during the slump, Storm Jameson (Mrs Guy Chapman) (1891–) chronicled the story of a Whitby shipbuilding family from the mid-nineteenth century to the 1920s in a trilogy of novels eventually issued as *The Triumph of Time*. Another Yorkshire-woman, Phyllis Bentley (1894–1977) from Halifax, did a similar service for the West Riding textile industry in *Inherit-ance* (1932), chronicling the story of a mill-owning family, the Oldroyds, from Luddite days to the post-war slump. But the historical texture is tenuous and the narrative padded with clichés. Romping through history and pronouncing the obsequies of once great Victorian industries supplied inter-war middlebrow novelists with a ready-made soundboard for plangent records of human pilgrimage from cradle to grave.

A somewhat sturdier social sensitivity stirred Winifred Holtby (1898–1935), from the East Riding, to portray Yorkshire life in *South Riding* (1936) with documentary fullness in respect not only of people's daily work and trials, but also of the public institutions and the local government machinery entangling their needs and efforts. The sociological density, with its obvious historical usefulness, far outweighs the pedestrianism of the work as a novel, for there is little imaginative intensity and the fictional inventiveness does not rise above the banal. Winifred Holtby represents, however, a generation of socially conscious women such as progressivist writers like Wells had championed. Her great friend, Vera Brittain (1896–1970), herself also a novelist, whose auto-biographical *Testament of Youth* (1933) gives an account of her own experience as a nurse during the First World War, tells in her tribute to Winifred Holtby, *Testament of Friendship* (1940), how Winifred served in France in the Women's Army Auxiliary Corps before turning journalist and becoming a director of *Time and Tide*. This literary and political weekly, founded by Lady Rhondda in 1920, attracted notable con-tributors.

Neither sketchy outlines of industrial history nor social documentation in tapestry woven of fictional banalities could express the deep disquiet of the inter-war years. The harsher notes of revolutionary disillusionment which were to ring out in the poetry of the 1930s were not loudly audible in the inter-war novel. But Walter Greenwood (1903–74), from Salford in Lancashire, knew at first hand the squalor and privations of life in depressed industrial areas as the number of unem-ployed rose to some three millions in the early 1930s. His novel, *Love on the Dole* (1933), put on record what the slump cost in human suffering and despair in the wastelands of the industrial north. His display of degradation in the world of dole-queues, demonstrations, the hated means test, the pawn-shops, and parish relief, stirred the public conscience. Greenwood achieves genuine pathos in handling the delicate cross-currents of reticence and strategic reservation in family intimacies against the background of the external indignities.

IV Popular writers

There was some degree of contemporary social awareness in *Angel Pavement* (1930) by J. B. Priestley (1894–), where the declining fortunes of a London firm of dealers in veneers and inlays are first dramatically revived, then utterly ruined by a big-scale adventurer. There is painstaking analysis of the human effects on various employees and their family circles. Priestley has a sense of humour and can turn a phrase, but he too often writes like an old-style essayist manqué. There is no theme that does not have its multiple variations intoned, and no human chatter is too unutterably vapid to escape record. Yet the authorial pose of J. B. P., the brusque, down-to-earth Yorkshireman from Bradford, growling out grumbles and bubbling with jocularity, self-opinionated taker-on of all the fortresses of cant and hypocrisy, became a national institution. *The Good Companions* (1929) was a runaway best-seller. A rambling novel in picaresque vein, it recounts the adventures of three characters who break out of their conventional roles in society and come together coincidentally to rescue a failing concert-party and revivify it as 'The Good Companions'. The break-out pattern of Wells's *Mr Polly* is here disinfected of social earnestness and given a dash of fairy-tale escapism by the idealisation of life on the boards. J. B. P., the Fieldingesque compère, his shoulders a-shake, helpfully nudges the reader, telling him when to laugh and when to cry.

Priestley the novelist never learned to restrain his own garrulity. When he turned playwright, theatrical exigencies pushed him some way towards the economy he lacked. *Laburnham Grove* (1933), *Eden End* (1935), and *When We Are Married* (1938) were among plays that established him as a domestic dramatist, amiably untaxing. The three plays setting out to probe the problem of time, *Dangerous Corner* (1932), *Time and the Conways* (1937), and *I have been here before* (1937), made suitably gentle demands on the audience's intellectual receptivity.

Another case of talent strained by over-production was that of Compton Mackenzie (1883–1972). *Sinister Street* (1913), a novel of growing up in the public school and Oxbridge milieu, was praised for its percipience by Ford and by Henry James. But by 1919 Virginia Woolf was slyly taking Mackenzie to task in the *Times Literary Supplement* for his facility in *Sylvia and Michael.*

The gifts which enable Mr Mackenzie to keep so large and various company in such incessant activity . . . are not negligible, although

whether they have anything to do with literature is an open question.
They include, to begin with, an astonishing swiftness of eye, so that he
has only to be in a room once in order to write a complete inventory of
its furniture.

More sympathetic critics have declared Mackenzie a kind of
English Proust for his skill in evoking the moods and atmosphere of the past, and indeed the six volumes of his *magnum
opus, The Four Winds of Love* (1937–1945), provide a
panoramic survey of the novelist's own times as experienced
by the central character. The ten-volume autobiography, *My
Life and Times* (1965–71), covers the same decades with
astonishing fullness of recall, but Mackenzie's popular reputation rests especially on his comic novels, such as the celebrated *Whisky Galore* (1947), one of his 'Highland romps'
which utilise the formulae of fictional farce with zest and
adroitness.

Hugh Walpole (1884–1941) also began auspiciously. His
short early novel, *Mr Perrin and Mr Traill* (1911), made its
point unforgettably in studying the claustrophobic tensions
and frustrations of the staff in a private boarding school. 'It
was the system, the place, the tightness and closeness and
helplessness that did for everybody.' The place is a breeding-
ground for madness and murderousness. Yet it is doubtful
whether Walpole ever again achieved a fully matching intensity
and thrust, though he was especially proud, and justly so, of
The Dark Forest (1916), the fruit of his experience in the
Carpathian campaign of 1915 in which he served with a Russian
medical unit before going to Petrograd as Director of the wartime British Propaganda Bureau there. *The Cathedral* (1922),
his Trollopian novel, is set in Polchester, a twentieth-century
Barchester, where a masterful, egocentric Archdeacon wreaks
personal havoc about him, ostensibly in dutiful pursuit of his
calling. But the moral point is made too heavy-handedly to
carry conviction. And, for all his expertise in narration and in
manipulation of characters, an air of laboured contrivance
hangs about Walpole's Lake District tetralogy, *The Herries
Chronicle: Rogue Herries* (1930), *Judith Paris* (1931), *The
Fortress* (1932), and *Vanessa* (1933). This family chronicle,
covering the last two centuries, reads suspiciously like a book
throughout. The formulas of the romantic novel are pressed
into service by an efficient marshaller of literary artifices.

There were less cumbersome ways of making a living than putting rugged Bradford or ruggeder Borrowdale on the literary map in *magna opera*. P. G. Wodehouse (1881–1975) concocted a recipe highly palatable to the public when he located in the supposed way of life of the wealthy and the aristocratic a world of hilarious make-believe, replete with country houses, leisured good-for-nothings, Bright Young Things, and forelock-touching village bobbies. In a series of novels which began with *My Man Jeeves* (1919) the moneyed bachelor, Bertie Wooster, an amiable chump with a talent for getting himself into a jam, and his unflappable valet, Jeeves, a more useful specimen of *homo sapiens* with a talent for putting other people in a jam, pit their combined resources against the prevailing empty-headedness of scheming spinsters, merciless aunts, dyspeptic peers, and various fatuous hangers-on. Here, and in the companion series of novels centring on Blandings Castle, Wodehouse created what seemed a riotously comic world where teetering on the edge of social disaster is a full-time occupation. What gives the books verve and originality is a rib-tickling idiom which stretches to absurdity recognisable idiosyncrasies of upper-class conversation, smart or slangy.

When the club-room habitués of the twenties and thirties were not chuckling over the capers of Bertie Wooster, they were rejoicing in the tough exploits of the chivalrous hero of *Bulldog Drummond* (1920), the 'demobilised officer who found peace dull' and figured dashingly in a series of novels by Sapper (pseudonym of H. C. McNeile) (1888–1937). That peace presented its challenges to many an ex-officer is evident from *Sorrell and Son* (1925), one of sixty novels by the best-selling writer Warwick Deeping (1897–1950). It is the story of a wounded ex-officer with a Military Cross who faces unemployment, starts at the bottom as a hotel porter, and struggles to affluence, all in the cause of giving his son a decent education. The book is a treasury of narrative clichés and middle-class snobberies, but it makes its point. Another club-room favourite was A. P. Herbert (1890–1971) whose comfortably innocuous irreverencies regularly took the mickey out of fashionable social tomfooleries in *Punch*. Prolific in prose and verse as arch-japester and wag, Herbert could assume the voice of the Modern Girl (see *The Topsy Omnibus*, 1949)

or outbard the Bard in Shakespearean burlesque at the drop
of a bowler. And while Father purred over A. P. H. at the
club, Mother was tucking the children up in bed after their
nightly dose of another *Punch* contributor, A. A. Milne
(1882–1956), who stumbled upon a new form of whimsy in
When We Were Very Young (1924) and *Now We Are Six*
(1927). The two volumes established his little boy, Christopher
Robin, as everybody's golden-headed youngster, happily and
healthily mixing up homely fact and exciting fantasy in nicely
tailored verses. The two prose books, *Winnie-the-Pooh* (1926)
and *The House at Pooh Corner* (1928), brought his toy animals
to life to assume characters consonant with their limpness,
their spareness, or their huggableness.

As for the young ladies, a lot of them were romping through
The Constant Nymph (1924) by Margaret Kennedy (1896–
1967). The numerous children of a composer, Albert Sanger
(he has a 'lordly relish for life'), are brought up in a liberated
bohemian atmosphere in Switzerland, to be left to find their
bearings when he dies. Tessa Sanger's girlish devotion to an
adult musician ('Innocence was the only name he could find
for the wild, imaginative solitude of her spirit') survives his
incongruous marriage into the philistine smart set, but she
dies when at last happiness is within her grasp. An unashamed
fantasia for plucked heart-strings, *The Constant Nymph* was
dramatised, filmed, and discussed everywhere.

Meanwhile maturer ladies were sighing over *Precious Bane*
(1924) by Mary Webb (1881–1927). This tale of early nineteenth-century farm life in a Shropshire village wrings the
heart for a girl with a hare-lip who nevertheless finds her
man. It renders dialogue in a craggy ruralese.

So when folk tell me of this great man and that great man, I think to
myself, Who was stinted of joy for his glory? How many old folk and
children did his coach wheels go over? What bridal lacked his songs and
what mourner his tears, that he found time to climb so high?

Such dialogue, rough-hewn names for persons and places, and
the reek of soil and dung created a recipe for homespun
peasant fiction that eventually provoked a hilarious backlash
from Stella Gibbons (1902–) in *Cold Comfort Farm* (1932).
Her doom-laden Starkadder family in their gloom-laden farm
are visited by a businesslike young lady who sorts them all
out.

Young men, of course, were reading detective stories. Agatha Christie (1890–1975) was beginning to turn out novels in rapid succession. *The Mysterious Affair at Styles* (1920) started the ball rolling. Agatha Christie's inventiveness in laying false trails and leading the reader up the garden path made for teasing mysteries that had to be solved at a sitting. There was a slightly more sophisticated literary flavour about the detective novels of Dorothy Sayers (1893–1957) which began with *Whose Body?* (1923) and included *Strong Poison* (1930) and *Murder Must Advertise* (1933). Her amateur sleuth, Lord Peter Wimsey, is that piquant phenomenon, an aristocrat with brains who is as conversant with the poets as with Debrett.

V Three Scottish poets

Meanwhile, on the poetic scene, latter-day Georgianism, the continuing productiveness of Yeats, the innovatory voices of Eliot and Pound, and the experimentation of Edith Sitwell, were not the only features of the 1920s and the pre-Auden 1930s. Three Scots justly came to prominence: Andrew Young (1885–1973), Edwin Muir (1887–1959), and Hugh MacDiarmid (1892–1978). Young could be classified as a Georgian in spirit. A naturalist, he published prose works on wild flowers. His verse publications began with small collections before the First World War. With *Winter Harvest* (1933), *The White Blackbird* (1935), and later, *Collected Poems* (1950), came recognition of a disciplined talent that combines directness with imaginative concentration. In 'The Swallows' the birds twist 'here and there / Round unseen corners of the air', they steeple-chase over a bridge, and become 'jugglers with their own bodies'. In 'The Shepherd's Hut' the sight of clothes drying outside a croft where there is no other sign of life, and bellying in the wind so that limbs take shape in them, sets the poet pondering where the shepherd's wife is.

> I thought, She little knows
> That ghosts are trying on her children's clothes.

Young wrote a long speculative poem about the after-life, *Out of the World and Back* (1958). In it the fruit of religious meditation is subject to the same careful craftsmanship that

marks his short nature poems, written in the tradition of
Edward Thomas and Robert Frost.

Young's poetry scarcely requires one to consult his biography: Muir's compels one to reflect on his. He came of an
Orkney farming family which was driven by poverty to Glasgow when he was fourteen. Bereavements and early privation
left their mark on him. A troubled, subjective writer with a
head full of strange dreams and manifestations from a too
assertive sub-conscious, he was helped by psychoanalysis and
found stability in a happy marriage. Muir and his wife, Willa,
lived much on the continent in the inter-war years, and among
their numerous translations they first presented the novels of
Kafka to the English public. Muir was in his thirties when he
began to write poetry with *First Poems* (1925). *Variations
on a Time Theme* (1934) followed. Muir often has recourse
to classical and Christian myth. He expresses his own experience of loss and exile, of poverty and squalor, by reference to
mythical archetypes, seeing an overall correspondence with
the Fall of Man, and using imagery of combat, of fallen cities,
of pilgrimage and imprisonment. The titles of later volumes
exemplify this: *The Narrow Place* (1943), *The Labyrinth*
(1949), and *One Foot in Eden* (1956). There is a kind of
ancient gravity, of monumental dignity, in Muir's frugal
diction and quiet rhythms. In *The Labyrinth* he pictures a
life of peace and harmony over which the gods converse in
tranquil voices 'above the untroubled sea' and this our life is
'as a chord deep in that dialogue'. This is contrasted with:

> the lie,
> The maze, the wild-wood waste of falsehood, roads
> That run and run and never reach an end,
> Embowered in error.

The former is the real world.

> I have touched it once,
> And now shall know it always.

In 'Scotland 1941' Muir attacked contemporary Scottish
materialism and bogus sentimental nationalism ('Burns and
Scott, sham bards of a sham nation') in a vein reminiscent of
Hugh MacDiarmid (pseudonym of Christopher Murray Grieve)

(1892–1978), who ridiculed the spectacle of starch-fronted London Scotties toasting Burns.

> Mair nonsense has been uttered in his name
> Than in ony's barrin' liberty and Christ.

MacDiarmid, the son of a postman from Dumfriesshire, burst on the literary scene with *Sangshaw* (1925), *Penny Wheep* (1926), and *A Drunk Man Looks at the Thistle* (1926). His invention of a literary Scots, a heady verbal diet compounded of vernacular vocabulary, idiom, and usage from different ages and localities, uniquely solved the problem of at once energising and de-sentimentalising the portrayal of Scots people and their experience on their home ground.

> Oh to be at Crowdieknowe
> When the last trumpet blaws,
> An' see the deid come loupin' owre
> The auld grey wa's.   ('Crowdieknowe')

Vigour and forthrightness, diversity of subject and mood, and tumbling abundance of idea and allusion made MacDiarmid's output one of the most distinctive literary achievements of the age. The sureness of verbal touch is such that it reaches the nerve even of the Sassenach reader for whom interpretation is half guesswork. MacDiarmid's membership of the Communist Party and his nationalistic Anglophobia did not endear him to all his readers. His eventual forsaking of Scots for English irritated chauvinistic admirers at home. It has to be accepted that the early freshness and concentration are rarely recaptured in *First Hymn to Lenin* (1931), *Second Hymn to Lenin* (1935), and subsequent collections. But MacDiarmid never ceased consciously to cultivate in his own way and on his own terms

> A speech, a poetry, to bring to bear on life
> The concentrated strength of all our being.
>   ('The kind of poetry I want')

6

Today the struggle
The 1930s and 1940s

I Introduction

The election of over a hundred Nazis to the German Reichstag
in 1930 marked the beginning of a fateful decade. In 1933
Hitler became Chancellor, the Reichstag was destroyed by a
fire blamed on the communists, and Germany left the League
of Nations. 1934 saw Hitler's bloody purge of his own party
in the 'Night of the Long Knives' and the foundation of the
out-and-out pacifist Peace Pledge Union in England by Dick
Sheppard, the Vicar of St Martin's-in-the-Fields Church,
London. The Spanish Civil War began in 1936, giving a sharper
definition to the opposite forces, extreme left and right, which
seemed to threaten to carve up Europe between them. As
Hitler reoccupied the Rhineland in 1936, annexed Austria in
1938, and then turned his threats on Czechoslovakia, the
British Prime Minister, Neville Chamberlain, who had succeeded Baldwin in 1937, set in motion a policy of 'appeasement' based partly, no doubt, on a British sense of guilt for
the supposed injustices of the Versailles Treaty in demanding
reparations from Germany and denying her a place in the
colonial sun. It was based also on a deeply ingrained conviction that a new war, in the age of chemical warfare, was un-
thinkable. Thus when Chamberlain flew to meet Hitler and
Mussolini in 1938 and to conclude the Munich Agreement
which conceded large tracts of Czechoslovakia to Germany
and left the country with virtually indefensible borders, there
was a distribution of gas-masks to the entire population of
the United Kingdom.

How far the policy of 'appeasement' was the product of
genuine pacific idealism, how far of covert preference for
fascist rather than communist domination of Europe, and

how far of cunning prescience that calculated on a war in which Nazi Germany and Soviet Russia would debilitate each other by mutual slaughter, the historians must decide. It has to be added, of course, that the Munich Agreement gave Britain a year in which to rearm. When Hitler began to threaten Poland in 1939, Britain and France guaranteed to come to Poland's aid in the event of German aggression, so that Germany's invasion of Poland in September of that year brought automatic declarations of war.

John Wain has praised the young writers of the 1930s for their 'wakefulness in the midst of apathy and inertia'.

In spite of the manifold troubles of that decade — unemployment, strikes, riots, the yells of dictators and the goose-stepping of storm-troopers — it was, in most Western countries, a period of superficial calm and plenty. A war was coming, food was being burnt and dumped in the sea to keep prices high, the unemployed were rotting in their mill-towns and mining villages: but, meanwhile, twenty cigarettes sold for less than a shilling, thirty-seven-and-six would buy a week-end in Brighton . . . . The cheaper newspapers ladled out sedative optimism . . . and popular taste in literature favoured the kind of novelist (Hugh Walpole, etc.) whose work . . . made no attempt to face the actual problems of the 1930s. Against this slumbrous background the younger and more alert writers sounded a constant Reveillé.

(Introduction to *Anthology of Modern Poetry* (1961).)

Among them were young men who recognised in Marxist condemnation of capitalism a judgment on social injustice which their experience of public school and Oxbridge provoked them to echo. The increasing power of Nazism and fascism in Europe, the evident failure of the League of Nations in the face of such challenges as Mussolini's invasion of Abyssinia in 1935, the apparent polarisation of left and right by the Spanish Civil War, promised a crunch which would squeeze out such luxuries as cultural values and the middle way. Thoroughgoing Marxists such as Christopher Caudwell (pseudonym of Christopher St John Spriggs) (1907–37), who wrote Marxist criticism, *Studies in a Dying Culture* (1938), as well as *Poems* (1939), and John Cornford (1915–36), whose poems include 'Before the Storming of Huesca' and 'Letter from Aragon', went to fight for the republicans in Spain and were killed.

II Poets of the thirties

The key figure among those who were to become known as the 'poets of the thirties' was W. H. Auden (1907—73). Auden was born in York but later his family moved to Birmingham. The urban wastes of the Midlands and the moorland wastes of the Pennines left lasting impressions on his mind.

> Tramlines and slagheaps, pieces of machinery,
> That was, and still is, my ideal scenery.
>
> ('Letter to Lord Byron')

It was also the 'peat-stained burns / That feed the Tyne and Tees' (*New Year Letter*). At Oxford, where Auden overlapped with Spender, Day Lewis, and MacNeice, he seemed pre-eminent among his contemporaries. His talents were hailed from the first with adulation. Yet he never posed as the Shelleyan legislator. He insisted that poetry is 'a game of knowledge', a game with rules and forms to be observed, but essentially the craft of a man in love with words. This does not mean that poetry is trivial, for the patterns and ritual of art may catch analogously the light of 'eternal fact'.

Auden does not don the mantle of the magus and yet the poetic *persona* has an assurance, a knowingness, an air of being fully in control, that commands readier, yet more distanced, responsiveness than poets who slip falteringly, if unreservedly, into the reader's confidence. Auden impinges on the reader's sympathies, not as bearer of intimate self-revelation, but as sharer of common feelings and experience. His skill at assembling the familiar bric-à-brac of life lived is telling even if sometimes it stirs admiration for talent instead of touching the nerve.

> The boarding-house food, the boarding-house faces,
> The rain-spoilt picnics in the wind-swept places,
> The camera lost and the suspicion,
> The failure in the putting competition,
> The silly performance on the pier . . .

Auden's objectivity is sustained by his sense of humour. Humour enables a poet to take poetry seriously without taking himself too seriously. Humour is the sense of proportion articulated. And Auden's sense of proportion enabled

him to grasp the social deprivations and spiritual malaise of
the 1930s, to measure the need for revolution and regeneration,
without losing his head to Marxism. He was active enough in
his left-wing sympathies, however, to serve with an ambulance
unit in Spain in 1937 and to assign to Medical Aid for Spain
the royalties of *Spain* (1937).

> Yesterday the installation of dynamo and turbines,
> The construction of railways in the colonial desert;
> Yesterday the classic lecture
> On the origin of mankind. But today the struggle.

Auden early collaborated with Christoper Isherwood
(1904–) in verse plays. *The Dog Beneath the Skin* (1936),
The Ascent of F6 (1937), and *On the Frontier* (1939) bear
traces of the influence of Brecht whom he met during a stay
in Berlin in 1928–9. The interest in the stage continued
throughout Auden's life, and he was to write opera libretti
for Benjamin Britten (*John Bunyan*, 1941), Stravinsky (*The
Rake's Progress*, 1951), and Hans Werner Henze (*The Bassarids,*
1966). But Auden's more significant work of the 1930s is
contained in *Poems* (1930), *Look, Stranger!* (1936) (*On This
Island*, New York, 1937), and *Letters from Iceland* (1937), a
verse and prose book written in collaboration with Louis
MacNeice. Auden has said in his critical book, *The Dyer's
Hand* (1963), that his first master was Thomas Hardy, but
decisive influences soon included T. S. Eliot, Edward Thomas,
Wilfred Owen, Anglo-Saxon and Middle English poets. The
early technique which captivated contemporaries included a
mastery both of epigrammatic crispness and of a conversational
tone winningly infectious in phrase and metre. The casual,
chatty manner was brought into service in contexts which
might have seemed to preclude such informality and the effect
was dizzyingly novel.

> About suffering they were never wrong
> The Old Masters: how well they understood
> Its human position; how it takes place
> While someone else is eating or opening a window . . .

So the poet reflects on Brueghel's *Icarus* in 'Musée des Beaux
Arts'. Auden was equally at home with rollicking ballad
metres and with flexibly drawn-out stanza forms. Clusters

of sharp descriptive imagery are deftly imposed without that
sense of strain which stanzaic sculpture so often conveys.

Auden and Isherwood went to the USA in 1939 and both
became American citizens in 1946. Auden's conversion to the
Christian faith as an Anglican gave his career an odd similarity
with Eliot's. Firmly established in reputation, he became one
of the most prolific poets of his age. In *New Year Letter*
(1941), a poem of some 1700 lines in octosyllabic couplets,
Auden ambles through reflections on the poet's calling and
function to make an analysis of the Devil's tactics in mislead-
ing men with humanistic dreams of earthly fulfilment that
misread the character of man's status. Auden places the
personal dilemma about what to do in wartime within the
context of a sketchy historico-philosophical account of the
genesis of 'Empiric Economic Man' of the machine age, and
the dawning realisation that 'Aloneness is man's real condition'.
There is some slackness of overall structure here, but the
moment-by-moment impact of the verse is characteristically
invigorating. *For the Time Being, A Christmas Oratorio* (1945)
is a more studiedly moulded work. Its voices include those of
St Joseph, the Virgin Mary, the Shepherds, the Wise Men,
Simeon, Herod, Soldiers, Chorus, and a Narrator. The debt to
Eliot is evident. Herod's prose *apologia* reminds the reader of
the Knights in *Murder in the Cathedral*. ('Why should He dislike me so? . . . I object. I'm a liberal. I want everyone to be
happy. I wish I had never been born.') The Narrator sometimes
sounds like Eliot's Chorus of Women, and there are passages
of gnomic generalisation reminiscent of *Four Quartets*.

> Alone, alone, about a dreadful wood
> Of conscious evil runs a lost mankind,
> Dreading to find its Father lest it find
> The Goodness it has dreaded is not good:
> Alone, alone, about a dreadful wood.

The Age of Anxiety, A Baroque Eclogue (1948) is a brilliant
if less rounded experiment. Four lonely characters, voicing
their thoughts in a New York bar, come together and move
off to an apartment. The interweaving of private monologue,
spoken dialogue (all in verse), and the detached prose commentary of a scene-setter, has a Joycean piquancy, though

the analysis of the age's condition tends to be half-smothered under an erratic superfluity of detail.

Yet Auden never ceased to be the poet of inspired snatches cumulatively irresistible. He is the anthologist's ideal poet. With a dozen different tones of voice at his disposal, he has equal mastery of baroque stateliness and chastely poised lyricism. To name representatively unforgettable poems is to produce a list of astonishing variety: 'Night Mail', 'Miss Gee', 'In Memory of W. B. Yeats', 'Sir, No Man's Enemy', 'The Shield of Achilles', 'The Cave of Making'. Only the greatest poets implant so much on the memory.

Christopher Isherwood (1904–), Auden's friend from schooldays, presented in his novel, *All the Conspirators* (1928), a record of struggle against the established agencies that conspire against youth's freedom. Isherwood has conceded that his writing is all fundamentally autobiographical. His experience of teaching English in Berlin from 1930 to 1933 provided the material for his celebrated fiction, *Mr Norris Changes Trains* (1935), *Sally Bowles* (1937), and *Goodbye to Berlin* (1939). The techniques of the documentary and the film studio are applied in giving 'shots' of significant developments at the time of Hitler's rise to power. Isherwood's autobiographical study, *Lions and Shadows* (1938), tells how he and a fellow Reptonian, Edward Upward (1903–), contemporaries at Cambridge, deliberately created a private world, 'Mortmere', which grew in elaboration and vividness 'to the gradual exclusion of the history school, the Pushocracy, the dons, the rags, the tea-parties . . . which formed the outward structure of our undergraduate lives'.

Of the many stories written about Mortmere for private amusement Upward's final one, 'The Railway Accident', dating from 1928, was eventually published. It is an extraordinary surrealistic study of mental and moral disorientation, a grotesque, lunatic vision delivered in scrupulously disinfected prose. Isherwood, introducing it to the public in *New Directions* in 1949, defined it as a 'farewell to Mortmere' and Mortmere as 'a sort of anarchist paradise in which all accepted moral and social values were turned upside down'. The next stage of Upward's pilgrimage was recorded in *Journey to the Border* (1938), an allegory of a middle-class young man's struggle of social conscience which is resolved by embracing

1. Coronation of King George V, 1911: the Procession

2. Coronation of King George V, 1911: Peers leaving Westminster Abbey

A memory of Henry James and
Joseph Conrad conversing at an afternoon party—
circa 1909.

max
1926

3. Henry James and Joseph Conrad, by Max Beerbohm

4. Arnold Bennett, by 'Low'

5. W. H. Hudson's 'Rima', by Jacob Epstein

6. Men leaving Calne, Wiltshire, for the Forces, 1914

7. The First World War: the Western Front

8. Dorothy Brett, Lytton Strachey, Ottoline Morrell, and Bertrand Russell

9. J. Middleton Murry, Frieda Lawrence, and D. H. Lawrence in 1914

10. Ford Madox Ford, James Joyce, Ezra Pound, and John Quinn in 1923

11. *T. S. Eliot,* by Patrick Heron

12. Unemployed hunger marchers in Trafalgar Square, 1932

13. The Second World War: *Tube Shelter Scene,* by Henry Moore

14. David Jones: Dedicatory Inscription in *The Anathemata* (1952)

15. *The Dancers,* by Mervyn Peake

PROLOGUE

This day winding down now
At God speeded summer's end
In the torrent salmon sun,
In my seashaken house
On a breakneck of rocks
Tangled with chirrup and fruit, ~~fear a price~~
Froth, flute, ~~brushwood and bracket~~ fin and quill
At a wood's dancing hoof,
By scummed, starfish sands
With their fishwife cross
Gulls, pipers, cockles ~~and~~ sails,
Out there, ~~riders~~ crow black, ~~men~~ alone,
~~men~~ Tackled with clouds, who kneel
To the sunset nets,
Geese nearly in heaven, boys
Stabbing, and herons, and shells
That speak seven seas,
Eternal waters away
From the cities of nine
Days' night whose towers will catch
In the religious wind
Like stalks of tall, dry straw,
At poor peace I sing
To you, strangers, (though song
Is a burning and crested act,
The fire of birds in
The world's turning wood,
For my sawn, splay sounds),
Out of these seathumbed leaves
That will fly and fall
Like leaves of trees and as soon
Crumble and undie
Into the dogdayed night.
Seaward the salmon, sucked sun slips,
And the dumb swans drub blue
My dabbed bay's dusk, as I hack
This rumpus of shapes
For you to know
How I, a spinning man,
Glory also this star, bird
Roared, sea born, man torn, blood blest.
Hark: I trumpet the place,
From fish to jumping hill! Look:
I build my bellowing ark
To the beat of my love
As the flood begins,
Out of the fountain head
Of fear, rage red, manalive,
Molten and mountainous to stream
Over the wound asleep
Sheep white hollow farms,

16. Dylan Thomas: Prologue to *Collected Poems* (1952)

17. Scene from television production of Samuel Beckett's *Waiting for Godot*

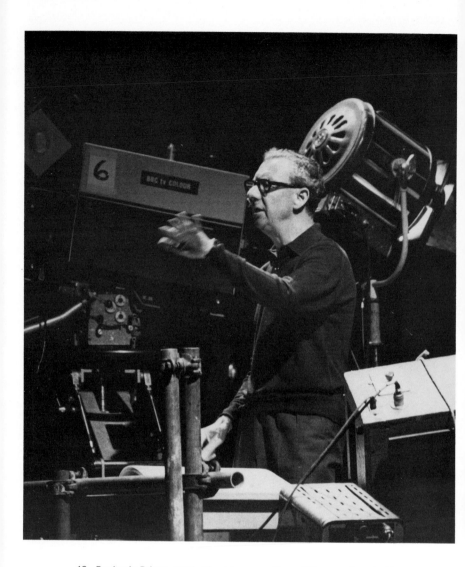

18. Benjamin Britten conducting his opera, *Owen Wingrave,* for television

the workers' cause. Upward was a member of the Communist Party for many years. After a lifetime of school-teaching, he re-emerged as a novelist with a trilogy eventually completed as *The Spiral Ascent* (1977), an arduously realistic and indigestibly detailed account of a communist couple's tortuous and tormented pilgrimage as Marxist–Leninists. The trilogy embraces the earlier novels, *In the Thirties* (1962) and *The Rotten Elements* (1969).

Stephen Spender (1909–) was only briefly a member of the Communist Party. The problem of reconciling communist social justice with liberal notions of individual freedom ultimately proved more taxing for him than was suggested in the sentimental romanticism of the left evident in his verse play, *Trial of a Judge* (1938). Spender's poetic career began with *Poems* (1933). The contents of several volumes such as *The Still Centre* (1939) and *The Edge of Being* (1949) were gathered together in *Collected Poems* (1955). His poem, 'The Pylons' ('those pylons / Bare like nude giant girls that have no secrets'), no doubt played its part in the choice of the label 'Pylon Poets' for the new generation of writers who were happy to use the gas-works or the pistons of a steam-engine as poetic imagery. However, as Louis MacNeice pointed out in *Modern Poetry* (1938), Spender himself tended to use 'stock mystical symbols – roses, crystal, snow, stars, gold' in his early verse. And his heady clarion call –

> Oh, comrades, let not those who follow after
> – The beautiful generation that shall spring from our sides –
> Let not them wonder how after the failure of banks,
> The failure of cathedrals and the declared insanity of our rulers,
> We lacked the Spring-like resources of the tiger . . .
>
> ('After they have tired')

proved less characteristic than gentler and vaguer invitations to humanity not to forget 'the essential delights of the blood' or to allow the traffic to smother 'the flowering of the Spirit'.

In his gossipy retrospect of the period, *World Within World* (1951), Spender spoke of Cecil Day Lewis (1904–72) as a literary traditionalist who had nevertheless given new sturdiness to Georgian forms by using the imagery of the factory and the slum. Day Lewis's ingenuity was exercised sometimes with a fine metaphysical sensitivity in his *Transitional Poem*

(1929), but his imagery soon began to reflect his communist preoccupation with the industrial world.

> Now shall the airman vertically banking
> Out of the blue write a new sky-sign;
> The nine tramp steamers rusting in the estuary
> Get up full pressure for a trade revival.
>
> ('Come out into the sun')

That is the imagery of rejoicing on the birth of a child in *From Feathers to Iron* (1931), a personal, domestic record. Strident imagery of track-laying and rock-blasting is used for gestation and childbirth. Hammer blows resound again in *The Magnetic Mountain* (1933), where the masses are called to the red flag.

> You shall be leaders when zero hour is signalled,
> Wielders of power and welders of a new world.
>
> ('You that love England')

Day Lewis's succeeding collections, *A Time to Dance* (1935), *Overtures to Death* (1938), and the rarer, post-war volumes reveal a poetic impulse that from time to time flamed in lyrics of touching directness (like 'The Album' or 'My Mother's Sister') which still speak with authority when the outcries of the troubled social conscience of the thirties have come to seem too raw, clumsy, and simplistic in their response to a complex civilisational malaise.

The temper of the time was more subtly registered by Louis MacNeice (1907–63), perhaps because he never simplified the current human condition into a political struggle between left and right. 'Young men were swallowing Marx with the same naive enthusiasm that made Shelley swallow Godwin', he noted in his autobiographical book, *The Strings are False* (1965). An Irishman from Belfast, he gave voice to native melancholy, wry mockery, and that double-layered irony which subjects the heavily critical self to a dose of its own medicine. MacNeice dipped into the new poetic bag of tricks,

> The jaded calendar revolves,
> Its nuts need oil, carbon chokes the valves,

in 'An Eclogue for Christmas' (from *Poems*, 1935) to express
his disillusionment with a stale civilisation; but to the question,

> What will happen when the sniggering machine-guns in the
> hands of young men
> Are trained on every flat and club and beauty parlour
> and Father's den?

his reply is that 'the whore and the buffoon / Will come off
best . . . reinstated in the new regime'.

The philosophic depth of MacNeice's imagination, his
scholarship, and his sense of the limitations of scholarship,
precluded the naivety of Spender and Day Lewis. Like Day
Lewis, he was a parson's son, and the air of lost faith pervades
his wriggling and wrestling as a human being caught up in
civilisational débâcle. There are few points of rest in MacNeice.
For all its humour, the rollicking balladry of the celebrated
'Bagpipe Music' —

> It's no go the Yogi-Man, it's no go Blavatsky,
> All we want is a bank balance and a bit of skirt in a taxi. —

is as rueful in its emotional dislocations as are the graver
ruminations in the *Autumn Journal* (1939). This poem,
justifiably MacNeice's best known, records his reflections
between August 1938 and the new year of 1939. The period
covers the Munich crisis, the sell-out of Czechoslovakia, and
the darkening prospect of war. The poem has the spontaneity
and frankness of a diary, mingling private personal concerns
with public issues. Its conversational naturalness is achieved
without any relaxation of workmanlike control. Whether
MacNeice then served his muse well by turning verse-play-
supplier for the new BBC Third Programme in the 1940s is
doubtful, but his later collections, *Solstice* (1961) and *The
Burning Perch* (1963), evidence again that, after Auden's,
his is the most stimulating poetic mind of the 'thirties group'.

If the work of the group began to seem like a concerted
movement, it was in part due to the attention they got in the
Faber Book of Modern Verse (1936), which institutionalised
fashionable poetic prejudice for an entire generation. Michael
Roberts (1902–48), himself a poet (see *Orion Marches*, 1939),
the editor, in trying to define modernity, excluded from his

anthology every poet, with the exception of Harold Monro, to whom the label 'Georgian' is generally applied. Even Edward Thomas was omitted, while Spender and Day Lewis got twenty-five pages between them.

> Every vital age, perhaps, sees its own time as crucial and full of perils, but the problems and difficulties of our own age necessarily appear more urgent to us than those of any other, and the need for an evaluating, clarifying poetry has never been greater . . . [Introduction].

Roberts's inclusions and exclusions suggest that he saw the 'evaluating, clarifying' function of poetry in social and political, or at least in public terms, and this predilection is symptomatic of the mood that swept away the Georgians, good and bad, to install the new men. The 'Auden group' were also energetically championed by their fellow-poet, Geoffrey Grigson (1905–), in the magazine, *New Verse*, which he founded in 1933 and edited until 1937. Grigson, who lambasted the Sitwells mercilessly, later recalled the heady controversy of the time rather ruefully in his autobiography, *The Crest on the Silver* (1950).

Two poets from South Africa who did not get into Roberts's anthology were Roy Campbell (1901–57) and William Plomer (1903–73). Campbell expressed a contemptuous anti-Georgianism in a satirical poem in heroic couplets, *The Georgiad* (1931). He could bluster in balladry like the best of the new breed:

> True sons of Africa are we,
> Though bastardized with culture,
> Indigenous, and wild, and free
> As wolf, as pioneer and vulture . . . .
>
> ('Poets in Africa')

But he put his swashbuckling aggressiveness at the service of the right and went off to fight for Franco in Spain. Plomer's satirical ballads are the work of a subtle practitioner who was seriously concerned with those moments of human experience when the frightening or the monstrous collides with the absurd or the trivial. In 'Father and Son, 1939' (from *The Dorking Thigh*, 1945) he neatly characterises the illusions of two generations and the outbreak of the war they helped to produce.

On a Sunday in September there were deck-chairs in the sun,
There was argument at lunch between the father and the son
(Smoke rose from Warsaw) for the beef was underdone
(Nothing points to heaven but the anti-aircraft gun) . . . .

Plomer, a widely talented writer, also produced short stories, and novels of African (*Turbott Wolfe*, 1926), Japanese (*Sado*, 1931), and English life (*The Case is Altered*, 1932). Among libretti which he supplied for dramatic and choral works by Benjamin Britten was that for the opera, *Gloriana* (1953).

Of other poets in this age group Ronald Bottrall (1906–) was highly praised for his early volumes, *The Loosening* (1931) and *Festival of Fire* (1934). Perhaps the reason for his subsequent neglect lies in his submission to the influence of Pound at a time when the taste for cosmopolitan allusiveness and oblique satire had been put out of fashion. Norman Cameron (1905–53), whose posthumous *Collected Poems* (1957) had an Introduction by Robert Graves, was a poet distinguished by epigrammatic precision and by skilful verse structure. There is sharp descriptive clarity in 'El Aghir' and wry moral commentary in 'The Firm of Happiness Limited'. The minor poet with no waste to explain away and no wayward enthusiasms to repent of sometimes offers a body of verse in substance able to match what remains of value when the dross is purged away from the corpus of seemingly larger writers. Cameron is such a poet.

III Romantics and visionaries

The Auden group certainly did not have it all their own way in the 1930s. By the time war came – even more by the time it ended – they were already outdated in many readers' eyes by the emergence of a younger generation of poets who leapt into prominence with notions of poetry that confounded their own: George Barker (1913–), David Gascoyne (1916–), and Dylan Thomas (1914–53). For these poets turned their backs on political man. The business of poetry lay not in the field of social commentary but with men as creatures of vision and spirituality. In Barker's *Thirty Preliminary Poems* (1933), *Calamiterror* (1937), *Eros in Dogma* (1944), and *The True Confessions of George Barker* (1950) an outgush of rhapsodic fervour streams from an oracular voice in whose tones the mystical and the erotic meet and collide. 'The image is what the imagination ascertains about the hitherto unimaginable,' Barker wrote. In a sonnet paying tribute to seamen lost overboard in a storm, the sea is a 'greedy bitch with sailors in her guts'. She spits at stars, gnaws at shores, and

> mad randy,
> Riots with us on her abdomen and puts
> Eternity in our cabins . . .

There lingers an air of somewhat coarse-grained flashiness about Barker's aural effects and his hectoring tone, but admirers have always applauded the largeness and boldness of a rhetoric which defies the prudent caution of versifying miniaturists and snapshot-takers.

David Gascoyne emerged first in *Roman Balcony* (1932) and *Man's Life is this Meat* (1936) as an exponent of surrealist method. Maturer work, from *Poems 1937–1942* onward, while retaining traces of the early imaginative overkill —

> But deep in the velvet crater of the ear
> A chip of sound abruptly irritates
>
> ('A War time Dawn')

— reveals an increasingly religious preoccupation with human anguish amid the desolation of war-torn cities and civilisational collapse. (See *A Vagrant*, 1950; and *Night Thoughts*, 1956.) The metaphysical confrontation with negation and grief evokes a vaguely Christian response. But there is perhaps surer analysis of man's spiritual need in the comparatively unnoted narrative poems of Gascoyne's contemporary, Francis Berry (1915–), *The Iron Christ* (1938) and *The Fall of a Tower* (1943), where a more academic cerebralism is at work both in the fashioning of image and in the articulation of a metaphysic.

The exalted stance and incantatory tone of Barker and Gascoyne was assumed most plausibly by the Welsh poet, Dylan Thomas. In Thomas the neo-romantics found their maestro and their martyr. Thomas's Celtic blood gave him his bardic exuberance. His life-long friendship with another Welsh poet, Vernon Watkins (1906–67), linked him with a man whose poetic vocation called out a religious dedication to prophetic revelation. 'I think him to be the most profound and greatly accomplished Welshman writing poems in English,' Thomas said of Watkins in a broadcast in 1946. Watkins's *Ballad of the Mari Lwyd* (1941) treated in dramatic, ritualistic form an ancient Welsh custom of taking a wooden Grey Mare from house to house on New Year's Eve. The best of Watkins's work, like 'Peace in the Welsh Hills', carries the disinterested authoritativeness of the visionary and the votary.

In introducing *Dylan Thomas: Letters to Vernon Watkins* (1957), Watkins described Thomas's method aptly. 'Dylan worked upon a symmetrical abstract with tactile delicacy; out of a lump of texture or nest of phrases he created music, testing everything by physical feeling, working from the concrete image outwards.' There is evidence in the poet's surviving notebooks that the nests of phrases accumulated in his early years continued to furnish material for much of his later work. *Eighteen Poems* (1934), *Twenty-five Poems* (1936), and *Deaths and Entrances* (1946) established Thomas for a time as the most celebrated living poet. Yet he remained a controversial figure. It is not difficult to point in his work to bad writing where emotive symbols are tossed off in a violence of rhythmic clamour, and where clotted imagery and contorted syntax produce congestion and confusion. Yet Thomas's method at its most scrupulous could blend infectious rhythmic pulse with dexterous conjuration of the magic inherent in word and image. The moving wartime poem, 'A Refusal to mourn the death, by fire, of a child in London', opens with lines that smack of Hopkins:

> Never until the mankind making
> Bird beast and flower
> Fathering and all humbling darkness
> Tells with silence the last hour breaking . . . .

Thomas laboured toilsomely at the task of stacking and shuffling words and images into rhetorical patterns of rare thrust and potency. As a result there are a handful of poems, like 'Fern Hill', 'Do not go gentle into that good night', and 'And death shall have no dominion' that justly captivated the new audiences for spoken poetry which gathered in the 1940s. For Thomas's arduous craftsmanship, his syntactical jugglery and verbal wizardry, operated alongside an imaginative sensitivity that could give his work subtlety as well as striking-power.

> Dawn breaks behind the eyes;
> From poles of skull and toe the windy blood
> Slides like a sea . . .   ('Light breaks where no sun shines')

Thomas frankly acknowledged his indebtedness to Joyce in the title of his *Portrait of the Artist as a Young Dog* (1940) with its vivid autobiographical sketches of his early life in Wales. There is the same intense vitality in the opening sections of his abandoned autobiographical novel, *Adventures in the Skin Trade* (1955). The Thomas of these books is a great comic writer, exuding wit and fun. So is the Thomas of the radio play, *Under Milk Wood* (1954), in which the listener eavesdrops on the thoughts and chatter of the inhabitants of a Welsh village, Llareggub (a reversible name). A riot of fantasy, it makes hay with a cheerfully over-Welshified Wales. Yet in his poetry a preoccupation with death, in his intimate letters evidence of a strangely unhappy uncertainty about the integrity of his work, and in his behaviour an almost frankly self-destructive addiction to alcohol, together present a tragic figure.

IV Dominant novelists

The comic sense and the tragic sense may be deeply inter-twined in a basically melancholy nature. The daemon that seized Dylan Thomas was more destructive than the daemon that turned Evelyn Waugh (1903—66) into a public caricature of artistic and 'aristocratic' idiosyncrasy. There is authority for using the word 'daemon'. After meeting Waugh over lunch in 1932, Belloc observed, 'He is possessed.' Waugh had leapt into prominence with his first two novels, *Decline and Fall* (1928) and *Vile Bodies* (1930). His gift for sharp social satire made him the rage with the Bright Young Things. But what gave rare spice to these novels was the strain of fantasy. Waugh was a master of the comic technique that smoothly edges recognisably telling portrayals of current folly and vice over the rim of plausibility into the maelstrom of farcicality. The final outcome is neither moral judgment nor social criticism but howling humour. The hero of *Decline and Fall* is the victim of corruption and bogusness that lay hold of him willy-nilly through his entry into upper-class circles as Oxford undergraduate, boarding-school master, and bride-groom-elect of a wealthy widow. Here is mockery disinfected of Huxley's priggish knowingness and Rose Macaulay's right-eous indignation. The writer who is loftily amused at human folly and wickedness and the writer who is magisterially indignant at it share a common detachment. The writer who is inebriated with mirth at the spectacle of absurdities which others might sneer at or castigate stands apart on a less certain footing in mental impregnability.

Waugh was scarcely, in the long run, a happy man. He had not the temperament to turn his talent for surrealistic comedy into a recipe for life-long productivity. His fourth novel, *A Handful of Dust* (1934), presents a different kind of victim—hero who loses wife, son, and home, and goes off to South America to die trapped in the jungle. The book could not sustain the kind of reputation the comic novels had established, but it was highly praised by the judicious. Waugh had been received into the Roman Catholic Church in 1930, and Catholic discipline and practice became key correctives for a personality desperately in need of anchorage. So Waugh is rightly grouped with writers for whom the struggle is ever-present. His novel, *Brideshead Revisited* (1945), made literary capital out of the conflict between secular and Catholic attitudes to marriage. By thrusting an agnostic hero into the lives of an aristocratic Catholic family Waugh sought to exemplify the collision between traditional doctrine and the modern liberal spirit. The personal cost of obedience to the Church's law is measured in emotional terms. If Waugh opened himself to the charge of vulgarity by over-playing his hand in this novel, the public found it compulsive reading.

The big work of Waugh's later years was a trilogy, *Sword of Honour*, designed to document the Second World War and its effect on those caught up in it. 'The Waugh to end Waugh', it was dubbed by those who preferred the young mocker to the old philosopher. The three novels, *Men at Arms* (1952), *Officers and Gentlemen* (1955), and *Unconditional Surrender* (1961), centre on the military career of Guy Crouchback, member of an old Catholic family but a man of such poor spirit and such pedestrian personality that lesser characters steal the limelight. It is indicative of Waugh's thinking that the war loses its glamour and the Allied cause its nobility when Germany invades Russia. 'It doesn't seem to matter now who wins,' Guy tells his father. During the long gap between the second and third novels of the trilogy Waugh wrote a remarkable fictional self-exposure, *The Ordeal of Gilbert Pinfold* (1957), in which a middle-aged writer suffers a nervous breakdown. Hallucination and persecution mania brought on by excessive use of alcohol and drugs were part of Waugh's own experience.

Waugh had handled a specifically Catholic moral dilemma in *Brideshead Revisited*, but he grew to dislike the book so much that he mocked it in *Unconditional Surrender*. It was his friend and fellow-convert, Graham Greene (1904–), who established a recognisably Catholic novel; and he did so under the influence of the French novelist, François Mauriac, whose theme was 'La misère de l'homme sans Dieu'. In a review of Mauriac's *La Pharisienne,* reprinted in *Collected Essays* (1969), Greene lamented that 'with the death of James the religious sense was lost to the English novel, and with the religious sense went the sense of the importance of the human act. It was as if the world of fiction had lost a dimension . . . .' In a search for a compensating 'importance' in deeper layers of personality, subjective novelists like Virginia Woolf, having already lost the spiritual world, lost the visible world also. Thus Greene goes on to describe the characters of Virginia Woolf and E. M. Forster as wandering 'like cardboard symbols through a world that is paper-thin'.

It was Greene's fourth novel, *The Stamboul Train* (1932), that brought him his first success and initiated a series of books, including *A Gun for Sale* (1936) and *The Third Man* (1950), which he labelled 'entertainments' and which stand apart from his serious 'novels'. Among the 'novels' were *It's a Battlefield* (1934), a satirical study of contemporary England, and *England Made Me* (1935), a study of incestuous love. But the central canon opens with *Brighton Rock* (1938), a book about gang-warfare and racketeering in Brighton. Pinkie, the young gangleader, is a study in depravity. He delights in inflicting pain. He marries Rose, a waitress, to prevent her from giving evidence against him, then tries to kill her. Both Pinkie and Rose have been brought up as

Roman Catholics and, for all the satanic ruthlessness of Pinkie and his apparently conscious commitment to damnation, the authorial voice keeps open the inexplicable mystery of God's possible destiny for him.

Greene's Catholic heroes confront a corrupted world. But *corruptio optimi est pessima*, and on this principle they are likely, if they fall, to touch the depths. Yet, knowing that the struggle entangling them is between God and the Devil, they have a point of judgment upon themselves which clarifies their own wickedness and which makes the ultimate and final sin of pride less easily embraced than it is by men and women whose ordinary decency has no roots outside the secular ethic. The divergence between the Catholic and the secular ethic — the former grounded in obedience, the latter oriented to altruism — opens up to sinners within the Church possibilities of heroism from which comparatively virtuous outsiders may be precluded. Greene's skill in skating on thin ice in the matter of his moral dispensations is notable. What he achieves positively is a sensitivity to the limited scope of worldly evaluations. The hero of *The Power and the Glory* (1940) is a 'whisky priest' in a Mexican state where the clergy were openly persecuted in the 1920s and 1930s. If he can escape to the next state he will be safe. A man of numerous unpriestly weaknesses — he drinks, has a daughter, and has been self-indulgent — he martyrs himself when he has already reached safety by re-crossing the border to minister to a dying man. In *The Heart of the Matter* (1948) Greene ran foul of orthodox Catholic opinion by pushing the theme of martyrdom-in-sinfulness over the edge of paradox into what could be defined as moral anarchy. Major Scobie, a Deputy Commissioner of Police in West Africa during the war, allows compassion for his wife to lead him into getting a dubious loan on her behalf, and compassion for a stranded, torpedoed widow to lure him into adultery. Finally his compassionate attempt to keep his wife from the painful truth leads him to take communion unabsolved and to kill himself, actively choosing damnation for the sake of wife and mistress, and offering it to God on their behalf.

Such a conclusion plays with more than one kind of fire. And Greene continued to produce protagonists who struck strange bargains in their commerce with God. Sarah, the heroine of *The End of the Affair* (1951), a married woman, prays for her lover's recovery when he is injured in a bombing raid, and vows in her desperation to give him up if her prayer is answered — as it is. In *A Burnt-Out Case* (1961), a success-worn celebrity and philanderer ends his days at a Catholic leper colony in the Belgian Congo, and his final act of self-sacrifice is to be killed for the one act of adultery which he did not commit.

Greene's numerous works include plays, such as *The Living Room* (1953) and *The Potting Shed* (1958), several volumes of short stories, books for children, and an auto-biography, *A Sort of Life* (1971). His unique status among novelists of our age is due to the personal weight of the human issues which he tackles and the dramatic tension that is brought to bear on them by a style of compelling economy and overpowering atmospheric suggestiveness. His studies of human conflict and suffering have provoked critics to compare his protagonists with the Greek tragic heroes.

There is one other novelist of the period whose human studies have caused critics to compare her works with Greek tragedies, and that is Ivy Compton-Burnett (1884–1969). Miss Compton-Burnett's fictional world may share the claustrophobic intensity of Greene's but her point of judg-ment is the reverse of his. She accepts the label 'amoral' for it, believing that crime often pays. Having rejected Christianity from childhood, she inevitably denied to her work that spiritual dimension in which Greene located the 'importance' of human action. Fascination by unpleasant aspects of human nature conjoined with pessimism about the effectiveness of virtue might seem to be a sure recipe for literary works of unbounded gloom. But Miss Compton-Burnett is a great humourist for whom the pretension, hypocrisy, and self-delusion in which the ravagers of human happiness vest themselves are target of a shrewd, ironic wit.

Miss Compton-Burnett's artistry imposes a restriction on locale as rigid as Jane Austen's. There are no forays into Mexico or the Belgian Congo. The titles of the main novels hint at the formalisation of content and presentation adopted: *Brothers and Sisters* (1929), *Men and Wives* (1931), *More Women than Men* (1933), *A House and its Head* (1935), *Daughters and Sons* (1937), *A Family and a Fortune* (1939),

Parents and Children (1941), *Manservant and Maidservant* (1947), and so on. The settings are generally country houses of the lesser gentry and the period is late Victorian or Edwardian. There are usually money problems in the families, and the demand for means to support the expensive establishments is a motivation for aggression, deception, and criminality. Domestic tyranny by the master of the house is a favourite theme. The exercise of power by the blackmail of invalidism, or of parental demand for filial gratitude and affection, is explored in all its forms. The trade in expressions of affection by which experts on the stock-exchange of personal relationships can play the market to boost their vanity and self-satisfaction has perhaps never been more subtly delineated, unless it be by Meredith. The astute profit-takers make emotional killings out of such natural disasters, afflictions, or needs as happily come the way of those whose shares in well-being they wish to buy up. Such is the jungle of life. And when you have been done down, you naturally want to get your own back. The practice of systematic adult bullying is permanently institutionalised. The pattern of hierarchical relationships between old and young, masters and servants, governesses and pupils, is an elaborate network of competitive victimisation. And behind a veneer of respectability crimes such as murder, forgery, and incest express the reality of the human condition.

Yet Miss Compton-Burnett's presentation threads humour through the fabric. The text is pared down to the minimum in respect of narrative and descriptive machinery. Characters converse and brood in a stylised dialogue choice in its phrasing, gently literary in its cadences, yet capable of delivering the most sophisticated hardware of assault and defence. Politenesses are resonant with ulterior overtones and gracious phrases flow smoothly over undercurrents of resentment and antipathy. Suavities that pull the rug from under bogusly virtuous self-dramatisation keep the pot of humour simmering. For the novels contain their quota of open-eyed commentators who can shoot sentimental postures to pieces by matter-of-fact dissection. The villains may get their way, but they are verbally transfixed before the reader's eyes. It is therefore doubtful whether the authorial claim to 'amorality' can be upheld.

The austere artistic detachment of Miss Compton-Burnett

reflects a notion of literary responsibility remote from that which drove the poets of the thirties to wave red flags. By and large the novelists of the inter-war period were not fore-runners of social revolution, but there was one writer who loaded his early novels with ammunition for the socialist cause, and that was George Orwell (pseudonym of Eric Blair) (1903–50). Orwell, an Etonian, served for five years in the Burmese Police, then violently rejected the values which his schooling and his role in imperial officialdom had represented. He turned working-class and shared at first hand the life of the unemployed, of tramps, and of menial workers. The earnest-ness of his role can be gathered from the autobiographical book, *Down and Out in Paris and London* (1933). Orwell's asceticism, his determination to know privation from the inside, his on-the-spot study of the depressed areas (in *The Road to Wigan Pier*, 1937), his experience in Spain where he supported a deviant communist group (as recorded in *Homage to Catalonia*, 1938), and finally his early death from con-sumption together guaranteed him a kind of secular canonis-ation by the leftists, and what Anthony Powell has called 'the Orwell myth' was launched.

Powell, with whom he was contemporary at Eton, has pin-pointed Orwell's limitation as a writer in his memoirs, *Infants of the Spring* (1976). 'His interest in individuals – in literature or life – was never great. Apart from various projections of himself, the characters in his novels do not live as persons...' Yet the books have interest for the social historian. *A Clergy-man's Daughter* (1935) follows the pilgrimage of a girl escaping a tyrannical father among tramps, hop-pickers, prostitutes, and the riff-raff of nocturnal London. *Keep the Aspidistra Flying* (1936) tracks the course of an idealistic hero whose revulsion against the prevailing money-ethic drives him to near martyrdom. *Coming up for Air* (1939) centres on a middle-aged insurance agent who seeks a holiday from sub-urban routine in the village where he lived as a child. His autobiographical record, spanning the previous forty years, has detailed glimpses of social conditions in pre-war and inter-war days. Fragments such as the record of a Left Book Club meeting have rare documentary value. But up to this point Orwell fails to convince the reader that he is by nature a novelist.

Yet he succeeded brilliantly when he turned from natural-istic fiction to allegory and fantasy. *Animal Farm* (1945) adopts the innocent form of a farmyard fable to satirise Russian communism. Farmer Jones has been expelled from his farm by the animals. They take over and, in their turn, the pigs cunningly establish their own selfish tyranny. The adjustment of propaganda to suit the tyrant's predilections is scathingly ridiculed. The revolutionary slogan, 'All animals are equal', is conveniently modified by the clause, 'But some are more equal than others'. Orwell had become well-known as a regular contributor to the left-wing journal, *Tribune*, and Powell has observed in his memoirs, *Infants in the Spring*, that it therefore took some courage in 1945 'to fire an anti-Communist broadside like *Animal Farm*' at genial Uncle Joe Stalin. *Nineteen-Eighty-Four* (1949), though equally power-ful, is a more sombre and disquieting book, an anti-Utopia in the tradition of *Brave New World*. It looks to the future to project a Britain submerged within a communist world power (one of three), Oceania. Techniques of surveillance by the party's central caucus and dictator Big Brother have been so refined that individuality and privacy have been virtually eliminated. Thought and culture are stifled in the grip of one big propaganda machine.

V Miscellaneous fiction

In his last ailing months Orwell, a widower, married Sonia Brownell, editorial assistant on the literary magazine, *Horizon*, which Orwell's fellow-Etonian, Cyril Connolly (1903–74) founded in 1939 and edited until it ceased publication in 1950. Powell speaks of the 'Connolly myth' as readily as he speaks of the 'Orwell myth'. The myth was born in the auto-biographical material in Connolly's *Enemies of Promise* (1938). It shows Orwell and Connolly as friends at prep. school and together winning scholarships to Eton. But, schooldays over, 'all is anti-climax, dust and ashes . . .'. Powell has an apt comment: 'Conviction of his own genius, that virus of the Twenties, had infected Connolly, too, at an early age.' He had an influential career as a literary journalist, but his own novel, *The Rock Pool* (1936), a study in a literary man's disintegration, already proclaims that 'whom the gods wish to destroy they first call promising', and *The Unquiet Grave* (1944) is an assembly of quotations and aphorisms significantly presented under the Virgilian pseudonym, 'Palinurus', Aeneas' pilot, who is lost overboard while the hero sails on to enterprise and achievement.

A curious case of genius that misfired, or perhaps of talent injudiciously applied, was that of L. H. Myers (1881–1944), another and much older rebel against the social ethos he had encountered at Eton, who turned communist. A writer of independent means who had had a *succès d'estime* with a long-pondered novel, *The Orissers*, as far back as 1909, he then devoted himself to the composition of a tetralogy, *The Near and the Far* (1940). It came out first as a trilogy, *The Root and the Flower* (1935), comprising *The Near and the Far*, *Prince Jali*, and *Rajah Amer*. *The Pool of Vishu* was added in 1940 to complete the work. The setting is sixteenth-century India in the reign of the Emperor Akbar, whose two sons are rivals for the succession. A complex pattern of personal and political intrigue carries a burdensome load of philosophical speculation. An interesting feature of this over-abstract and verbally devitalised work is the satire of Bloomsbury in the portrayal of a pleasure camp established by a homosexual prince.

The success Orwell achieved with fable is noteworthy, for public reaction to non-naturalistic fiction is notoriously capricious. Rex Warner (1905–), for instance, who in later life turned historical biographer, tapping the vein opened up by Robert Graves, had started his literary career with a fable, *The Wild Goose Chase* (1937), in which three brothers leave their homeland in pursuit of the symbolic Wild Goose, representative of goodness and justice, and find a land of totalitarian slavery whose idol is a stuffed goose. A second allegory, *The Professor* (1938), reflects more precisely on the contemporary political condition of England, the alternatives offered by fascism and socialism, and the apparent ineffectiveness of pacific idealism in the face of tyranny. Warner was contemporary at Oxford with Day Lewis and plainly has affinities with the poets of the thirties, but the symbolical technique put him out of key with literary fashion. This may have been no great loss so far as the first two novels are concerned. *The Wild Goose Chase* is too misty and diffuse, *The Professor* too heavily didactic. But *The Aerodrome* (1941) is at once economic, artistically controlled, and as disturbing in its drift as *Nineteen-Eighty-Four*. A village, representative of English life, easy-going and threaded through with corruption, has an air-force base planted nearby which stands for a brutal new organisational thoroughness that will replace individuality by tyranny. Warner here achieved the unique distinction of getting something like an English equivalent of Kafka (in *The Castle*). Yet the impact of the work has been negligible.

In the matter of literary quality inadequately recognised no case is more striking than that of James Hanley (1901–), author of over twenty novels and several volumes of short stories, a novelist highly praised by Auden and E. M. Forster, by Faulkner and Henry Green, by Herbert Read and C. P. Snow. Born in Dublin, Hanley went to sea and spent ten years in the merchant service before settling down in Wales to write. His impact on the public has never measured up to his real stature. The total output may include much that is below the level of his best work, but that best has rare power and intensity. As early a novel as *Boy* (1932), a sombre study of a Liverpool stowaway who escapes the tyranny of home and shipyard for the even more brutal and vicious persecutions of sea-mates, is a compassionate, highly pressurised study. For Hanley's concern is with what happens in the human mind, the worries and hopes, the dreams and obsessions, that turn even the externally unspectacular into the stuff of tragedy. Forty-six years after *Boy*, Hanley was being congratulated by the *Times* reviewer of a new novel, *A Kingdom* (1978), for what he has done 'to open our eyes to the extraordinary human animal, ourselves'.

The output from the intervening decades includes an epic pentalogy, *The Furys* (1935), *The Secret Journey* (1936), *Our Time is Gone* (1940), *Winter Song* (1950), and *An End and a Beginning* (1958). The cycle chronicles the lives of Denis Fury, a seaman, his wife, Fanny, and their son, Peter. In this saga, as elsewhere, Hanley achieves a universal status for his protagonists. No more than in the case of Conrad is it adequate to label him a 'novelist of the sea' without noting how experience on board merely gives a sharper edge to the testing struggles of man in nature and man in society. *The Closed Harbour* (1952) is a harrowing account of the escalating moral and mental collapse of a French seaman who has lost his captain's ticket through returning alive almost alone from the sinking of his ship. His own nephew was among those who went down, so that his mother and his sister reinforce at home the scathing and suspicious judgment of the authorities.

Something of the same claustrophobic intensity of personal suffering and the same awareness of the enmity of the sea is found in the novels of Neil Gunn (1891–1973), the son of a Caithness crofter. In *The Grey Coast* (1926) he depicts the meanness of life for crofters and fishermen on the coast of the Moray Firth where 'existence became possible as a dour test of endurance, body and soul jealously self-contained'. The analysis of the suffering and frustration of the orphan heroine, Maggie Sutherland, is unsparing in its detail, though a happy ending is contrived. *Morning Tide* (1931), *Young Art and Old Hector* (1942), and other novels register comparable experience with a vividness of detail that is to some extent due to Gunn's striking imagery. Gunn achieved perhaps his greatest success by turning back in *The Silver Darlings* (1941) to the time of the Highland Clearances in the early eighteenth century, when evicted crofters moved from the glens to the coast to build up the herring-fishing industry. The tale has epic stature and the young hero is appropriately named 'Finn'. Gunn's rejection of dehumanising developments assumed rather a romantic than a political colouring and, in later novels, such as *The Well at the World's End* (1951), sharp observation gives ground to an insubstantial strain of mysticism.

The romantic spirit drove T. H. White (1906–64) to set his Arthurian tetralogy, *The Once and Future King*, in a background of imaginary mediaevalism rich in detail but unfettered by strict historicity. The technicalities of hawking, jousting, tilting, and the like are thoroughly explicated, but an element of sheer fantasy intrudes in the unashamed wizardry of Merlin, who has a walking mustard-pot, is moving backwards through time, and has nineteenth-century relics like the *Encyclopaedia Britannica* at his disposal. In the matter of background White rolls the Middle Ages up into a bundle and picks out what he wants to fashion an ideal 'Merry England'. He selects from Malory and makes Malory's position his starting-point. The whole represents the kind of past presupposed by Malory with a lot of extras thrown in. *The Sword in the Stone* (1938) deals with Arthur's youth and preparation for kingship. *The Queen of Air and Darkness*, originally called *The Witch in the Wood* (1940), deals with the establishing of the great work of Chivalry in the order of the Round Table, and also with Agravaine and Mordred (Arthur's illegitimate sons) who are to prove Arthur's undoing. *The Ill-Made Knight* (1941) tells the story of Launcelot and Guenever, and the quest of the Holy Grail. *The Candle in the Wind* (1958) tracks the collapse of Arthur's work.

The moral pattern that emerges logically from this reconstruction shows Camelot established through unselfish application of the chivalric code. The rot begins to set in when the code, having served its civilising purpose, turns into a pointless game. Arthur's diagnosis of the demoralisation is that a spiritual end is needed, and he therefore initiates the quest of the Holy Grail. T. H. White's shedding of the historical straitjacket is congenial to the Matter of Britain. Cheerful anachronisms of tone and temper enable him to embody in Arthur and in his codes an ethic plainly relevant to the struggle between discipline and lawlessness, order and decomposition, in every age.

White, whose other books include *Mistress Masham's Repose* (1947), a novel about descendants of Lilliputians brought home by Gulliver, and *The Goshawk* (1952), an account of his own experience in training hawks for falconry, earned a sympathetic biography from an admiring fellow-novelist, Sylvia Townsend Warner (1893–1978), a woman of many gifts who was also an eminent musicologist and expert on Tudor music. In her first novel, *Lolly Willowes* (1926), Laura Willowes, a respectable spinster aunt, discovers her true vocation as a witch and makes a compact with the Devil. The lucid prose, the gentle irony, the measured cadences make a sharp point about woman's lot. For the 'old employment of being Aunt Lolly' was empty. 'One doesn't become a witch to run around being harmful, or to run around being helpful either, a district visitor on a broomstick. It's to escape all that — to have a life of one's own, not an existence doled out to you by others . . .' A fuller study of a woman's breaking out is made in *Summer Will Show* (1936), in which a spirited Dorset Lady of the Manor sees through 'the rational humanitarianism which forbids that any race should toil as slaves when they would toil more readily as servants', rejects the tedious role assigned to her by society, and finds fulfilment at the Paris barricades in the 1848 Revolution. The more ambitious novel, *The Corner that Held Them* (1948), portrays the life of an English priory of Benedictine nuns in the fourteenth century with the express purpose of enabling the Marxist approach to 'get its teeth into the religious life'.

VI Irish writers and others

If there is a hint of Jane Austen in Miss Townsend Warner's amused, ironic detachment and in her deftly poised prose, there is perhaps even rarer Austenian subtlety in the way Elizabeth Bowen (1899–1973) registers the finer absurdities of the social comedy. No one could more adroitly capsulate, for instance, the psychological complexities of a family's response to an unexpected call by a too eager visitor. But Miss Bowen's central terrain is that of the stricken heart. Her own experience, as a product of the Anglo-Irish ascendancy with a family home in County Cork, involved an emotional dislodgement during the Irish Troubles that was compounded by more personal afflictions (her father's illness and her mother's death) and fully accounts for her concern with the fragility of happiness, the sense of loss, and the capacity to suffer. But she restricted herself in her novels to the privacies of life and judged it no business of the writer to mount a pulpit or a platform. Miss Bowen's acute awareness of people's most sensitive social and emotional antennae, and her brooding reflectiveness on the day-to-day awakenings of the human pilgrimage, are salted in her best work by an ironic gift for comic exaggeration that saves the atmosphere from becoming too sombre or claustrophobic.

Loss of innocence is such a pervasive theme that Miss Bowen has been compared with Henry James. *The Hotel* (1927) traces the bruising of a vulnerable girl who tries to find refuge from loneliness among the shallow, drifting characters assembled at an Italian resort. In *The Last September* (1929) the lonely heroine, an adolescent orphan, is in the Big House owned by her aunt and uncle in Ireland at the time of the Troubles (1920). The parallel psychological insecurity, personal in the case of the girl, public in the case of the

English—Irish adults, is investigated by a writer who had felt both. Elizabeth Bowen's two strongest studies of youthful vulnerability bruised are *The House in Paris* (1936) and *The Death of the Heart* (1938). Both show the sins of the fathers visited upon the children. Adults freeze out their children, not necessarily by wickedness or ill-will, but by sheer inadequacy and insensitivity. The illegitimate boy, Leopold, in *The House in Paris* goes to a Paris house at the age of eleven for the purpose of seeing his real mother for the first time, and is bitterly disappointed. It turns out that the house was where his mother stayed as a girl when he was conceived. The source of the boy's misery is located in youthful rebellion a generation back. More telling, because less ambivalent in the focus of its sympathy, is the story of Portia Quayne in *The Death of the Heart*. The chance product of a silly affair that ended her father's marriage and led him to a nomadic life with an unbecoming partner, Portia is orphaned and then shunted at sixteen on to a step-brother whose home can offer nothing in the way of congeniality, let alone of affection. Hungry for acceptance, Portia falls prey to a shallow, ostentatious fellow by whom she then feels herself betrayed. There is social comedy in the portrayal of personalities at loggerheads as well as penetration in the study of Portia's awakening.

Within a few years of Elizabeth Bowen's birth in a Big House in County Cork, Frank O'Connor (pseudonym of Michael O'Donovan) (1903—66) was born in a tenement in Cork city; by the age of fifteen he was in the IRA, and he fought with the republicans in the Civil War. But the new Ireland did not satisfy him. He worked in London during the Second World War and spent many years in the USA afterwards. O'Connor's autobiographies, *An Only Child* (1961) and *My Father's Son* (1968), fascinating records of Irish upbringing, experience in the Civil War, and management of the Abbey Theatre, register the scrupulous integrity which precluded identification with any cause tainted by fanaticism, intolerance, or small-mindedness. O'Connor found his fulfilment as a writer of short stories. There were nearly two hundred of them, many of them first published in journals such as *The New Yorker* and later collected in book form. The first volume, *Guests of the Nation* (1931), contains in the title story his most celebrated piece about the execution

of English soldiers held hostage by republicans in the Civil
War. O'Connor's stories of Irish life are not problematical,
but put reality before the reader with local vividness and
universal applicability.

O'Connor ran into Sean O'Faolain (1900–) while fighting
against the Free State forces in 1922. O'Faolain too came
from Cork. His father was a loyal constable in the RIC while
O'Connor's had been a bandsman in the British Army.
O'Faolain used his inside experience of the Troubles in a
somewhat sensational collection of short stories, *Midsummer
Night Madness* (1932). Three subsequent novels of Irish life,
A Nest of Simple Folk (1933), *Bird Alone* (1936), and *Come
Back to Erin* (1940), focus on rebellious heroes. But O'Faolain,
like O'Connor, did his best work in short stories, where the
tone is quieter and more philosophical (see *Selected Stories*,
1977). Meanwhile a writer who lived through all the Troubles
without being obsessed in her work with the Matter of Ireland
was Kate O'Brien (1898–1974). Her novel, *Without My
Cloak* (1931), chronicles the life of a Victorian small-town
family, the Considines, with a Galsworthian nostalgia and a
Galsworthian vein of erotic sentiment.

The Matter of Ireland was of course dislodged from British
consciousness by the Matter of Germany when war was
declared in 1939. It was not a good time to write a first novel.
Beckett's *Murphy* (1938) was submerged, but Beckett lived
to achieve acclaim in the late fifties and sixties. Flann O'Brien
(pseudonym of Brian O'Nolan) (1911–66) was less fortunate
with his comparably experimental novel, *At Swim-Two-Birds*
(1939). Submerged by events, republished over twenty years
later, it won enough attention to get his novel, *The Third
Policeman* (1967), into print only posthumously. O'Brien's
reputation during his lifetime was as Myles na Gopaleen, who
contributed a regular comic column, the 'Cruiskeen Lawn', to
the *Irish Times* from 1933 to 1966. *The Best of Myles* (1968),
a selection drawn largely from the war period, is worth consulting if only for its mock-pedantic study of clichés. In *At
Swim-Two-Birds* an author's own characters turn on their
creator in vengeful counter-authorship. The narrator's biography further complicates a hilarious exercise in tearing the novel
form to pieces from the inside. *The Third Policeman*, written
soon afterwards, is a tighter and more sombre fantasy that

follows a murderer's pilgrimage into the afterlife. Kafkaesque symbolism and teasing dialogue convey preternatural menace. *The Dalkey Archive* (1964), which made use of some of the material in the then unpublished *The Third Policeman*, is a less homogeneous though superficially more naturalistic novel.

The Irish fondness for parody and for multiple irony can sometimes give a work an ambivalent status. The dividing line between mocking parody and appreciative pastiche is a fine one. The dramatist, Denis Johnston (1901–), put on his play *The Old Lady Says No* in Dublin in 1929. It contrasts the romantic story of the rebel, Robert Emmet, with the living reality of Irish life for what would appear to be a sharply satirical purpose, yet the rhetoric of revolution can be received sympathetically. Perhaps the ambivalence explains the comparative neglect of Johnston. *The Moon in the Yellow River* (1931) focuses on an incident in the Civil War in which the irregulars destroy a power plant and emerge as machine-wreckers. ('This is no country. It is a damned debating society,' says the German engineer.) Most controversial of all Johnston's plays is *The Scythe and the Sunset* (1958), which turns the tables on the 'myth' of the 1916 rising. Johnston's view is that the rebel leaders would have been universally laughed off as absurd by their countrymen had not the British given them a serious military status by turning big guns on them.

Johnston received his later education in Edinburgh and Cambridge; he worked for the BBC during the Second World War, and held university posts in the USA in the 1950s and 1960s. The Irishman who studies and works abroad will naturally bring a different understanding to bear on the Matter of Ireland. Or he may well ignore the Matter of Ireland. No doubt he is more likely to ignore it if he comes from the British north than if he comes from the republican south. Helen Waddell (1889–1965) is a case in point. The daughter of a Protestant missionary from County Down, educated first in Belfast, Helen Waddell left Ireland for Oxford and London when she was nearly thirty. A scholarly mediaevalist, she produced a fascinating historical study, *The Wandering Scholars* (1927), and then managed to capture in fiction the figures of Abelard and Heloise with a roundness that does full justice to the diverse impulses of passion, learning, and piety that made them what they were. *Peter Abelard* (1933) is remarkable for the fullness of its historical detail, concrete and intellectual, and for the sure artistic instinct that made Abelard's moral pilgrimage an epitome of spiritual man's dilemma in time.

In the post-war Oxford to which Helen Waddell went to study in 1920, a compatriot from Belfast had settled down to work after service in France, and he had like literary gifts and scholarship. C. S. Lewis (1898–1963), for long years a Fellow of Magdalen College, was one of those rare literary personalities around whom others cluster to form a recognisable group with its own place in literary history. Lewis was eminent as a critic and a literary historian. His lucidity and vigour as a writer of Christian apologetic made him perhaps the most listened-to prophet of Anglo-Saxon Christendom. He brought literary imagination to bear on his theological output and theological insight to bear on his fiction to equally fruitful effect. *The Screwtape Letters* (1942), a little masterpiece of irony, is one side of a confidential correspondence between devils about their task of ensnaring a human soul. The trilogy of science-fiction (*Out of the Silent Planet*, 1938; *Voyage to Venus*, 1943; *That Hideous Strength*, 1945) looks at space exploration and technological imperialism in terms of the cosmic status of the fallen human race. The *Chronicles of Narnia*, a cycle of seven stories for children, beginning with *The Lion, the Witch, and the Wardrobe* (1950) and ending with *The Last Battle* (1956), ransacks a lifetime's garnering of riches from fairy-tale and the lore of past story and legend, and weaves together the natural and the marvellous, the stuff of fantasy and of myth, into adventures shot through with mystery and resonant with moral and spiritual overtones.

At the centure of the Lewis group were J. R. R. Tolkien, whose major work did not hit the public until a later decade, and Charles Williams (1886–1945), a fellow-Anglican who combined literary with theological interests. Williams turned to the Matter of Britain in two cycles of poems, *Taliessin through Logres* (1938) and *The Region of the Summer Stars* (1944). The Arthurian material is treated with probing exploration of its mythical and religious centre. The Grail Quest is seen in terms of the need for the return of Christ to a Britain

(Logres) under the Byzantine imperium. The work has intellectual intensity and a rather angular liturgical splendour. Its
episodes are flashed before the imagination like a series of
slides. Taxingly economic in presentation, the poetry makes
no concession to current modes of ensnaring the reader's
confidence, yet there is a verbal discipline sometimes lacking
in the more accessible novels. These, once more, set the lives
of the characters in the context of supernatural conflict
between the powers of good and evil. The attempt to give
cosmic dimensions on the Miltonic scale to the daily lives of
men and women in twentieth-century England was of course
to challenge the *Zeitgeist* head-on. But the novels, which
include *Many Dimensions* (1931), *The Greater Trumps* (1932),
Descent into Hell (1937), and *All Hallows' Eve* (1945), reveal
Williams's remarkable imaginative ingenuity in exploiting
knowledge of the occult on the one hand, and the resources
of mystical understanding on the other, for the purpose of
making the salvation or damnation of human souls an immediate issue on the contemporary scene. Williams was also involved
in the revival of poetic drama, religious in substance, that
stemmed from the production of Eliot's *Murder in the
Cathedral*; but his plays, of which the best known is *Thomas
Cranmer of Canterbury* (1936), are too metaphysically complex in thought for easy communication between stage and
audience.

The Scots dramatist, James Bridie (pseudonym of O. H.
Mavor (1888–1951)), opened a vein more palatable to the
theatre-going public when he hit on the idea of dramatising
some slightly off-centre Biblical stories in updated idiom. In
Tobias and the Angel (1930) he turned first to the Book of
Tobit in the Apocrypha for the charming story of how blind
old Tobit's son, Tobias, is despatched on a journey to collect
now much-needed repayment of a long-standing debt. The
angel Raphael joins him in the disguise of a porter and aids
him in outwitting a demon who repeatedly strangles a nubile
young lady's husbands on their wedding night. Bride and
fortune accrue to Tobias. An unaffected, uninterfering
theatrical sense applied to this tale and subsequently to other
biblical tit-bits, *Jonah and the Whale* (1932) and *Susannah
and the Elders* (1937), gave them a fetching ingenuousness on
stage. But well-staged narrative is not necessarily notable for

dramatic cohesion, and when Bridie worked on subjects nearer home weaknesses of structure emerged. His dramatisation of the Burke and Hare murders in *The Anatomist* (1931) was effective simply by virtue of its built-in interest of content. *Mr Bolfry* (1943) has surer craftsmanship and gained Bridie credit as the creator of 'problem plays'. Young men and women, gathered at a highland manse, attempt conjuration as a lark, and the Devil ('Mr Bolfry') joins them. Next morning, they believe they must have shared a common nightmare until the umbrella left by Mr Bolfry walks out belatedly after him.

Among submerged books published on the eve of war was *Lark Rise* (1939), the first volume of the trilogy of lightly fictionalised autobiography by Flora Thompson (1873–1947). It was followed by *Over to Candleford* (1941) and *Candleford Green* (1943), and the trilogy was reissued as *Lark Rise to Candleford* (1945). Candleford is Buckingham. Flora Thompson began this work in her sixties. A village girl who started work in a post office at the age of fourteen and married a post office clerk, she had a direct style, acute observation, and a delightful openness of mind to everything about her. Her trilogy, covering a country upbringing in the 1880s and 1890s, is a valuable historical document as well as a movingly evocative record. In the decade of renewed European struggle Flora Thompson cast her mind back to the frugal routines of the agricultural labourer, the primitive practicalities of domestic toil, and the lore of the country mind, as they existed before the First World War.

7
After firing
The 1940s and 1950s

I Introduction

THE course of the Second World War was such that British
troops were involved in campaigns in the Far East, in Africa,
and in Italy as well as just across the British Channel. Indeed
the land operations across the Channel were restricted to the
few first desperate months of failure to resist the German
advance into France, which culminated in the surrender of
France in 1940 and the swift evacuation of British troops
from the ports and beaches, and to the massive landings of
invasion forces in Normandy four years later for the steady
advance into Germany that brought about Hitler's defeat. In
the interim the Second World War was a matter of bombing
and counter-bombing from the air, of service in far-off fields,
and of convoy-running over seas mined and infested with sub-
marines. Sir Winston Churchill assumed a personal authority
as Prime Minister from 1940 which enabled him, with his gift
of rhetoric, to give passing events the character of movements
in a shapely drama whose issue was that of civilisation's
survival. As the dismal withdrawal from France in 1940 gave
place to the air Battle of Britain by day and the bombings of
our cities by night, there was not much to sustain public
morale except Churchill's stirring phrases about what was
owed to the few by the many and the privilege of serving the
nation in its finest hour. But the entry of the United States
into the war in 1941, Montgomery's victories in North Africa
in 1942, the rash German invasion of Russia in 1941 and the
consequent surrender of a Germany army at Stalingrad in
1943 were all developments that made Nazi power seem less
invincible, while the news that began to filter through of the
horrors of the concentration camps corroborated the enemy's

evil status and gave the Allies' case increasingly the flavour of a crusade. Once the long preparations were over and the Anglo-American landings in Normandy were successfully effected, the last act of the drama played itself out with a steady predictability that military adventures rarely manifest.

There was during the war some anticipation of a post-war world very different from the world of the thirties. Sir William Beveridge's *Report on Social Security and National Insurance* was published in 1942 to become the blue-print for the establishment of the post-war Welfare State. R. A. Butler's Education Act of 1944 made secondary education compulsory for all. And after the war the India Independence Act of 1947 began the process of final withdrawal from imperial and colonial responsibilities that marked the succeeding decades. But a legacy of war which was to cast a shadow over subsequent decades was the invention of the atom bomb. When the Americans dropped it on the Japanese cities of Hiroshima and Nagasaki in 1945 the unprecedented material and human damage it inflicted made immediate Japanese surrender inevitable. Britain built its first nuclear reactor in 1947 and Russia effected its first atomic explosion two years later. By 1954 the hydrogen bomb had succeeded the atom bomb. The theory of nuclear deterrence became the obsession of the world's super-powers, and the threat of nuclear extinction became an issue which literature could not ignore. It led to protest movements with which writers and other thinkers were often associated. Einstein, whose discoveries had directly opened the door to nuclear research, came to regret where his work had led. He was one of many Jewish and other political refugees who had left Nazi Germany and came to enrich the culture of the countries they adopted. There were those too, such as the conductor Arturo Toscanini, who left Mussolini's Italy for the USA. Einstein came first to England before settling in America: among those who settled in England were the Hungarian writer, Arthur Koestler, the Austrian artist, Oskar Kokoschka, and the Austrian philosopher, Ludwig Wittgenstein.

The immediate post-war years under a Labour government which had taken office in 1945 after an electoral landslide were inevitably years of austerity. The tasks of demobilisation, rebuilding bombed cities, and restoring an economy weakened by the cost of war and in particular the loss of overseas investments, coincided with the need to console a war-weary civilian population and reintegrate among them a body of servicemen, many of whom were eager to see a society from which pre-war injustices had been banished. Shortages of goods continued and it was over five years before all rationing was finally abolished. In the new decade the Festival of Britain in 1951 and the Accession of Queen Elizabeth II in 1952, as well as such events as the conquest of Everest by Sir John Hunt's party in Coronation year, 1953, brightened an atmosphere disturbed by the descent of the 'Iron Curtain' of distrust between the East-European Communist bloc and the Western democracies.

II Servicemen poets

It was early in the war that the popular press began to ask, Where are the war poets? There seemed to be a general expectation that the new conflict ought to be inspiring matching pieces to Brooke's 'The Soldier' and Grenfell's 'Into Battle'. But paradoxically it was the First World War which prevented the Second World War from having the psychological and emotional effect on writers that was being looked for. The educated young men who went off to fight in 1939 and 1940 had been brought up under the shadow of the First World War. They had read Owen and Sassoon and seen *Journey's End*. They had also seen human wrecks left over from Passchendaele and had listened to soured ex-servicemen, often jobless, angrily denouncing the wickedness of the war and the hypocrisy of those who had directed it, glorified it, or profited by it. Awareness of the gigantic waste of the First World War, conjoined with hatred of Nazi tyranny, determined the mood of the new servicemen. The war could neither be glorified nor evaded. And it could not this time be mistaken for a monstrously unique aberration. In this respect the war was perhaps kinder to artists than to poets. Graham Sutherland became an official war artist and made a dramatic record of the devastation; Henry Moore, another official war artist, made a celebrated series of drawings of Londoners sheltering from air-raids in the London Underground stations. Their task was not different from that of their predecessors in the First World

War, and indeed Paul Nash was an official artist in both conflicts. But the experience of Owen and Sassoon could not be
repeated.

It was difficult for the young servicemen who turned to
poetry to escape self-consciousness in this respect. Sidney
Keyes (1922—43) calls one poem 'War Poet':

> I am the man who groped for words and found
> An arrow in my hand.

Keyes went to Oxford in 1940, joined up in 1942, and was
killed in North Africa a year later. He saw his first volume
of poems published, *The Iron Laurel* (1942), but not his
second, *The Cruel Solstice* (1944). Death was a concern from
the start. 'The Foreign Gate' puts Keyes's vocation of sacrifice
into the context of the demands made by historic battles,
and this is the way of David Jones. For Keyes war is not an
incongruity in itself. Rather it intensifies the prevailing human
condition — the greed and destructiveness that unfit men for
peace. And it reflects and enlarges the inner conflict of the
individual:

> Until you have crossed the desert, and face that fire
> Love is an evil, a shaking of the hand,
> A sick pain draining courage from the heart.
>
> ('The Wilderness')

Alun Lewis (1915—44), a Welsh graduate, had had time to
begin his career as a teacher before he joined the army in
1940. He was sent to India in 1942 and killed in Burma.
Raider's Dawn (1942) and the posthumous *Ha! Ha! Among
the Trumpets* (1945) contains his verse, and there was also
a volume of short stories, *The Last Inspection* (1943). Lewis's
most famous poem, 'All Day It Has Rained', describing a wet
Sunday in a bell tent, summed up for reluctant conscripts
the drabness and the boredom which loomed so large in the
lives of servicemen. The title poem of *Raider's Dawn*, describing an air-raid —

> Blue necklace left
> On a charred chair
> Tells that Beauty
> Was startled there —

focuses, like 'The Soldier' and 'Goodbye', on wartime experience as real to the civilian as to the serviceman. India elicited
from Lewis poems of remarkable descriptive accuracy and
sometimes of penetrating insight into the lives of the Indians.
He captured the pitiably bewildered lostness of a struggling
beggar and likewise of a 'landless soldier lost in war' ('The
Peasants') and he saw a parallel between the social and economic fears that tangled lives on the home front, and the jungle
in which the Burma war was fought ('The Jungle').

Keith Douglas (1920–44) studied English at Oxford under
Edmund Blunden, who was to write an Introduction to his
Collected Poems (1966), before serving in the tank corps in
North Africa. He was killed in Normandy. For him war intensified and purged the sombre integrity of an already wounded
spirit, ruthless in its rejection of shallow consolation and of
easy verbalism. His early awareness of death, sharpened by
battle experience, gave a sense of urgency to his work that
left no time for cultivation of grand or lyrical graces. 'My
object', he wrote in a letter in 1943, '. . . is to write true
things, significant things in words each of which works for its
place in a line . . . . I see no reason to be either musical or
sonorous about things at present'. 'Dead Men' shows corpses
eaten by dogs in the desert at night, 'Russians' depicts a whole
standing battalion frozen stiff, 'Vergissmeinicht' ponders the
picture of a girl-friend found on an enemy corpse. There is
no moralising. And there is no surprise or awakening at a
revelation effected by war as opposed to peace. There is rather
metaphysical probing of the teasing human reality that war
evidences, the paring off of all accretions to the bone beneath
the skin. 'Remember me when I am dead / And simplify me
when I'm dead,' his most celebrated poem demands.

> As the processes of earth
> Strip off the colour and the skin;
> take the brown hair and blue eyes
> And leave me simpler than at birth
> when hairless I came howling in . . .

An equally widely known poem is 'Soldiers Bathing' by
F. T. Prince (1912–), a South-African born poet who served
in Intelligence and subsequently became a university teacher.
'Soldiers Bathing' stands in contrast to 'Simplify Me When

I'm Dead', for the sense of doom is replaced by probing analysis which patiently digs delight and gratitude out of contemplating soldiers stripped bare and escaping briefly in the sea waves the

> . . . terrible pressure that begets
> A machinery of death and slavery.

The poet's recall of Italian paintings of men stripped in battle is no doubt the kind of accretion which Douglas strove to peel away, but it leads Prince to see the rage and bitterness of 'war's horrible extreme' as a commentary on the Crucifixion. Prince, a poet of fastidious discipline, gathered his work to date in *Doors of Stone: Poems 1938–1962* (1963).

The increased mechanisation of warfare bound millions in servitude to the machinery Prince lamented — 'Each being a slave and making slaves of others'. For every man who saw corpses in the sand there were thousands who trained on parade grounds and received stereotyped instructions from NCOs. One of the aptest and most popular commentaries on the war was the satirical poem, 'The Naming of Parts', by Henry Reed (1914–), which at the outset cunningly parodied Auden's *Spain*:

> To-day we have naming of parts. Yesterday,
> We had daily cleaning. And tomorrow morning,
> We shall have what to do after firing. But to-day,
> To-day we have naming of parts . . . .

But no one voiced the tedium of service life more sardonically than Roy Fuller (1912–), who served in the Navy from 1941 to 1946.

> For what is terrible is the obvious
> Organisation of life: the oiled black gun
> And what it cost, the destruction of Europe by
> Its councils: the unending justification
> Of that which cannot be justified, what is done.
>
> ('What is Terrible')

Fuller's dry acerbity and his ironic detachment from the folly of war and the sloganising that accompanies it (see 'Spring 1942' and 'Autumn 1942') arise from a clarity of outlook that rejects consolatory blur of feeling or thought. *Collected Poems 1936–1961* (1962) is the work of a man who has rigorously moulded verse reflections on what life presents and searchingly analysed his own responses. There is a lack of emotional intensity, and sometimes an air of remoteness hangs over poems in which feverish brainwork seems to be trying to compensate for lack of driving impulse. But Fuller has been regarded as a key figure in poetic history for his role in handing on the ironic Audenesque astringency of the thirties to the 'Movement' poets of the fifties.

III Scottish and Irish poets

There were poets among the servicemen whom no one would be tempted to label 'war poets'. G. S. Fraser (1915–80) served in North Africa, but his early poetic affiliation was to a briefly fashionable movement associated with the anthologies, *The New Apocalypse* (1940), *The White Horseman* (1941), and *The Crown and Sickle* (1944). The movement reacted against politico-social relevance in favour of a new romantic concern with the personal realities of love and death, and against machinery in favour of myth, but few of the 'Apocalyptics' proved to have staying power. Norman MacCaig (1910–), however, who wrote *Far Cry* (1943), was to shake off his apocalyptic affiliation and make a new start with *Riding Lights* (1955), the first of a series of collections extending over the 1960s and 1970s in which he emerged as a poet of fresh perceptiveness, able to alert the brain and tease the senses with descriptive imagery finely conceived and deftly phrased.

> In a salt ring of moonlight
> The dinghy nods at nothing.
> It paws the bright water
> And scatters its own shadow
> In a false net of light.   ('Moorings')

MacCaig is a thinker too, speculating metaphysically on things seen, delighted to give a surprise twist to his perception, an unpredictable bonus of wit and insight. MacCaig's contact with his reader does not falter. This cannot be said of his fellow-Scot, W. S. Graham (1918–). The verbal bravura of

Graham's early volumes of the 1940s has been tamed, but his continuing preoccupation with the problem of utterance and the fluidity of identity scarcely allows him to be intelligibly open to his reader. In addition to the long title poem, *The Nightfishing* (1955) contains seven 'Letters' in which Graham experiments tellingly with a three-foot line. Imagery of the sea, fishing, the shore, a cottage, and related reflections on his personal past and the nearness of life to death come across with a sustained musical infectiousness and a fitful emotional intensity that make the reader hungry for more companionableness and clarity.

There is no failure to get across — to the Scots at least — in the poetry of Sydney Goodsir Smith (1915–75), a New Zealander with a Scots mother and a distinguished father who became Professor of Forensic Medicine at Edinburgh University and wrote an autobiographical book, *Mostly Murder* (1959). Smith came to Edinburgh and enrolled under Hugh MacDiarmid's banner. Steeping himself in Scottish literature, he learned to use the language of the Makars and their successors with the energy and thrust of a restless, rebellious intelligence. The English reader needs a glossary. But Smith was not culturally insular. He was well-read in many literatures. His *Collected Poems* (1975) and his Joycean novel, *Carotid Cornucopia* (1947), are the product of a rich mind and a boisterous spirit. Perhaps Smith is seen at his best in *Under the Eildon Tree* (1948), a collection of 'elegies' on love. This volume appeared in the same year as the *Collected Poems* of a Scots poet already dead, William Soutar (1898–1943), which has an Introduction by Hugh MacDiarmid. Soutar had had a tragic life, going from service in the Navy to Edinburgh University, and soon succumbing to a spinal disease which left him bedfast for the last thirteen years of his life. On his bed he kept a journal from which excerpts were published in *Diaries of a Dying Man* (1954). And from his bed he issued volumes of poems in Scots and in English. He was not a master of metrical variety and innovation, but his use of the ballad and of simple stanza forms for lyrical, satirical, and comic purposes was telling. Robert Garioch (1909–81), like Soutar, did his main work in Scots. Though his output includes some war poems, he is better known as a comic poet, a racy commentator on follies and pretensions who can debunk good-

humouredly. Targets like the Edinburgh Festival are shot at
with infectious relish.

> Americans wi routh of dollars,
> wha drink our whisky neat,
> wi Sassenachs and Oxford Scholars
> are eydent for the treat
> of music sedulously high-tie
> at thirty-bob a seat;
> Wop opera performed in Eyetie
> to them's richt up their street . . .
>
> ('Embro to the Ploy')

Garioch published *17 Poems for 6d* as early as 1940. His
Selected Poems of 1966 is the work of a versatile craftsman.
He can use the fable like Henryson ('The Twa Mice') and can
rollick in ridicule as jauntily as any flyter and without loss of
magnanimity. (See 'In Princes Street Gardens' or 'Heard in
the Canongate'.)

It may seem odd to the Sassenach that the Lallans poet,
Garioch, exudes the sophisticated urbanity of the capital
city, Edinburgh, while George Bruce (1909–), a regional
poet who puts vividly before him the stark realities in the
lives of fishing folk on the North East Scottish coast in such
collections as *Sea Talk* (1944), for the most part uses standard
English. In the one case critics speak of indebtedness to
Henryson, Fergusson, Burns, and MacDiarmid: in the other
case they speak of indebtedness to Eliot, Pound, and Yeats.
These are the inheritances between which the modern Scottish
poet must choose. Maurice Lindsay (1918–), whose work
Bruce championed by selecting from his past poetry and
introducing it in *The Exiled Heart* (1957), wrote first in
Lallans in *The Enemies of Love, Poems 1941–1945* (1946),
but gradually came to feel the unreality of concentrating on a
declining language spoken by fewer people every year. 'I
therefore turned my attention to writing in the tongue I, and
the majority of Scots, actually speak; a kind of Scotticised
English.' Lindsay's poems are undemonstratively neat and
graceful, quiet of voice but genuinely observant.

> She moved among the sour smell of her hen's droppings,
> her cheeks rubbed to polish, her skirts bustled
> with decent pride; alone since the day the tractor
> hauled itself over the hill and toppled
> her man away from her . . .   ('Farm Widow')

Poets of the Scottish and of the Irish Renaissance have faced comparable problems in moulding standard English to their needs. Austin Clarke (1896–1974) strove for over fifty years to give his English poems essential Irish qualities. Clarke, who left a lively account of his Dublin childhood in *Twice Around the Black Church* (1962), scarcely foreshadowed in his early narrative and lyrical verse the poet who came to light in *Night and Morning* (1938), where he began to tackle social and religious aspects of contemporary Ireland. After a seventeen-year gap, during which he was preoccupied with revitalising verse drama in Dublin, Clarke returned to pure poetry with *Ancient Lights* (1955). The collections of subsequent years, including *Flight to Africa* (1963) and *Mnemosyne Lay in Dust* (1967), exploit technical devices derived from Gaelic poetry with bracing bluntness and pithiness, and with an expertly controlled rhythmic punch.

> The hasty sin of the young after a dance,
> Awkward in clothes against a wall or crick-necked
> In car, gives many a nun her tidy bed,
> Full board and launderette. God-fearing State
> Provides three pounds a week, our conscience money,
> For every infant severed from the breast.
>
> ('Living on Sin')

Clarke's range covers poems of wry autobiographical reflection, of lively portraiture, and of packed description. There is history and anecdote, protest and celebration, comedy and painful inner self-scrutiny. Through it all runs a current of energy that few poets have sustained so consistently.

While Clarke was preoccupied with drama, Patrick Kavanagh (1905–67), the son of a country cobbler from County Monaghan, was gaining the reputation in Dublin of being Yeats's successor. His rural upbringing, with its years of hardship on a farm, supplied the material for two works of autobiographical fiction, *The Green Fool* (1938) and *Tarry Flynn* (1948). Having published *Ploughman and Other Poems* (1936), Kavanagh had made his way to Dublin to throw himself into the pub life which was to destroy Flann O'Brien, Brendan Behan, and himself. His poem, *The Great Hunger* (1942), depicting the lot of the poor farmer struggling against physical hardships and against the inhibiting effects of the Irish moral climate on feeling and imagination, is accounted one of the great poems of the age.

Patrick Maguire, the old peasant, can neither be damned nor glorified:
The grave-yard in which he will lie will be just a deep-drilled potato field
Where the seed gets no chance to come through
To the fun of the sun.

But Kavanagh, who turned against the pioneers of the Irish literary movement for falsely romanticising the Irish peasantry ('I no longer need Yeats. I have outgrown him . . .'), became hypercritical too of his own early dreams and poetic aspirations, and in subsequent volumes, *A Soul for Sale* (1947) and *Come Dance with Kitty Stobling* (1960), he achieved a devastating verbal ruthlessness in peeling off every trace of veneer or pretence. Disillusionment with 'the insincere city' and its readiness to lionise the peasant poet and sentimentalise the life he represented sharpened Kavanagh's talent for irony and wry self-scrutiny.

The career and output of the Dubliner, Denis Devlin (1908– 59), stand in sharp contrast. Social and cultural distances separated the schoolteacher-turned-diplomat who finished up as Irish ambassador to Italy, from the rough boy from Mucker. Devlin, an Irish Catholic schooled in European culture, published *First Poems* in 1930 and *Lough Derg* in 1946. A fellow-poet, Brian Coffey (1905–), edited and introduced his posthumous *Collected Poems* (1964). Devlin cultivated the craft of poetry with that overt respect for the artefact itself which poets like Kavanagh strive to bypass in their pursuit of down-to-earthness. Thought-out speculation, fed on the fruits of learning and phrased with careful artistry, may aspire to sublimity without precluding genuine feeling, as Devlin's work proves.

IV Other poets and verse dramatists

The poet who assays the heights does his image no harm if he sometimes relaxes. Humour has a way of authenticating seriousness. John Heath-Stubbs (1918–) has been aware of this. Heath-Stubbs, who collaborated with the South-African born poet, David Wright (1918–), in editing the *Faber Book of Twentieth-Century Verse* (1953), is a man of erudition, master of an assured and flexible expertise, but he has a delightful vein of humour.

> Mr Heath-Stubbs as you must understand
> Came of a gentleman's family out of Staffordshire
> Of as good blood as any in England
> But he was wall-eyed and his legs too spare.
>
> ('Epitaph')

The amusing title poem of *A Charm Against Toothache* (1954) is neatly fabricated of nice artifices. Twenty-five years later 'Send for Lord Timothy' from *The Watchman's Flute* (1979) burlesques typical detective-novel material hilariously. Such poems, like the meatier efforts of Gavin Ewart (1916–), seem to stand, by sheer concentration of substance, securely on the upper side of the boundary separating comic poetry from 'light verse'. Yet often Heath-Stubbs's readiness to draw material from recondite areas of classical, historical scholarship, from the world of art and music, together with what a later poet, Edward Lucie-Smith (1933–), calls his 'consciously literary, highly wrought, rather unspontaneous' manner, limit his appeal.

Heath-Stubbs had come under the influence of C. S. Lewis and Charles Williams when he was at Oxford and he published a study of the latter, *Charles Williams* (1955). Another, and older, poet on whose beliefs Lewis exercised a decisive influence was Ruth Pitter (1897–), a craftswoman in fancy goods by profession who has also been a life-long craftswoman in verse. She early gained the recommendation of Hilaire Belloc, and over forty years later collected her poems to date in *Poems 1926–1966* (1968). An observer of nature and of people, endowed with a sense of mystery, she has recorded moments of mystical exploration which have led critics to compare her with Traherne. She can combine sculptured grace with rhythmic naturalness.

> But for lust we could be friends,
> On each other's necks could weep:
> In each other's arms could sleep
> In the calm the cradle lends . . .   ('But for Lust')

A woman poet of comparable religious orientation but whose personal and spiritual pilgrimage has been ostensibly more turbulent is Kathleen Raine (1908–). Miss Raine read natural science at Cambridge where she met the poet and sociologist, Charles Madge, who became for a time her husband. She has told her personal story in the autobiographical trilogy, *Farewell, Happy Fields* (1973), *The Land Unknown* (1975), and *The Lion's Mouth* (1977). It is a chronicle of one who came 'under the influence of the spirit of the time which equated the search for truth . . . with the rejection of all truths from the past' and then herself rejected the 'illusion that the "freeing" of the artist from tradition can lead to anything except the end of civilisation as such'. She sees the cult of self-expression as destructive of personality and believes that 'only in a supernatural context does the natural thrive'. In her *Collected Poems* (1956) and subsequent volumes she stands therefore as a poet in the neo-Platonic tradition as it has come down in Blake, Shelley, and Yeats. The emphasis on human spirituality and her use of an appropriate symbolic vocabulary have not endeared her to the critical school for whom social man is the central reality, but the sheer lyrical beauty of her poetic line, the frankness of her voice, and the fastidious shaping of rhythm and stanza, command attention.

> A Gaelic bard they praise who in fourteen adjectives
> Named the one invisible soul of his glen;
> For what are the bens and the glens but manifold qualities,
> Immeasurable complexities of soul?   ('The Ancient Speech')

G. S. Fraser has set Kathleen Raine's joint scientific and mystical interests alongside her enthusiasm for the work of abstract artists and sculptors such as Henry Moore, Barbara Hepworth (who illustrated her first collection, *Stone and Flower*, 1943, with drawings), and Ben Nicholson, suggesting that these artists too were 'seeking in outward nature archetypal forms or Platonic ideas'.

No reference to matters so elevated would be required to characterise the poetry of Stevie Smith (1902–71), who from the time of her first volume, *A Good Time Was Had By All* (1937), turned out verse with a charm and oddity all its own. Miss Smith manipulates a kind of inspired idiocy to comic and sometimes to profound, or near-profound, effect. She can accumulate naiveties whose sequence or conjunction is disturbingly hilarious if not hilariously disturbing. She focuses on the space between tragedy and triviality which terror and laughter dispute. The uncomfortable title poem of *Not Waving But Drowning* (1957) has justly been a favourite with anthologists. The image of the hand raised from the waves in distress and mistaken for a hand raised in greeting is eloquent with ambiguities. ('I was much further out than you thought.') In more patently frivolous vein Stevie Smith has a curious agility with nonsense verse whose nonsensicality may or may not conceal a cutting edge, but whose ingenuous reiterations will not leave the reader satisfied only to smile. Some poems are anecdotal, some comment on topicalities, while others play tricks in jingling doggerel that cunningly radiates suspicion of its surface inoffensiveness.

The minor poet whose gift is as eccentric as Stevie Smith's may steal attention from steadier talents. A woman poet especially, who steers clear of idiosyncrasy, apocalyptic claim, or public platform, and fastens on the world of things domestic and personal, may find her quiet meditations overlooked. E. J. Scovell (1907–) published three volumes of verse in the 1940s and her collected poems, *The River Steamer*, in 1956. She reflects on events of home life, on parenthood, on growing old, with a fine delicacy of touch and with a pervasive sense of wonder. Similarly Anne Ridler (1912–), in *Nine Bright Shiners* (1943), *A Matter of Life and Death* (1959), and *Some Time After* (1972), has recorded her reflections on love, marriage, parenthood, and the passing events of family life with an open-hearted candour and fervour rooted in Christian belief. Anne Ridler has also written verse plays on religious themes. An early play, *The Shadow Factory* (1946), a nativity play whose setting is a modern factory, was put on at the Mercury Theatre in the season of new plays directed by E. Martin Browne. The same season saw the first productions of *This Way to the Tomb* by Ronald Duncan (1914–), and *A Phoenix too Frequent* by Christopher Fry (1907–).

Duncan's play juxtaposes in masque and anti-masque the martyrdom of the fourteenth-century hermit, Saint Anthony of Zantë, with a gathering at his shrine of reporters and television crews for the anniversary on which he is supposed to put in a miraculous reappearance. Riding on the tide created by *Murder in the Cathedral*, Duncan cunningly developed the cross-reference between history and modernity used by Eliot.

Benjamin Britten composed music for the play, and in the same year Britten's opera, *The Rape of Lucretia*, for which Duncan wrote the libretto, was put on at Glyndebourne. In subsequent plays, such as *Nothing Up My Sleeve* (1950) and *The Catalyst* (1958), Duncan experimented increasingly with flexible conversational rhythms, insisting that in verse drama poetry should evolve from the action and not clutter it with decoration.

It was not Duncan, however, but Fry who was to inherit Eliot's mantle in the theatre. He had written a pre-war festival play, *The Boy With a Cart* (1937). It presents episodically the story of the Cornish Saint Cuthman who, on his father's death, pushes his mother around in a cart in search of a place to build a church. After the war, in *A Phoenix too Frequent*, Fry dramatised a story from Petronius of a young Ephesian widow, determined to die in her husband's tomb, who thinks better of it after encountering a vigorous young soldier on guard. The tragedy, *The Firstborn*, performed at the Edinburgh Festival in 1948, studies Moses' dilemma in being called upon to free his captive people from the Egyptians, a course which involves striking at the Pharoah's family with whom he was brought up. But it was *The Lady's Not for Burning* (1948) which pushed Fry into the front rank of English dramatists. The setting is mediaeval. Jennet Jourdemayne has been condemned to be burnt as a witch. Thomas Mendip is determined to be executed for supposed murder. The coming together of the two transforms both. Fry's poetry has here a dancing buoyancy: it scintillates with metaphor and bravura. The distinctive air of his imaginative terrain derives from his conviction that we live in a world 'in which we are all poised on the edge of eternity, a world which has deeps and shadows of mystery . . .'

Fry has shown that this awareness can undergird actions in which the overtly religious content is minimal or nil. *Venus Observed* (1950) presents the human situation as warranting joy and gratitude and correspondingly demanding humility and self-surrender. The scene is a country mansion. The Duke of Altair, a middle-aged widower with a sexual history, is teased by the need to find stability amid the teeming variety of female attractions. He is also a researcher of the heavens by telescope. Bedroom and observatory are one, and the restless search for stability by phallus and telescope is symptomatic of man's lot in time. The Duke has to learn that impermanence must be accepted; that peace lies on the further side of acceptance. His armour of self-satisfaction is punctured at some sacrificial cost when a resentful former mistress sets fire to his home. The vitality of Fry's dialogue, his sense of humour and of paradox, enable him to skate gracefully on the thin ice of symbol-laden serio-comedy.

The Lady's Not for Burning and Venus Observed were conceived as the spring and autumn pieces in four 'Comedies of the Seasons'. A graver religious play, A Sleep of Prisoners (1951), intervened before the winter comedy, The Dark is Light Enough (1954), was produced, and the historical play about Henry II and Becket, Curtmantle (1961), intervened before the summer comedy, A Yard of Sun (1970), completed the series. Long before this, changed theatrical taste had driven Fry into film-script work. But he also made successful translations and adaptations of two French dramatists whose technique he found congenial, Anouilh's L'invitation au Château as Ring Round the Moon (1950), his L'alouette as The Lark (1955), and Giraudoux's La guerre de Troie n'aura pas lieu as Tiger at the Gates (1963). Anouilh's drama inhabits an area where naturalism and stylisation, reality and make-believe overlap, and Giraudoux bypasses psychological realism in favour of symbol and archetype. Fry's poetic virtue lies in what Derek Stanford calls the 'baptismal' power of his words to 'immerse his subject in a dimension which gives to them a new and added significance'.

V The realistic novel

Literary careers play strange tricks with chronology. A novelist who did his important work in the 1940s and later, L. P. Hartley (1895–1972), had served in the First World War when some of the poets of the 1940s were in their infancy or not even born; and some of them were dead by the time his first significant novel, The Shrimp and the Anemone (1944), reached the public. It proved to be the first novel of a trilogy, Eustace and Hilda, which chronicles the lives of a middle-class brother and sister. The swallowing of a shrimp by an anemone symbolises the central theme. Brother and sister have lost their mother in childhood. The strong-minded Hilda, the elder, to whom Eustace turns in admiration as a surrogate mother, makes excessive emotional demands upon him which prove ultimately stifling. By coincidence her compulsive moral pressure on him as a child entangles him in a net of practical as well as emotional obligations to her. The two try to go their own ways in the second novel, *The Sixth Heaven* (1946), but eventually, in the third novel, *Eustace and Hilda* (1947), Hilda, whose itch for dominance has frightened off the man Eustace wanted her to marry, breaks down from shock and becomes paralysed. The blackmail of suffering levers Eustace back to her to push her about in a bath-chair. Hartley has both pathos and humour at his finger-tips. There is some subtlety in his presentation of the child mind and its distorted sense of proportion. His analysis of the psychological impoverishment effected by Hilda's dominance is telling. But the trilogy suffers increasingly from diffuseness, and passionate intensity is lacking.

Hartley scored a popular success with *The Go-Between* (1953), in which Edwardian society life in a country house is the background for a beautiful young woman's furtive affair with a common farmer. Hartley's angle of vision gives the book its distinction. The tale is narrated in middle age by a friend of the family who was on a boyhood visit to the house at the time of the crisis. He was used as a messenger boy between the girl and the farmer. Since, as a child, he idealised both the girl and the official fiancé neglected for the farmer, the full discovery of what the offending couple are about is as much a psychological shock for him as it is a social shock for the family. Of Hartley's later novels the two complementary books, *The Brickfield* (1964) and *The Betrayal* (1968), jointly investigate a story of youthful guilt, life-long in its legacy though largely imaginary in its substance, which transforms the timid, dejected young Hartleyan hero of earlier novels into a morbid adult hag-ridden by calamity.

Hartley, at that time a well-known reviewer, gave encouraging notices to the early novels of Anthony Powell (1905–), whose social background was similar to his own. The most impressive of Powell's pre-war novels, *Afternoon Men* (1931), belongs alongside Huxley's and Waugh's satires of fashionable bohemian life in the 1920s. But Powell's manner and tone of voice are unique. There is nothing of Huxley's intellectual flamboyance or Waugh's hammer-blows of ridicule. Powell quietly dissects human silliness by letting it speak unexaggeratedly for itself. His method is to assemble the fragmentary pieces of experience that life and observation jumble together, with all the thinness of utterance which so much human intercourse consists in, and to leave the detection of vapidity to the reader.

After the war Powell decided to abandon as wasteful the practice of writing separate novels in which the novelist is for ever starting again, and to write a single long work in a series of volumes. The eventual result was the twelve-volume sequence, *A Dance to the Music of Time*, in which the narrator, Nicholas Jenkins, chronicles the lives of a group of contemporaries over the period of Powell's own life, and his career parallels Powell's own. These personal courses are unfolded against the sketchy background of important public events such as the hunger marches of the thirties, the Spanish Civil War, the Abdication, the Second World War, post-war political change, and the Burgess—Maclean affair. Walter Allen has defined Powell's geographical and spiritual terrain as centred on the point where Mayfair meets Soho. Powell's artistic plan was feasible because, as Bernard Bergonzi has said in *Anthony Powell* (1962):

The segment of English society that Powell writes about is one in which, in a loose sense, everyone knows everyone else, where Oxford, Cambridge, the public schools, all have connections with the principal London foci of intellectual, professional, and business life, to form a fairly coherent network.

This interconnection of people at the top applies especially to the 1920s and 1930s, the period of the first six novels: *A Question of Upbringing* (1951), *A Buyer's Market* (1952), *The Acceptance World* (1955), *At Lady Molly's* (1957), *Casanova's Chinese Restaurant* (1960), and *The Kindly Ones* (1962). The titular image of a dance defines the choreographic structure in which the careers of Jenkins's contemporaries are interwoven by successive personal appearances and, when absent, by the relentless flow of gossip. Marriages, re-marriages, and liaisons provide a catch-all network for hauling ever more families on deck. The manipulation of time-shifts and the proliferation of anecdote give dimensional fullness and textural density. The two later trilogies cover respectively the Second World War and the post-war world up to the 1970s: *The Valley of Bones* (1964), *The Soldier's Art* (1966), *The Military Philosophers* (1968), *Books Do Furnish a Room* (1971), *Temporary Kings* (1973), and *Hearing Secret Harmonies* (1975). Over the work as a whole the lack of philosophical reverberations is to some extent compensated for by the implicit evidence of the 'disintegration of society in its traditional forms', more especially the breakdown of marriage morality from the top, and the advent of cynicism. Much hinges on the central contrast between Nick's unassumingness and sensitivity, and the crude, unimaginative ambition of his foil, Kenneth Widmerpool, the man of drive, whose career counterbalances Nick's. But Powell's title invites comparison with Proust, and such elements of cohesion scarcely add up to an organic rhythm of inner design comparable to that provided by Proust's current of philosophical reflection, his absorbing analysis of love, and Marcel's intense self-exploration. It is the notational fullness of Powell's documentation which gives the work its solidity.

Powell has now embarked on a multi-volume series of memoirs, *To Keep the Ball Rolling*, of which volumes I and II (*Infants of Spring*, 1976, and *Messengers of Day*, 1978) cover school and university days and early years in London. A much-mentioned contemporary at Eton and Oxford is the novelist, Henry Green (pseudonym of Henry Yorke) (1905–73). Powell records how he and Green 'shared the discovery of Proust at Oxford', and how Green placed his first novel, *Blindness* (1926), with a publisher while still a student. Green went into business and became Managing Director of a Midlands engineering firm, and the next novel, *Living* (1929), explores the drab lives of men working at a Birmingham factory. The attempt of the daughter of one of them, Lily Gates, to escape by elopement with a showy and shallow young fellow peters out in a pathetic yet comic anti-climax. 'By dislocating syntax, by compressing and eliminating articles, and by dealing in indirect discourse, Green achieves a colloquially crabbed ungainliness which epitomises the lives of the workers,' Robert S. Ryf has written in *Henry Green* (1967).

Certainly economy of style was Green's passion. He shared

Powell's laconic detachment and his cool deliberation in under-playing his hand, but he differed in occupying a fictional terrain stripped of culture. This bareness conspires congenially with the stylistic terseness to emphasise the aridity and in-security of contemporary life in *Party Going* (1939), a novel in which a party of society butterflies find themselves fog-bound at Victoria station when they should be on their way to a holiday in France. While the packed masses of delayed commuters fret angrily in the background, the aimless upper-class idlers in the station hotel fill the unexpected parenthesis with their customary vapid gossip and self-indulgent personal interplay. Glimpses of human oddity and human need else-where on the station represent a moral judgment on them as the frustrated commuters represent a social judgment on them. To this extent perhaps *Party Going* is the surest of Green's novels in thrust and cohesion.

Caught (1943) is based on Green's wartime experience of the Fire Service and is evocative of the London Blitz; *Back* (1946) follows the return to civilian life of a war veteran damaged in mind and body. *Concluding* (1948) reminds the reader now of Orwell, now of Kafka. Set in the future, it pictures a state institution in the country for training girls at a time when the dead hand of refined officialdom has smothered the natural life out of people, even their sexuality. Two girls who run away, an old scientist called 'Rock' who resides on the estate and is immovably representative of lost freedoms, and his daughter who falls in love — these are some of the deviants who challenge the prevailing sterility. There is distinction in the dialogue, upon which is focused the most complex tangles of conflicting motivations. Yet, for all the suggestiveness, detail by detail, of Green's symbolism, his idiosyncratic portraiture and plotting, he remains enig-matically aloof from the probing of the thoroughgoing ex-egete.

There are no enigmas or unfathomable depths in the work of C. P. Snow (1905–80), born in the same year as Powell and Green but not into their social class. He rose from a humble home in Leicester through local grammar school and university college to a Cambridge fellowship and thence, via the Civil Service and the Ministry of Technology in Harold Wilson's first Labour administration, to a life peerage as

Lord Snow. A scientist, he set himself the task of breaking through the barrier between science and literature, a barrier he lamented in 1959 in a public lecture, *Two Cultures and the Scientific Revolution*. His *Strangers and Brothers* is a series of eleven novels tracing the personal career of Lewis Eliot, and the stories of various characters who impinge on it, in his progress from the provinces to Cambridge, to the Bar, and to Whitehall. The period covered is from 1914 to 1968, but the books are not in strict chronological sequence. The first novel, *Strangers and Brothers* (1940), later re-titled *George Passant*, is set in an unnamed Leicester. *The Masters* (1951) is the story of Senior Common Room intrigue over the election of a new Master at a Cambridge college. *The New Men* (1954) looks at an atomic research establishment and the moral issue of dropping the nuclear bomb. *Corridors of Power* (1964) records intrigue at Cabinet level over the nuclear deterrent policy. The series suffers from a deficiency of intensity and of imaginative sensitivity to the stuff of life. Prosaic registration flattens out dimensions of human feeling and awareness. Even Lewis Eliot's anguish is minuted rather than felt. A consequent air of enervation often makes comparative youngsters sound like premature old men. The proficient yet strangely arid *opus* suggests a dichotomy in Snow himself. For while the control of English life appears to be in the hands of small-minded men whose brains are continuously lubricated with alcohol, the system and its criteria are treated with what at bottom is a disturbingly naive respect.

In the central decades of the century public appetite created a market not only for pulp fiction but for well-made novels of daily life, readably undemanding, handling with simplistic conviction the limited range of moral and emotional conflicts that the modern media allot to suburban man and touching sometimes on those human dilemmas which supply footnotes for psychological textbooks. Snow's wife, Pamela Hansford Johnson (1902—81), served this market, with its predominantly female readership, in a series of novels, varied in genre and background, in which the themes of ill-matched lovers, frustrated love, or abused love, recur along with problems of conflicting loyalties and over-strained family bonds. Miss Johnson's trilogy, *Too Dear for My Possessing*

(1940), *An Avenue of Stone* (1947), and *A Summer to Decide* (1949), covers the period between the early 1920s and the late 1940s and moves between Belgium and London, between peace and war, effectively intertwining the lives of people from different milieux and registering many aspects of life at the time. Miss Johnson's output includes a later, loosely linked satirical trilogy, *The Unspeakable Skipton* (1959), *Night and Silence Who is Here?* (1963), and *Cork Street, Next to the Hatters* (1965), in the first of which David Skipton is modelled on Frederick Rolfe, the novelist. Miss Johnson has been praised for her insight into masculine character and for a detachment and objectivity more associated with men novelists than with women. By contrast Rosamond Lehmann (1905–), another novelist born in the same year as Powell, Green, and Snow, is decisively feminine in her outlook. Stephen Spender describes her in *World within World* (1952) as a woman who had great personal warmth and impulsiveness alongside 'a cool self-control and the egoism of the artist'. Her novels illuminate the vignette. They have analytical depth over the area of feminine feelings and interests and adroit management of presentational techniques. Miss Lehmann has Virginia Woolf's awareness of the nuances of inner emotional life. Her *Dusty Answer* (1927), a study of girlhood, has been compared with Elizabeth Bowen's *The Death of the Heart*, while *The Echoing Grove* (1953), the story of a love triangle between two sisters and the husband of one of them, has been compared with Miss Bowen's *The Heat of the Day* because the personal story is unfolded against the public background of the 1930s and 1940s; but this background is sketchily realised. The emphasis is on the finer exploration of the two sisters' emotional reactions, where Miss Lehmann moves with assurance.

To turn to Nancy Mitford (1904–73) is to swallow a breath of fresh air. No one would compare Nancy Mitford with Virginia Woolf or Elizabeth Bowen. Instead she has been compared with Evelyn Waugh for her mockery of pretentiousness and with Anthony Powell for her way of handing over the stage to her *dramatis personae*. Miss Mitford came of a highly eccentric aristocratic family. Daughter of Lord Redesdale, she had to watch one sister turn communist, another sister marry the British fascist leader, Oswald Mosley, and a third sister, Unity, turn ardent admirer of Hitler. Her early novels of the 1930s were frivolous farces, but she produced two novels in the 1940s, *The Pursuit of Love* (1945) and *Love in a Cold Climate* (1949), which register upper-class life with a fidelity to speech, manners, and codes that calls for no authorial intrusion to make it at once valid documentary and high comedy. Miss Mitford draws on her own experience of a family at once personally eccentric and stereotyped in social ethos. She has only to allow an empty-headed young woman of the aristocracy to describe left-wingery in her own terms to bring the house down. The authentic aristocratic voice rings repeatedly with unconscious self-parody. 'I have seen too many children brought up without Nannies to think this at all desirable.' 'I think I may say we put India on the map.' The powers of mimicry give brilliance to the text. Miss Mitford is good too at registering the inconsequential 'logic' of children, their delightful way of levelling the weighty and the trivial, and their gleefulness in confederacy.

Nancy Mitford's concern was with a social order that had already become a matter of historical interest. Contemporary public crises do not concern her. 'I only ask the 50s to be as heavenly as the 40s — for me,' she wrote to Evelyn Waugh at the turn of the decade. Yet the war of the forties cast its shadow over Powell's *opus*, disrupting the ballet of the thirties with the touch of death, and it shifted Green's angle of vision from the Firbankian mockery of *Party Going* (1939) to the deeply felt concern with human brokenness and need voiced in *Back* (1946).

The Second World War was not just something happening overseas like the First, sending home its wrecks in troop-trains and dispatching its knock-out blows in yellow telegrams. It was a matter of rationing, evacuation, and air-raids at home as well as of burnt-out tanks and torpedoed ships far away. And war produces, as well as air-raids, difficulties like separation and shortage of food which quite pacific circumstances might cause. Elizabeth Taylor (1912–75), in her first novel, *At Mrs Lippincott's* (1945), looks at the life of an officer's wife who tags on behind him in a furnished house when he is posted at a distance from home. Living in a furnished house is not in itself an experience peculiar to wartime, yet the novel carries an exact flavour of the 'home front'. Critics have compared Elizabeth Taylor to Jane Austen. She limits herself to her familiar milieu, very often the homes of affluent commuters, but she knows about those who do not fit in as well as those who do. She is affectionately amused by the incongruities of the human comedy. Kate Heron, of *In a Summer Season* (1961), marries the human opposite of her deceased first husband with whom she shared a delightful community of cultural interests, and the new husband is his junior by ten years. A compassionate and congenial widower next door, a long-standing family friend, pulls her back mentally towards a life unknown to her present husband, as of course do her own two children. Miss Taylor handles this kind of situation with fastidious artistry, keeping an eye focused on the inner life of each character. The economy of her method in mingling dialogue with reflection and adroitly filling out the canvas is a rich economy.

At the back of people's minds in Miss Taylor's novels are questions of making meals, getting to work, dealing with the weather, the garden, the drains. These are current realities, whatever the condition of Europe. At any given point in our century the literature of the moment mingles the private and the public, the immediate and the remoter past. 1945, which saw the publication of literature about the very recent past such as *At Mrs Lippincott's*, Sidney Keyes's *Collected Poems*, Alun Lewis's *Ha! Ha! Among the Trumpets*, Waugh's *Brideshead Revisited*, and Orwell's *Animal Farm*, saw also the publication of Nancy Mitford's *Pursuit of Love*, Sassoon's far-flung *Siegfried's Journey 1916–1920*, and Flora Thompson's further-flung *Lark Rise to Candleford*. And echoes from Irish history resounded in Sean O'Casey's *Drums Under the Window* and Mary Lavin's novel, *The House in Clewe Street*. For O'Casey was reliving the years leading up to the Easter Rising of 1916, while Mary Lavin (1912–) was tracing the family history of the Coniffes, small-town property owners in Castlerampart, whose orphan heir, Gabriel, is brought up by two spinster aunts only to break away from their tyranny. There are no drums under the window. The public scene is ignored. Miss Lavin's avowed object was to look closely into the human heart. She can define the minor dilemmas of domestic sociability with delicious irony. She makes a serious examination of the nature of one person's influence on another.

Known especially for her short stories, Miss Lavin has humour, a sense of drama, and a gift for epigram.

The public world impinges thus diversely on the fiction of the age. But there is always the novelist for whom the public world is the *raison d'être* of his work. Arthur Koestler (1905–), Hungarian-born journalist, worked for the Communist Party in the 1930s, became disillusioned, and took British citizenship after the war. His *Spanish Testament* (1938) tells of imprisonment by the Nationalists when he was reporting on the Spanish Civil War, and *Scum of the Earth* (1941) of imprisonment in France in 1939. In polemical works such as *The Yogi and the Commissar* (1945), as well as in fiction, Koestler has represented the plight of modern man under the burden of totalitarianism. *Darkness at Noon* (1940) tracks the agony of a member of the Bolshevik old guard, Rubashov, one time idealist revolutionary, whom party loyalists arrest and interrogate during the Stalinist purge. The power and subtlety of the book lie in the awakening of doubts in Rubashov over the human cost of what he has done in the cause, and his suppression of these self-questionings under brainwashing. 'Sympathy, conscience, disgust, despair, and atonement are for us repellent debauchery,' his former comrade-in-arms, Ivanov, reminds him. Mind and body are worn down step by step until Rubashov signs a false confession which ensures execution.

Another powerful novel, *Arrival and Departure* (1943), no doubt closely reflects Koestler's own experience in telling how a disillusioned Balkan Communist, Petya Slavek, who has been tortured, escapes in 1941 to Neutralia (Portugal) where he ponders his next step. Surrounded by the nationals of various warring states, he achieves a comprehensive view of the meaning of the conflict. 'There was now a war in triangle; one side was utopia betrayed; the second, tradition decayed; the third, destruction arrayed.'

If Koestler is the ardent prophet, P. H. Newby (1918–) is the painstaking artificer. Newby plots skilfully, he is a fine ironist, and he finally enjoys turning the tables. He makes the reader aware of the cracks in the surface of life. This theme of insecurity represents a serious commentary running through novels whose presentation of external incongruities and psychological illogicalities is often rich in farce. Newby began with *A Journey to the Interior* (1945), a quest novel portraying a broken widower's pilgrimage to a corrupt sultanate and calling up memories of Conrad and Greene. Newby was a lecturer in English at Fouad Awal University in Cairo during the war and the Anglo-Egyptian novels of his middle years, *The Picnic at Sakkara* (1955), *Revolution and Roses* (1957), and *A Guest and his Going* (1959), recall the head-on confrontation of racial attitudes, grave and comic, in E. M. Forster and Joyce Cary. Critics have augmented the confluence of indebtedness by detecting in Newby traces also of the influence of Waugh and Powell. The distinguishing mark in Newby is the relationship in his central characters between loss of external footing and less explicable inner dislocations. Edgar Perry of the Anglo-Egyptian trilogy, a university lecturer at Gizeh, is nonplussed and exasperated by the maddening devotion of his pupil Muawiya, and Muawiya is detailed by the Moslem Brotherhood to shoot him. The farce of mutual incomprehension is efficiently contrived. Yet somehow the contrivance attenuates the imaginative dynamic by which character is concretely realised.

VI Morality and fantasy

How such material could be transmuted into the stuff of vibrant tragi-comedy had been shown some fifteen years earlier in the African novels of Joyce Cary (1888–1957). Cary, an Irishman from Donegal, had served as a District Commissioner in Nigeria before settling down in Oxford in the 1920s to write. The African novels, *Aissa Saved* (1932), *The African Witch* (1936), and *Mister Johnson* (1939), throw African notions into hilarious and tragic collision with the ethics and beliefs of white administrators and missionaries. Ingenuous eagerness by natives to embrace the ways of the whites causes the message of the West to be farcically distorted as it is subsumed into the framework of native lore and superstition. Not that imaginative self-deception is the monopoly of the negro. Rudbeck, the English administrator in *Mister Johnson*, pictures himself as a great road-builder, while his mission-school-educated clerk, Johnson, throws himself with naive exuberance and with dreams of unbounded self-glorification into emulation of alien ways which ends in catastrophe.

Cary's irresistible gusto sweeps the reader into eager align-
ment with his narrative drive. His eye for human oddity, the
busy pace of his narrative, his prevailing high-spiritedness,
and his Irish fluency have called out comparisons with eighteenth-century novelists such as Smollett and Defoe, as well
as with Dickens. But this debt to classic fiction is only half
the story of Cary's effectiveness. Walter Allen in *Joyce Cary*
(1953) has noted his success 'in grafting on to the trunk of
our traditional fiction, with its stress on story, action, and
broadly conceived character, technical devices first used in
the experimental novels of this century, by Joyce, Lawrence,
and Virginia Woolf . . .' In these writers the reader is not
distanced from the characters by the intervening author, as
in classic fiction, for these novelists are 'intent on rendering
the moment of consciousness in itself'. They involve the
reader for much of the time 'in what may be called a con-
tinuous present'.

Cary wrote two trilogies, the first comprising *Herself
Surprised* (1941), *To Be a Pilgrim* (1942), and *The Horse's
Mouth* (1944). The six novels of the two trilogies are first-
person narratives, and Cary's skill in assuming varied roles,
male and female, has the panache of verbal wizardry. Sara
Munday, the narrator of *Herself Surprised*, is a cook who has
married her employer's son, has been widowed, and become
the mistress successively of an artist, Gulley Jimson, and a
lawyer, Mr Wilcher. She writes in prison, having been convicted
of stealing from Mr Wilcher, and with Moll Flanders's moral
aim of commending her case as an object lesson to others.
But contrition is swamped under the tide of her self-disclosure
as essential woman, mother and mistress of mythic stature,
incurably susceptible to the needs of the male. Tom Wilcher,
the narrator of *To Be a Pilgrim*, is now an old man near the
edge of senility and under some restraint from his doctor
and his niece after an incident of self-exposure. He would
like to escape surveillance and go off to marry Sara, his house-
keeper and mistress. He is living in the past, and the earlier
decades of the century are evoked nostalgically through his
eyes. Wilcher has been an over-cautious, fussy man, who has
never broken out, and for him Sara remains a symbol of
gaiety, enjoyment, domestic sensuality, and devoted service.
But Gulley Jimson, the narrator of *The Horse's Mouth*, is a

man of different breed. A visionary painter of invulnerable self-confidence who has no time for the inhibiting codes of respectability or moral responsibility, he yet endears himself by ruthless vitality in pursuit of his artistic vocation. A riotously comic character, he sustains imaginative plausibility by sheer personal thrust. For him Sara becomes the symbol of predatory womanhood with designs on his prophetic independence, a man-catcher out to make her nest and tame her victim.

The second trilogy, *Prisoner of Grace* (1952), *Except the Lord* (1953), and *Not Honour More* (1955), has a similar basis in a triangle. Chester Nimmo, a radical politician, sees himself as a divinely ordained reformer. His religious sense of vocation gives him a self-confidence as overweening as Jimson's, and it carries him through political manoeuvres and tergiversations that in others might seem like hypocritical opportunism. His wife, Nina, tells the story in the first novel. She married Nimmo because she was pregnant by her cousin, Jim Latter, only to be gripped by her husband's messianic magnetism. In *Except the Lord* Nimmo, now an old man, gives an account of his Devonshire upbringing as the deeply religious son of a non-conformist pastor. ('I tried to get at the roots of left-wing English politics in evangelical religion,' Cary said.) *Not Honour More* is Jim Latter's death-cell confession after he has murdered Nimmo in jealousy. The conflict between the charismatic statesman of working-class origin and of chameleonlike adaptability, and the stolid middle-class soldier with his rigid sense of duty is a hinge upon which a perceptive glance at fifty years of national history seems to swing.

In the inter-war years, while Cary was living in Parks Road, Oxford, struggling to keep his family by his pen and taking his daily walks in the Parks, another family man, J. R. R. Tolkien (1892–1973), Professor of Anglo-Saxon, was cycling up and down the Banbury Road between his home in North Oxford and Pembroke College where he held a fellowship. Both men were to win literary acclaim in their sixties. Cary had fought in the Cameroons in the First World War and Tolkien had been on the Somme. Both were throughout their lives indefatigably accumulating mountains of material from which great books were to be knocked into shape. Cary's African novels came out before the war and so did Tolkien's

The Hobbit (1937). It tells how Bilbo Baggins, under the fitful supervision of the wizard Gandalf, joins a company of dwarves in a journey to the far-off Lonely Mountain where the evil dragon Smaug holds the treasure and kingdom that properly belong to the dwarf, Thorin Oakenshield. The hobbit is a small creature whose hairy, tough-shod feet are his only non-human characteristic. Bilbo's adventure takes him from a comfortable home in the Shire through terrifying perils of mountain and forest. A world of elemental wonder and risk is peopled by hostile creatures such as trolls, goblins, and wargs, as well as by friendly elves and eagles. The upshot of this tale is that Bilbo gets home safely with a magic ring which is an evil key to power, and safe in hobbit hands only in so far as hobbits are small, brave, ingenuous, peace-loving creatures, content with simple natural comforts like eating, drinking, and yarn-spinning. In the hands of vain, self-centred, and possessive beings, the ring is the means of tyranny and total corruption. The hobbit has to forego rightful attachment to home comforts and put all he has at risk in the adventure that alone can guarantee freedom from the tyranny of evil.

The theme clearly lends itself to magnification and reduplication. For a writer who thinks in terms of Fall and Redemption and has survived wars against tyranny to observe the encroachment of mechanical and administrative technology upon a green and pleasant land, logical elaboration of the quest to wrest the means of ultimate domination from the powers of darkness will be something more than fairy story. Tolkien created a vast world of myth and legend to do justice to the ramifying interpenetration of the natural, the homely, and the innocent by the corrosive infection of evil. *The Hobbit* turned out to be only the vestibule of entry in the fantasy world of the trilogy, *The Fellowship of the Ring*, comprising *The Lord of the Rings* (1954), *The Two Towers* (1955), and *The Return of the King* (1956). This heroic romance chronicles the history of Middle Earth in the Great Year of the Third Age. Continual allusion, corroborated by appendices, erects a fabric of history complete with annals, legends, memoirs, chronological tables, and genealogical trees, that give the density of patiently researched documentation to the invented world. Even the language of ancient records and related tongues spoken by beings of old are described in philological detail. The gist of the central adventure is that Frodo has inherited the magic ring from Bilbo. Sauron, the evil Lord of the land of Mordor, covets the ring in order to conquer the whole of Middle-Earth and enslave its creatures. There is only one place where the ring will be safe from his grasp. It must be thrown into the Cracks of Mount Doom in the desolate land of Mordor. Sam, Merry, and Pippin set out with Frodo, a quartet of hobbits, to accomplish this feat. Their respective adventures soon reveal how vast and multifarious is the creeping menace of evil confronting Gandalf the wizard, Aragorn the rightful lord of the usurped, metallised, and mechanised city of Isengard, the tree-like ents, the elves, and the men.

Tolkien disliked strict allegory for the interpretations it imposed. But he did not undervalue the function of symbols. 'Just as speech is invention about objects and ideas,' he said, 'so myth is invention about truth.' After his death, his son Christopher prepared for the press a work called *The Silmarillion* (1977) which relates to events of a deeper past, the Elder Days or First Age of the World, and the ancient drama to which characters in the trilogy look back. The book is a compilation of legends from the great mass of often multi-versioned writings left by Tolkien and setting forth the entire history 'from the Music of Aimer in which the world began to the passing of the Ringbearers from the Havens of Mithlond at the end of the Third Age'.

The will to invent a mythology so comprehensive represents a creative impulse of totally different cast from that which registers the life of the passing decades. There is comparable cosmic inventiveness in the genius of Mervyn Peake (1911–68), artist and novelist, whose pictorial range had been enriched by early years in China and by work as a war artist — for he recorded the human spectacle that confronted the Allies when they moved into Belsen. Peake's great work, *The Gormenghast Trilogy*, consists of *Titus Groan* (1946), *Gormenghast* (1950), and *Titus Alone* (1959). There is nothing primaeval about Peake's world. It does not map forests, caves, and mountains, but a topography of man's fabrication, an immense castle, a gigantic conglomeration of halls and corridors, cellars and stairways, turrets and roofs, large and varied enough to contain within its compass a peopled microcosm of decaying civilisation. Earl and Countess are surrounded by relations, hangers-on, and a full panoply of graded dignitaries and menials, from the Keeper of the Hall of Bright Carvings and the Master of Ritual down to the eighteen Grey Scrubbers whose hereditary duty is 'to restore each morning to the great grey floor and lofty walls of the kitchen a stainless complexion', and whose expressionless, slab-like faces and traditional deafness attest the effect of age-long proximity to stone walls. Peake's visual percipience and his mastery of a vocabulary for transferring pictorial vividness to the printed page enable him to project a gallery of animated portraits embodying a system dominated by ancient ritual and moribund hierarchy which lies like the hand of death on the spirit of the young heir, Titus.

Drear ritual turned its wheel. The ferment of the heart, within these walls, was mocked by every length of sleeping shadow. The passions, no greater than candle-flames, flickered in Time's yawn, for Gormenghast, huge and adumbrate, out-crumbles all.

Titus's restless urge to escape is counterbalanced by the cunning of a rebel kitchen-boy, Steerpike, who sees and seizes the opportunity for a career of evil and destruction by deceptively manipulating the weaknesses of the system and its practitioners. The rise of Steerpike, his crimes, his unmasking, and his pursuit to the death by Titus occupy the first two novels, and the third, in which the tone is sourer, takes Titus to a nightmare world of iron servitude from which the absurd, tradition-soaked ways of the castle look innocuous enough. Peake is master of the farcical, the bizarre, and the grotesque. The panoramic fullness of design and the pervasive sense of involvement in a drama whose off-stage reverberations touch the roots of a human dilemma implicit in the character of civilisation itself endow Peake's work with a largeness that generally appertains to masterpieces. His slighter books, like *Mr Pye* (1953), have a less strenuous, more whimsical wryness.

Tolkien's route into his fictional world lay through linguistic scholarship, Peake's through art. Malcolm Lowry (1909–57) took the more tortuous way of alcohol addiction. Between school and university he had joined the crew of a freighter on a journey from Liverpool to the east, and the painful initiation it represented provided material for his first novel, *Ultramarine*

(1933). His great novel, *Under the Volcano* (1947), is the testament of an irredeemable alcoholic. It traces the tragic end of Geoffrey Firmin, British consul in Mexico, whose escalating addiction has driven away his desperately loving wife, Yvonne. She returns unexpectedly in 1938. The central theme is Yvonne's offering of love and help, and Geoffrey's inability to respond except self-destructively. Lowry described Firmin as one who has misused the divine gift of wine, symbolically and blasphemously. In his yearning for a return to purity and innocence he bears the burden of human guilt. A final Spanish epigraph presses home the correspondence with the Fall of Man. 'Do you like this garden which is yours? We evict those who destroy it.' Prefatory epigraphs from Sophocles, Bunyan, and Goethe underline man's mortal dilemma. The quotation from Bunyan's *Grace Abounding* speaks of the sinner's envy of the ·animal for having 'no soul to perish under the everlasting weight of Hell and Sin' and his added burden of not being able to 'find with all my soul that I did desire deliverance'.

An alcoholic haze hangs over the book, but outer and inner worlds are fused with tortuous vividness as Firmin increasingly loses contact with things external. Lowry's technical skill in entangling threads of sequential reasoning with the onrush of delirious fantasy and in registering the alcoholic's fitful semi-contact with other persons inevitably calls out comparisons with Joyce, and there is evidence of a network of symbols and correspondences conceived with Joycean interest in multi-layered interpretation. Lowry's posthumous publications include short stories, *Hear Us O Lord from Heaven Thy Dwelling Place* (1961), and *Selected Poems* (1962). In the latter there are confessional poems of searing self-revelation such as 'He Liked the Dead':

> The grass was not green nor even grass to him;
> nor was sun, sun; rose, rose; smoke, smoke; limb, limb.

There appeared in the same year as *The Volcano* a novel, *The House of Sleep* (1947) (republished as *Sleep Has His House*, 1948) by Anna Kavan (1904—68), whose output cries out for comparison with Lowry's. A heroin addict for the last thirty years of her life, she too powerfully registered the cost of her addiction. *The House of Sleep* is a sequence of dream-like fantasies elaborating a number of sketchy, factual, and seemingly autobiographical events 'in the development of one individual human being'. The dream, which allegorises the addict's choice of Hell, is at once devastatingly detached and suffocatingly personal. 'Once you're on the way down the machinery takes charge of you, you're caught, trapped, finished for good and all.' And the renunciation it implies pre-echoes Lowry's poem above. 'You'll never feel the sun warming you any more. You'll never hear the birds. No bird could live in this atmosphere, this *ersatz* air that eddies here in stale and fetid artificial gusts.' The prose has imaginative intensity, at one moment drenched in delirious richness, at the next moment measuring out doses of ironic humour. There is mock-logic anticipatory of Beckett, there are conflations of incongruous imagery that smack of Joyce, and the influence of Kafka is pervasive. A late novel, *A Scarcity of Love* (1956), has qualities that link Miss Kavan with Peake. The initial background is a castle exuding Gothic atmosphere whose mistress devotes herself to self-admiration with a demonic dedication that gives her larger-than-life stature and surrounds her with a palpable aura of alienation from human sympathy. Anna Kavan's posthumous short stories, *Julia and the Bazooka* (1970), mostly revolve around addiction to the syringe and various moods of separation from rationality it induces.

VII History and criticism

Alongside its sad cases of addiction, twentieth-century literary history contains an instance of alcoholism conquered. Alfred Duggan (1903–64), a dipsomaniac in the Oxford of the 1920s whom Evelyn Waugh claimed to have rescued, turned in middle age into a sober and productive historical novelist, working on some of the less documented periods of history. *The Lady for Ransom* (1950), for instance, deals with the Byzantine empire in the eleventh century, and *Conscience of the King* (1951) with Britain in the fifth to sixth centuries at the time of the coming of the Saxons. For all their lack of dramatic intensity and human passion, Duggan's novels are rich in historical detail. So is *The Man on a Donkey* (1952), by

H. F. M. Prescott (1896–1972), a *tour de force* which fastens on the history of a small priory at Marrick in Swaledale in order to chronicle the northern resistance to Henry VIII's impositions that culminated in the Pilgrimage of Grace in 1537. Historical fiction brings historical judgment into play in varying degrees. The market for costumed romance has been a profitable one as the successes of Naomi Mitchison (1897–) in the 1920s and of Mary Renault (pseudonym of Mary Challans) (1905–) in the 1950s and 1960s show. Both of them set their tales in the classical and ancient world. But fiction such as that of Duggan and Miss Prescott, whose substance is intrinsically interesting *qua* history, obviously has a different relationship with pure history. G. M. Trevelyan (1876–1962), a leading historian, argued the importance of Scott's Waverley novels in changing historians' representation of people of the past. Trevelyan was himself one of those historians whose literary gifts enhance their scholarship, and he gained a large public for his *English Social History* (1944). Another gifted historian, Veronica Wedgwood (1910–), a member of the celebrated Staffordshire pottery family, whose works include *The King's Peace* (1955) and *The King's War* (1958), has specialised in seventeenth-century studies and the English Civil War, while A. L. Rowse (1903–) has specialised in the Elizabethan period. More recently A. J. P. Taylor (1906–) has written stimulating studies of the twentieth century and the two world wars, including *The Origins of the Second World War* (1964).

While pure historians such as these operate outside the strict boundaries of 'English Literature', there are writers whose work in fiction and non-fiction overlaps the boundaries. Rebecca West (pseudonym of Cicily Fairfield Andrews) (1892–), one-time companion of H. G. Wells by whom she had a son, produced her best work of fiction, *The Fountain Overflows* (1957), with its penetrating autobiographical evocations, late in her career when she had behind her only some rather indisciplined early novels, but was justly celebrated as a critic and a thinker in journalism and in books. Another writer who came into his own only when he recaptured his past late in life was the essayist and novelist Richard Church (1893–1972), who uncovered a powerful vein of evocative nostalgia in the autobiographical trilogy beginning with *Over the Bridge* (1955). Church, like Miss West, is one of those writers who might readily slip through the net of literary history with its properly predominant concern for major achievements in the novel, poetry, and drama. It is easy to overlook the less aptly classifiable writers such as the poet and novelist L. A. G. Strong (1896–1958), the poet and editor James Reeves (1909–78), the poet, playwright, and literary biographer Robert Gittings (1911–), and the literary biographers and critics, Lord David Cecil (1902–) and Peter Quennell (1905–). Critics who have catered for a wide public are to be distinguished from rigorously academic ones such as the controversial Cambridge English don, F. R. Leavis (1895–1978), who founded the critical quarterly *Scrutiny* in 1932 and moulded the minds of a generation of students to the notion that the discipline of English studies should be geared to the preservation of moral and intellectual integrity at a time when popular values are debased by the mass media. *Scrutiny* ran for nineteen years and was reissued in twenty volumes in 1963. Critics and thinkers who claim attention too for their work in poetry or fiction include the short-story writer V. S. Pritchett (1900–) who for long had regular space in the weekly *New Statesman*, the novelist Rayner Heppenstall (1911–81), and the poet David Holbrook (1923–).

8

Post-modern reassessment
The 1950s and 1960s

I Introduction

NOT until ten years after the end of the war did the most striking changes in social *mores* and external fashions take place which were to give the post-war world a totally distinct set of attitudes from those of the thirties. Under the shadow of the hydrogen bomb the Campaign for Nuclear Disarmament was launched in 1958 and the first of the protest marches to Aldermaston was organised. The crushing of a Hungarian rising by Russian tanks in 1956 had added to the fear of Soviet intentions, while the Anglo-French invasion of Egypt in the same year provoked in the so-called 'Suez crisis' a bitter national schism between those who, like Sir Anthony Eden, the Prime Minister, believed in putting dictators such as President Nasser of Egypt in their place, and those who felt that British action of this kind was a throw-back to the bad old imperial days. Such political issues bred a smouldering sense that there was a lot of hard-bitten old prejudice to deal with in the British mind. It was fanned in the moral field by the controversy surrounding the publication in 1957 of the Wolfenden Report on Homosexual Offences which prepared the way for legalisation of homosexual practices between consenting adults, and by the unsuccessful prosecution of the publishers of Lawrence's *Lady Chatterley's Lover* under the Obscene Publications Act in 1960. Meanwhile the setting up of new universities less committed to traditional English educational thinking, and the transformation of the United Kingdom into a multi-racial society by the vastly increased rate of immigration from the coloured Commonwealth, were perhaps also factors making in their different ways for the shaking of foundations which brought about the return of a Labour government under Harold Wilson in 1964 after thirteen years of unbroken Tory rule.

Literature reflected this shaking of foundations, and the drama most violently. Several new dramatists had their first plays performed in the second half of the 1950s, and though these writers, who include Beckett, Osborne, Whiting, Arden, Behan, and Pinter, differed widely in the content of their plays and in the techniques they used, they all combined to break with the theatre of upper-middle-class comedy and romantic fantasy as thoroughly as Eliot and Fry had broken with it — but in a totally different direction. The theatre of the fifties and sixties exploited to the full the artistic reaction against the proscenium stage, the removal of theatre censorship, the fashionable cult of supposed two-way communication between actor and participating audience, the demand for art to commit itself frankly to political and social causes, and the lifting of inhibitions on sexual candour. It would be easy to exaggerate the wider social significance of what happens in the theatre, which readily lends itself as a hot-house for neurotic self-expression, and therefore theatrical claims to represent wholesale shifts of the public mind have to be treated with caution. The decade that produced Wycherley's *The Country Wife* produced also Bunyan's *The Pilgrim's Progress*. The decades that saw kitchen-sink drama succeeded by shock-the-audience sex and violence on the capital's stages also witnessed the general reading public gripped successively by Tolkien's innocent hobbits and Richard Adams's righteous rabbits. Nevertheless the 'Revolution in the Theatre' involved a vital and stimulating upsurge of innovation whose effects have still not fully run their course.

II The new drama

Apart from the second wave of the verse drama revival represented by Fry, the new drama had little to compete with. Middlebrow West-End drama was represented by Terence Rattigan (1911–77), remembered for *The Winslow Boy* (1946), which dramatised a *cause célèbre* of 1910 concerning a naval cadet falsely charged with forgery, and *The Browning Version* (1948), an intimate portrayal of a public-school master who is a failure. Rattigan's easy accommodation of a not-too-strenuous audience attention in neatly tailored pieces, and his frank defence of this practice, made him the spokesman for theatrical unadventurousness and a ready target for the *avant-garde*. Shortly before the theatrical storm broke, London audiences were applauding the comedies of N. C. Hunter (1908–71). *The Waters of the Moon* (1951) is set in a decayed country mansion in Devonshire run as a boarding house for decayed gentlefolk. It is a gentle exercise in teaching stay-at-homes not to be mesmerised by impossible dreams of possible change, and it was followed, in *A Day by the Sea* (1953), by a display of nearly breaking out and marrying on the part of a work-numbed diplomat. These diluted Chekovian plays are thick with slice-of-life dialogue, and they throb with tepidity.

There is no tepidity in the work of the key dramatist of the new movement, Samuel Beckett (1906–). Beckett, born in Dublin, a modern languages graduate of Trinity College, went to France, became a friend of James Joyce, and edited *Our Exagmination* . . . (1929), a collection of essays by Joycean disciples on the 'Work in Progress' which was to become *Finnegans Wake*. It was many years later, in middle life, that Beckett came to the theatre, and he insists that he is primarily a novelist. His first novel, *Murphy* (1938), shows dissatisfaction with standard fictional recipes by mocking them. Through an ironic burlesque of fictional plotting the hero, whose bent is towards savouring the quintessence of effortlessness, moves in quest of peace to employment in a lunatic asylum and self-immolation in an armchair. *Watt*, written during the war but not published until 1953 in Paris and 1963 in London, reflects the desperate circumstances of its composition. Beckett had settled in Paris and when war came he joined the French Resistance. Narrowly escaping capture by the Gestapo, he fled to Unoccupied France where he worked as an agricultural labourer and where the writing of *Watt* served as a therapy on the edge of breakdown. Autobiographical memories of personal frustration and inner obsessions are projected in a raw, clinical disconnectedness that leaves the task of digestion to the reader. But Beckett lit upon the ideal form for his therapeutic self-exploration in the monologues of his trilogy, *Molloy, Malone Dies*, and *The Unnamable*, which were first written in French and whose

English versions appeared in 1958–9. The quest for reconciliation between appearance and reality, the pilgrimage in search of identification and relationship, the *reductio ad absurdum* of man's imprisonment in a defective body with a totally inadequate machinery of action at his disposal, and the utter paucity of those things upon which he must rely for satisfaction – these themes are adumbrated in outpourings undoctored to the requirements of accepted narrative presentation.

When Becket turned to the stage he was compelled by the nature of the medium to carve his material into blocks of more recognisable cohesiveness. *Waiting for Godot* (1955) represented a theatrical revolution in that it scrapped indentifiable locale, social setting, and temporal placement, and brought to the stage a new verbal idiom, nothing less than a ransacking of all idioms for the purpose of ironically discrediting them. Since established verbal currencies undergird the stances by which men and women keep their footing in their numberless personal, occupational, social, and ideological roles, the effect of Beckett's irony is to pull the carpet from under their feet. And since all verbal currencies have their fair share of pretentiousness and shallowness, devaluation of them can be comically effected. Devaluatory riposte and ironic come-back are the stuff of knockabout farce as well as of cynical disillusionment. Beckett's greatness lies in his recognition that the sense of humour is the mind's most potent safeguard against despair.

So Vladimir and Estragon, looking like a couple of tramps, seemingly homeless and rootless, wait fruitlessly for undefined Godot with no explicit purpose, and their back-chat, littered with the bric-a-brac of cliché and logic, is a fitter accompaniment to their music-hall clowning than to any more serious human purpose. Indeed, since they make no claim on human prerogatives, they call out no social protest at humanity oppressed and disfigured. Again, in *Happy Days* (1962), where dialogue is conducted between a woman buried up to her waist in sand and a man who can only crawl on all fours, no comment is called for on the atomic holocaust which appears to lie behind this reduction of the species. Limitation is accepted as being of a piece with the human lot. The absence of any reference to it emphasises its unremarkableness. Beckett's implication that you can screw up the pegs of human impotence indefinitely without breaking the strings, so accustomed is the instrument to frustration and negation, constitutes his most powerful ironic shaft. So to the chair-bound hero and his dustbin-bound parents in *Endgame* (1958), and other such exercises in organised nullity.

While Beckett projected impotent man, John Osborne (1929–), in *Look Back in Anger* (1956), presented Jimmy Porter, the archetypal 'angry young man'. Porter, a university graduate, has contracted out of any predictable social role to run a sweet-shop. His wife Alison hails from the middle class, buttress of the once supposedly secure social fabric which is both nostalgically recollected and savagely condemned. Porter vents the fury of the personally and socially alienated on self, wife, and system. Osborne's fluent rhetoric of abuse gives the play its vitality. Its setting is a drab Midlands flat and its concern with quarrelsome domesticity around the ironing-board and over the Sunday papers gave currency to the label 'kitchen-sink drama'. But the play survives as only a negative symbol of the early 'Protest' movement in that the central impetus resides rather in temperamental self-indulgence than in any concern for current public issues. *The Entertainer* (1957) probed further the erosion of Edwardian stability and purpose-fulness into empty sentimentality by presenting the career of a failed and aging former music-hall comedian as symptomatic of British decline, but Osborne's venture into historical chronicle, *Luther* (1961), is a disjointed piece of work which fails to get to grips with its subject.

John Whiting (1917–63) observed with dismay the infection of a great literary tradition by kitchen-sink drama. Versed in the work of Eliot, and influenced by Shaw, Fry, and Wyndham Lewis, he left a significant *corpus* of work behind him in two volumes of *Collected Plays* (1969), but the theatre was not utterly unjust to him in failing to provide him with adequate box-office response. *Marching Song* (1954) and *The Gates of Summer* (1956) are perhaps the most intellectually rewarding plays of the decade for today's reader, but the personal pilgrimages explored — that of a disgraced general in a defeated European country who is required to fake a public front for political ends, and that of a disillusioned philanderer — are not articulated in clear, let alone vivid, dramatic projection. The contrast between romantic fiction and reality is forcefully made. There is epigram, paradox, and humour. Whiting keeps the reader's brain active. But the discrepancy remains between the level of reflection and the degree of technical alertness to theatrical practicalities. *The Devils* (1961), based on Aldous Huxley's *The Devils of Loudon*, was Whiting's one public success.

If Whiting wrote plays for the library, John Arden (1930–) wrote them exclusively for the stage. Whiting lamented the possible silencing of the dramatist's individual voice by the chorus of the collective: Arden came eventually to lament the tyranny of the play-text and to lust after a theatre like a fair-ground with people walking in and out while a perform-ance lasting half a day takes place. Arden's main success was *Sergeant Musgrave's Dance* (1959), which attempts epic chronicle in the manner of Brecht. It is set vaguely in the late nineteenth century. Four deserters from a colonial war bring back the corpse of a comrade to his home town in mid-winter. It is a mining town and the workers are on strike. Musgrave's purpose is to arrange a recruiting meeting, tell his audience what war is really like, display the skeleton, charge the people with the guilt of national complicity, and then turn guns on them in retribution. Dramatic development is interrupted by songs. The cast is large. Arden likes big scenes, and the impact of the action, moment by moment, is effective. But neither in overall dramatic cohesion nor in sureness of moral thrust does the play carry conviction. Arden's *The Workhouse Donkey* (1963) mocks the corruptions of local government in a gallimaufry of presentational idioms — naturalism, burlesque, verse, song — whose ambivalence of tone is inten-tional. Arden admires the Jonson of *Bartholomew Fair*, and his extravaganza, which he called a 'vulgar melo-drama', evidences his desire for drama with 'essential attributes of Dionysus'. *Armstrong's Last Goodnight* (1965) is based on a mediaeval Scottish ballad about taming a rapacious Border chieftain in the reign of James V. The contrast between cultured, sophisticated commissioners and primitive clansmen, and the treacherous subterfuges involved in well-intentioned statecraft, are sturdy dramatic material and Arden experi-ments appropriately with a contrived Scottish idiom, but sustained intensity is lacking.

'Mannered comedy, grotesque farce, period problem play,

autobiographical allegory, ballad opera, community drama, epic chronicle, mime, play, melodrama — he has experimented in all these forms, and several hybrids besides,' Simon Trussler observes of Arden's continuing experimentation (*John Arden* (1973)). By contrast, Brendan Behan (1923–64) has the stylistic identity of a single voice. An Irish republican from Dublin, he was sent as a boy to Wormwood Scrubs and thence to a Borstal institution after arrest in Liverpool while on IRA service, and his fictional autobiography, *Borstal Boy* (1958), tells the story with a good deal of amusing exaggeration. His play, *The Quare Fellow* (Dublin 1955, London 1956), registers life in Mountjoy Gaol, Dublin, during the last day before a murderer's execution — the 'quare fellow' with whom the rest of the prison community are temporarily obsessed. Gruesome preparations for the hanging overshadow the inmates' day. Pious hymn-singing is counterpointed with detailed instructions for ensuring that the drop-door is just right for the victim's weight. The hangman has to check up on his neck-size. There is a humane, plain-spoken warder to touch the conscience. Above all there is irresistibly comic dialogue among the old lags. ('Do you mean we're getting food with our meals today?') Behan's second play, *The Hostage* (1958), is set in a Dublin brothel where IRA men are holding a British soldier hostage in the attempt to rescue a comrade from execution in Belfast. The cockney captive falls in love with a young Irish kitchenmaid. He is finally killed in a police raid, but not before Behan has wrung laughter and tears out of O'Casey's contrasts between causes and people, bloodshed and love, abstract idealism and the realities of life.

Behan's plays illustrated that verbal brilliance can give vitality even to a conventionally conceived or loosely structured play; in short that the good dramatist is a good writer; that drama remains primarily literature. If Behan made the point, Harold Pinter (1930–) rammed it home. He devised a dialogue as distinctive in its own way as Eliot's or Fry's, Shaw's or Wilde's, yet totally original and unique. He did not bring to the theatre the social commitment of a Shaw or the moral assurance of an Eliot. He did not bring the sophistication and wit of a Wilde, nor the rich native legacy of a Behan or an O'Casey. Nor did he, like Beckett, make a style out of everybody else's styles by a judiciously incongruous application of a system of 'Pick 'n' Mix'. He listened to living conversation, he seized on the most prosaic idioms of vernacular usage, he planted them in contexts so ambiguous that they acquire mystifying resonance, he arranged them in sequences so perseveringly innocuous that inoffensiveness is smothered under its own weight, and he punctuated them with pauses so fraught with breathtaking dubiety that what is unuttered by Pinter reverberates more clamorously than what other dramatist shout. He did all this and made it funny.

There is a ceiling to the neural disturbance that can be felt by an audience whose own mental footing vis-à-vis the play-world is secure. If clearly articulated action is replaced by hint and mystery, by menace undefined, so that the audience has difficulty in deciphering motive or even distinguishing friend from foe, their unsettlement becomes palpable. In *The Birthday Party* (1958), Stanley, a nervous, reclusive lodger in a seaside resort, is visited by two seeming old friends ostensibly bent on giving him a birthday celebration. But what gradually leaks through to the audience when they get him alone is that he has betrayed some organisation and that they are going to deal with him. Hints of IRA terror and torture make Stanley's collapse explicable, but the character of his involvement and most of what is meant by 'plot' remains a mystery. Similarly the one-act play, *The Dumb Waiter* (1960), presents two men in a basement hide-out who, it seems, are criminals with a job to do and awaiting instructions from some boss above. Pinter gives solidity to their worried dependence by .making the dumb-waiter their source of food and the link with their controller. When a long-awaited directive arrives, it orders one of the pair to kill the other. In *The Caretaker* (1960) Aston, who has had a brain operation that has left him mentally obtuse, takes home a dim-witted tramp, Davies, to a seedy room in a derelict house. Aston's brother, Nick, is more pretentiously idiotic, and lives largely in a world of make-believe. The riddling lack of even vestigial clarification in this play makes it perhaps the sharpest exemplar of Pinter's claim that an audience must not always expect verification and that characters without defined history, intentions, or motive are as legitimate as any. What does emerge in the dialogue of these three mentally deprived men is how tenuous may be the contacts by which people break out from their isolation and subjectivity. There also comes through, to be set beside the menace of undefined retribution for undefined guilt explored in earlier plays, the menace of the intruder and the potential supplanter. *The Homecoming* (1965) again leaves the audience's minds agog with questions to fire at the inaccessible author. Like Beckett, Pinter has moved towards greater spareness and economy, becoming no less inscrutable, but re-emphasising his central concern with human impotence and frustration, guilt and insecurity, isolation and doubt, above all with man's susceptibility to teasing worries about his place in the scheme of things.

Other and lesser writers in the late 1950s extended the scope of drama by carrying it into theatrically unexplored corners of English life. Arnold Wesker (1932–) put a Jewish East-end family on stage in *Chicken Soup with Barley* (1958). The action extends from 1936, on the day of a fascist march by Mosley that is met with violence from left-wingers, to 1957 when the Hungarian rising has been ruthlessly suppressed by the Red Army. Wesker's characters respond variously to the lessons of an experience which brings the communist cause into question and sheds doubt on the relative importance of political and personal interests. The play was the first of a trilogy. In *Roots* (1959) and *I'm Talking About Jerusalem* (1960) Wesker successively elaborates dichotomies inherent in the collision between left and right. He could not isolate the struggle for equality from the need for culture as opposed to media-fed illiteracy, for free-range ruralism as opposed to urban depersonalisation, and for individual craftsmanship as opposed to mass technology. Later plays (*Chips with Everything*, 1962; *Their Very Own Golden City*, 1966; *Friends*, 1970) suggest increasing frustration both with the conformist pressures of the establishment and with the impracticability of idealistic reform.

Shelagh Delaney (1939–) from Salford put a working-class Lancashire family on stage in a lodging house in *A Taste of Honey* (1958), if mother, daughter, and art student can be called a family. Mother goes off to have an affair and daughter is pregnant by a long-departed negro sailor. The social implications of the feckless scramble for happiness are evident. The vitality of the piece derives from the sure ear for local conversation — not just Lancashire usage, but ironic northern

modes of self-protection and the subtle ways of being aggres-
sively affectionate. John Mortimer (1923–), a barrister, takes
counsel into the cell of a condemned murderer in *Dock Brief*
(1958) for an ironic encounter with a man who is resigned to
his lot, having finished off an intolerably tyrannous wife. It
transpires that a successful outcome of the case, in the form
of a reprieve, is of great moment to the barrister and of no
interest to his client. Mortimer's concern in this one-act play
is not only with the gap of understanding between simple
victim and sophisticated would-be rescuer, but also with the
isolation of the legal mind and the legal system from the
human realities they draw into their net, a concern he returns
to in his full-length play, *The Judge* (1967).

N. F. Simpson (1919–) called out comparisons with Beckett
and with dramatists of the Absurd when his short play,
Resounding Tinkle (1958), appeared, its action revolving
around the delivery of an elephant to a semi-detached house.
But surrealist anarchy can justify itself only by reference to
secondary inference lacking here. Simpson's full-length play,
One Way Pendulum (1959), has a fitful crazy validity: to
install parking meters round the lawn and to stand for an
hour in order to get one's money's-worth from one of them is
a shade less remote from the accepted fooleries of modern
man than trying to teach Speak-Your-Weight scales to sing
the Hallelujah Chorus. But the comic-strip farce of *The Cresta
Run* (1966), which burlesques the antics of counter-espionage,
seems nearer to the Marx Brothers than to Beckett or Ionesco.
Similarly Joe Orton (1933–67) pursued the lure of farcicality
beyond the reach of real human interest. *Loot* (1966) is a
witty play that eschews plausibility. Horse-play with a coffin
and a corpse is perhaps just sufficiently related to the audience's
sense of death to be awarded the label 'sick'. *The Good and
Faithful Servant* (1968) has fun at the expense of factory
personnel, welfare services, and professional do-goodery.

III Protest fiction

As the dramatists of the 1950s, whether with soap-box
rhetoric, wry clownery, or ruminative projection of man's
limited articulacy, thus variously portrayed our social and

metaphysical unease, a group of novelists conveniently arose to corroborate the journalistic projection of a rebellious literary movement of 'angry young men'. The fictional protagonists, or anti-heroes, whose pot-shots at institutionalised conformities gave substance to the projection are by no means simply a collection of Jimmy Porters. Some at least of the novelists realised that, without social commitment, protest can degenerate into disgruntlement and must therefore be held in ironic focus. William Cooper (pseudonym of Harry Summerfield Hoff) (1910–) portrayed an early anti-hero in *Scenes from Provincial Life* (1950). Joe Lunn, Leicester schoolmaster, can adapt neither to the classroom grind nor to the codes of romantic monogamy. He tells his own story, ironically debunking himself as well as downgrading anything and everything that is of no selfish personal use to him, and the effect of cynicism at odds with society is comic. Indeed a later novel, *Scenes from Married Life* (1961), shows Lunn captured by the civil service machinery and by woman, a helpless victim of success and matrimony. No doubt this is light-weight stuff from which the real substance of life is left out; but so are the novels of Kingsley Amis (1922–) whose Jim Dixon in *Lucky Jim* (1953) was quickly accepted as the archetypal angry young man of fiction. A university lecturer with a built-in resistance to the pretentiousness, social and cultural, to which his status requires him to subscribe, he is conducted through slapstick capers that Amis's deftly comic prose renders highly entertaining. In *That Uncertain Feeling* (1955) John Lewis is a librarian who can contemplate his vanities and inadequacies with ironic self-mockery, but again his pursuit by a wealthy married woman is pantomime stuff. The hero who is up against phoneys so patently phoney that they could deceive no one yet is himself devoid of ideals and solidity, who is lazy, undemanding, and stirred to enthusiasm only by drink and female breasts, is a new fictional formula rather than a projection from experience. But Amis's technical equipment is considerable, and he has turned an adroit hand to a variety of fictional genres in subsequent novels.

Charles Lumley in *Hurry on Down* (1953) by John Wain (1925–) has a working-class background and a university education and in conjunction the two equip him with passports to nothing. He drifts from window-dressing, hospitalportering, and the like to drug-running, until finally the 'running fight between self and society ended in a draw'. Wain lacks Amis's technical polish and, as steady 'middle-class' respectability is battered, a trickle of indiscriminate authorial distaste for people seeps through the fabric of the critique. Of Wain's subsequent novels *The Smaller Sky* (1967) deals neatly and piquantly with a scientist who wants to be left alone and settle down to life on Paddington Station, but *A Winter in the Hills* (1970) and *The Pardoner's Tale* (1978) are cliché-ridden in substance and clumsy in presentation.

Room at the Top (1957) by John Braine (1922–) has greater social validity and moral thrust than *Lucky Jim, Hurry on Down*, or, for that matter, *Look Back in Anger*. Joe Lampton, a working-class war orphan in the West Riding, faced by social snobbery and stimulated by the spectacle of wealth enjoyed, decides to beat the top people by joining them. Father and mother were destroyed by a German bomb. A warm human personality is correspondingly destroyed as Lampton allows the conscious machinations of ambition to devalue personal affection. Sexual relationships become a means of cerebral satisfaction and of climbing the social ladder. It is Joe's frank reflections on himself that give psychological depth and moral force to the study. His story is continued in *Life at the Top* (1962) in which he glimpses what climbing the ladder has cost him.

Amis's Jim and Wain's Charles have to contend with the provocative blessings of university education, and even Braine's Joe has enough education to get a white-collar job and worm his way into a middle-class dramatic society, but Arthur Seaton, the hero of *Saturday Night and Sunday Morning* (1958) by Alan Sillitoe (1928–), is a factory mechanic who has no intellectual dissatisfaction to contend with. He escapes to heavy drinking at the week-ends and keeps two married sisters on a string. The sharp focus on working life in the Midlands, the discontent with the social framework, and the consciousness of violence and brutality ready to erupt into daily life have called out comparisons with D. H. Lawrence. But though the later novels extend the range of Sillitoe's social critique by involving more sophisticated characters, like Arthur Seaton's elder brother, Brian, in *Key to the Door* (1961), the basic contrasts between drab routine and breaking

out, static conformity and decisive change, are too simplistic-
ally articulated to acquire philosophic weight.

The 'angry' movement is usually interpreted in terms of discontent with the stereotyping of material conditions affected
by the post-war Welfare State and the continuing impregnability of the ostensibly rich. If it lacked corroborative idealism
it also for the most part lacked authenticating venom. Somehow inter-war protest had been meatier and rawer, no doubt
because it had the iniquities of the slump to gun for instead
of the provisions of bureaucratised welfare. A novelist whose
work in some ways bridges the gap between the social and
political reformism of the poets of the 1930s and the less
coherent personal and cultural rebelliousness of the 1950s is
Doris Lessing (1919–). Mrs Lessing, who herself became a
communist for a time, has complained of the parochialism
and pettiness of the anti-heroics of the 'angry' fifties. Certainly,
as an angry young woman, she did not have to invent targets
for assault. Brought up in Southern Rhodesia, she came to
England with a disgust of racialism and with a broken marriage
behind her to chronicle the experience of a quiveringly vital
young woman, comparably experienced, in a quintet of
novels, *Children of Violence*. They are *Martha Quest* (1952),
A Proper Marriage (1954), *A Ripple from the Storm* (1958),
Landlocked (1965), and *The Four-Gated City* (1969). Mrs
Lessing calls the whole 'a study of the individual conscience
in its relation with the collective'. It records a long struggle to
find sexual and political fulfilment and inner self-knowledge.
It begins with Martha's African childhood, depicting the inter-
racial situation and the spectacles of inequality, exploitation,
and deprivation with which it surrounds her. The power and
vividness of the descriptive evocation gives the work undoubted
imaginative status. Mrs Lessing proceeds to track the passions
and griefs of Martha's love life, an aspect and product of her
spirited rejection of conventional *mores* that fetter political,
social, and moral self-expression. Martha lacks the generosity
and capacity for self-criticism which would bind the reader in
continuing sympathy with her, but her career is a forceful
registration of the feminine impulses behind left-wing ideol-
ogies of the 1930s and 1940s. In *The Golden Notebook*
(1962) Mrs Lessing attempted to reorganise the various
themes, personal and socio-political, which the quintet

explored so sprawlingly. She has latterly turned to fantastic fiction. Her projected cosmic chronicle, *Canopus in Argos: Archives*, began with *Shikasta* (1979).

Meanwhile the 1960s brought to light an older woman writer from abroad who had been almost forgotten for thirty years. Jean Rhys (1894–1979) was born in Dominica, the daughter of a Welsh doctor and a West Indian. She came to England at sixteen, started life as a chorus-girl, then married a Dutchman. She lived in Paris, where she was actively encouraged as a writer by Ford Madox Ford, and finally settled again in England. Her fiction of the 1920s and 1930s includes *After Leaving Mr Mackenzie* (1931) and *Voyage in the Dark* (1934) as well as the short stories *The Left Bank* (1927). Her often embittered heroines are victims who suffer by virtue of their race, their poverty or dependence, and their sexual susceptibility, for, like Doris Lessing, she made fiction of the stuff of her deeply felt trials and dissatisfactions. When she published *Wide Sargasso Sea* (1966), a novel which cunningly tells the untold story of Mr Rochester, the hero of Charlotte Bronte's *Jane Eyre*, and his mad wife from the West Indies, she won instant recognition.

IV The post-war novel

While fashionable theatre and fiction thus restlessly or wryly, angrily or mockingly, projected our social and spiritual discomfiture, a novelist appeared who turned the tables on modernity by analysing our condition in terms of Original Sin. Man is sick, 'not exceptional man, but average man'. He is a fallen being with a sinful nature and his spiritual state is perilous. William Golding (1911–) proclaimed himself unashamedly a moralist for whom the novel is a fit vehicle for pressing upon fellow creatures the reality of their mortal condition. *Lord of the Flies* (1954) overturns the glib assumptions of the conventional boys' adventure story in which schoolboys marooned on an island rise virtuously to the occasion. R. M. Ballantyne's Victorian story, *The Coral Island*, provided the model to be rejected. Golding's schoolboys, victims of a wartime air disaster, revert to savagery. Meagre attempts to sustain the rationale and organisation of civilised beings give way gradually, under corrupt leadership, to hunting, killing, and barbarous rituals. A Christ-like boy, Simon, is killed sacrificially. To trace through a boy's eyes, as Golding does, the dawning understanding of man's fallen nature is the more disturbing because childhood is such an apt emblem of the innocence lost.

In his next fable, *The Inheritors* (1955), Golding goes back to the time when our progenitor, *homo sapiens*, is taking over from Neanderthal man. The Neanderthalers, 'the people', have strong primary sensations but cannot conceptualise or pattern their experience in art or ritual. They have a simple piety, will not kill for food, and live together amiably and unselfishly. It is at first a shock to the reader to learn that the 'new men', who eventually destroy them, are our ancestors and that the primitive beings whom evolutionary progress is assumed to have displaced were not ogres. The 'new men' can conceptualise, can see themselves from offside, and can deceive themselves. Their relationship to the Neanderthals is that of the fallen to the innocent. Many, including Golding himself, regard this as his finest book. Certainly the imaginative and verbal ingenuity involved in getting inside the primitive consciousness is unique.

Golding's moral patterning is locked into the central fabric of his novels like hidden foundations. In *Pincher Martin* (1956) (published in the USA as *The Two Deaths of Christopher Martin*, 1957) a naval lieutenant is tossing in mid-Atlantic after a torpedo attack on his ship. He climbs on to what appears to be Rockall to put up an apparently courageous, almost superhuman fight for survival. The events of the past float through his mind. Images call up mythic archetypes of heroic endeavour, including Prometheus and Robinson Crusoe. But it transpires that Martin's will to live is rooted in a fundamentally shallow self-dramatisation on the part of one who has cheated and bullied and exploited others in making his way. Finally it is revealed that all has taken place in the man's mind in the few moments before he drowned. This time Golding upends the story of Robinson Crusoe, the pious, resourceful individualist, into a study in damnation of a man whose self-will has pitted him against God.

Ballantyne and Defoe yield place to Dante as seminal influence on *Free Fall* (1960). Lost in the blackness of middle life, Sammy Mountjoy seeks to recall how he came to be where he is. His autobiographical recollections gradually track down the point of his fall. Childhood freedom was lost in his treatment of Beatrice Ifor with whom he fell in love. He wanted to possess and subdue her: he seduced, degraded, and forsook her. In rediscovering the image of what she first revealed to him he learns to identify the moment of his fall. But when he sees her again, she is a lunatic in an asylum, paying the price. *The Spire* (1967) is a more complex study in human wilfulness. It is based on the actual history of the construction of the spire at Salisbury Cathedral. It goes back to the fourteenth century to study a Dean, Jocelin, whose ruling passion to erect a spire in defiance of architectural practicalities is at once a vocation served with costly zeal and dedication, and an expression of wilful personal obsession with stamping his phallic image against the sky. The ambiguity inherent in Jocelin's dual motivation brings angel and demon into conflict for his soul.

Golding has also written a play, *The Brass Butterfly* (1958), a collection of short stories, *The Scorpion God* (1971), and three further novels, *The Pyramid* (1967), *Darkness Visible* (1979) and *Rites of Passage* (1980). Certain limitations in psychological portraiture and some stiffness in registration of the social scene are evident in his work, and his structural patterns are worked out with a challenging thoroughness, but the poetic insight and the moral sturdiness carry an immense authority.

As theology supplied Golding with his structural motifs, so Muriel Spark (1918–), a Roman Catholic convert, found that Catholicism enabled her to see life as a whole 'rather than as a series of disconnected happenings' and gave her a key to artistic control of her material, 'a norm from which one can depart'. Two of Golding's fictional locations are islands recalling Ballantyne's and Defoe's, and Mrs Spark's *Robinson* (1958) clearly brings Crusoe to mind. For Robinson is a mystery-man, half-Crusoe, half-Prospero, helpful yet remote host, healer, and governor in relation to three survivors of a plane crash on what is called 'Robinson's Island'. Robinson and his island are both endowed with mythic status. The story is told by January Marlow, one of the survivors. Her two male companions in distress, together with Robinson and his adopted orphan, Miguel, individually redefine aspects of the experience, personal and mental, which has been the substance of January's past life. This localised renewal of problematical relationships recalls the refurbishing of the old conspiracy that occurs on the spot in *The Tempest*. A keystone of the symbolic pattern is Robinson's temporary disappearance (planned, it would seem, rather like the Duke's in *Measure for Measure*), which takes a repressive lid off and allows destructive urges to surface in the survivors as they do in Golding's schoolboys.

Mrs Spark's method is to focus on a small group of people subjected to the strain of abnormal circumstances. But the abnormality, which produces an obsessional angle of vision and wrenches participants from their habitual composure, only magnifies and intensifies aspects of the human condition that are ultimately inescapable. Thus *Memento Mori* (1959) is a study of aged people who are individually subjected to anonymous telephone calls announcing, 'Remember you must die.' The novel explores the various ways by which people of different temperament and profession try to assimilate the message among their established personal obsessions. The irony is that those actually so near to death should try to exclude the fact of mortality from their reckoning. *The Prime of Miss Jean Brodie* (1962) studies a female thorn in the flesh of authority, an Edinburgh schoolmistress, progressively-minded after the fashion of the 1930s, who grooms too familiarly a group of personable girls with aesthetic tastes and social sensibilities that will make them *'la crème de la crème'*. Miss Brodie involves them in her own sex life in a way that ultimately leads to her dismissal. The mental and emotional life of growing girls is registered with subtlety. And Mrs Spark has turned her microscope on a maturer age group in *The Girls of Slender Means* (1963) to bring the personal lives of girls resident at a London hostel and their boy-friends to crisis point when the detonation of an unexploded bomb sets fire to the hostel. *The Mandelbaum Gate* (1965) is set in Jerusalem at the time of the trial of Adolf Eichmann and makes the division between Jew and Arab symptomatic of wider dualities. Mrs Spark is a witty stylist whose dialogue is vital and whose satiric scrutiny of human aberration is effected in precise and telling prose. The comic sense is acute, and the serious estimate of human significance which informs her work is unobtrusively articulated.

Iris Murdoch (1919–) is a professional philosopher. The

progress of her main characters tends to be towards a freedom found in unselfish acceptance of life's contingency and variety. But there is a lack of compelling force to give their experience dramatic exposure. In *Under the Net* (1954) John Donoghue, a stage Irishman who lives by his wits, is conducted through a tumbling series of comic capers. The reader who has yawned over the humourless long-windedness of Doris Lessing and judiciously skipped the protracted descriptive coloratura of Lawrence Durrell hesitates to pass solemn judgment on a writer who can be as funny as Miss Murdoch, but her attempt to support a full-length novel on a practical joke in *The Bell* (1958) issues in patent contrivance. She has inventiveness, she is verbal mistress of the externalities of place and action, but her set-pieces are over-plotted.

What skilled plotting can achieve was manifested for the 1950s by Lawrence Durrell (1912–). Durrell called himself 'an angry young man of the thirties' for his blistering attack on English smuggery and respectability in *The Black Book* (Paris, 1938) whose sexuality made it unpublishable in England. The book harks back to the ethic of Forster's *Where Angels Fear to Tread* in its contrasting polarities of England old and devitalised and the Mediterranean sunny and alive. Durrell was posted to British Information Offices in Cairo and Alexandria during the war, and this provided him with material for his *Alexandria Quartet*, a tetralogy of over-lapping novels: *Justine* (1957), *Balthazar* (1958), *Mountolive* (1958), and *Clea* (1960). It is a many-stranded record of life in a lushly evoked Alexandria where Darley, a schoolteacher and the narrator of *Justine*, is first involved with Justine, the wife of a wealthy Copt, Nessim. Balthazar is a doctor, Mountolive is the British Ambassador and former lover of Nessim's mother, and Clea is Darley's eventual mistress. Gradually it transpires that Nessim and Justine are smuggling arms to Palestine, while Darley is a secret agent. By superimposing the spy-plot on to a complex shifting pattern of sexual liaisons, Durrell achieves an impressive feat in the unfolding of narrative. His technique is to allow each succeeding novel to amplify and correct its predecessors by fuller information derived from different participants. Recurring reinterpretation for ever cancelling out assumptions arrived at from limited stand-points makes a highly readable if often over-written *opus*.

Durrell, who is also a poet, has continued to write novels but his fiction of the 1950s represents his powers at their peak, and there are those who question whether academic criticism has exaggerated the gap between his tetralogy and less pretentious works by writers who have served the mass market for spy stories with frankly commercial zeal. They point to Ian Fleming (1908–64) with his stories of James Bond, Britain's super-hero of a violence-ridden, sex-spiced world of espionage, and to John Le Carré (pseudonym of D. J. M. Cornwell) (1931–), whose stories of cold-war intelligence exploits portray a world of chill brutality. Both writers have the kind of deft narrative craftsmanship that the modern sophisticated public for spy stories and crime stories demands. Its challenge lured the poet Cecil Day Lewis to write detective novels for thirty years under the pseudonym 'Nicholas Blake', and it lured the Oxford don, J. I. M. Stewart (1906–) to turn aside from literary criticism and from fictional chronicling of university life under his own name, to produce over thirty books of crime fiction as 'Michael Innes'.

Angus Wilson (1913–), like Durrell, did his best work in the 1950s. He began with short stories sharply observant of the social scene, *The Wrong Set* (1949) and *Darling Dodos* (1950). He then wrote a group of novels on a broad canvas, believing that the current need was for thoughtful registration of the social scene, such as George Eliot had provided for her day in *Middlemarch*, but recognising that post-Freudian analysis could not be contained within nineteenth-century fictional frameworks. 'We are on the threshold of a psychology for which older novel forms do not provide,' he said. He thus purposely set out to combine breadth with depth in a way appropriate to the age. A central theme in *Hemlock and After* (1952) is the relation between public and private life, between high-minded liberal humanism and inner integrity. Bernard Sands, a successful novelist, achieves his aim of establishing a government-supported country house for writers, Vardon Hall, and simultaneously gets a glimpse of himself, a married man who is practising homosexuality, as susceptible to sadistic excitation. The revelation undermines his confidence and his liberal–humanist conviction, he publicly destroys his own image at the opening of Vardon Hall, and triumph turns to disaster. The obsession with the disturbed humanist conscience persists in *Anglo-Saxon Attitudes* (1956) in the central figure, Gerald Middleton, a retired professor of mediaeval history, aware of his failure as husband, father, lover, and also as historian in that he has long suspected a celebrated archaeological discovery to have been a fraud perpetrated by the now dead husband of his mistress, and has taken no action. The crisis of conscience ultimately drives him to act, but not before, in the characters of numerous persons involved in his public and private affairs, Wilson has portrayed a variety of types representative of cultural currents in English life from high-powered scholars to second-rate novelists, from the disciples of Bloomsbury to those of Wyndham Lewis. The skill with which Wilson controls the dialogue of bores and asses and frauds, and his fullness of documentation in unfolding the course of archaeological hoax and detection cannot wholly compensate for the lack of dramatic intensity and the failure to project the issues raised in the restricted milieu on to a screen of wider applicability. Contrasts have been drawn between the complacency of E. M. Forster and Angus Wilson's agonised scrutiny of the Forsterian ethic. Wilson's novels, however, appear to represent a sustained confrontation with his own neurosis. *The Wild Garden or Speaking of Writing* (1963) sheds light on a sensibility which can find that 'cocktail parties, Christmas dinners, and social functions still represent the hell of human failure to communicate.'

The novelist has to get across to a public that can think of tortures more agonising than these. Anthony Burgess (1917–), for instance, having behind him half-a-dozen novels including a trilogy on post-war Malaya, turned in *A Clockwork Orange* (1962) to an exercise in sub-Orwellian, anti-Utopian fiction which subjects liberal humanism to rougher treatment than Wilson's hag-ridden heroes encounter. Burgess projects a future England where Alex is gang-leader of teenage delinquents who terrorise people with theft, rape, torture, and murder. Captured, Alex is taken from gaol under humane, liberal legislation, for Reclamation Treatment, and is transformed into an emotionally neutered creature for whom art, music, and sex, as well as violence, are sick-making. He has become a piece of machinery, a 'clockwork orange'. Liberal humanitarianism and totalitarian conditioning are both the objects of Burgess's satire. The delinquents' lingo, 'nadsat', based on Slav roots, is ingenious. Indeed Burgess's strength lies partly in verbal virtuosity that is heavily derivative from Joyce. The gift for linguistic mimicry is one aspect of an assimilative talent which makes much of Burgess's work unmistakably imitative. There is comic entertainment, however, in the portrayal of the middle-aged poet, Enderby, in *Inside Mr Enderby* (1963), who can compose only on the lavatory seat and who figures again in *Enderby Outside* (1968) and *The Clockwork Testament* (1976).

Linguistic virtuosity also marks the novels of Nigel Dennis (1912–), in particular *Cards of Identity* (1955). The Identity Club holds an annual conference at an English country house. 'Identity is the answer to everything.' The club distributes appropriate identities to unreal, 'self-painted' people ('We give our patients the identities they can use best'), and the case-histories under survey subject aspects of contemporary life – public, political, religious, sexual – to extravagant satire. In substance and style the work is directed at an informed readership aware of current trends in culture and in social analysis, and responsive to literary parody and pastiche. If there is Joycean exuberance in the comedy of *Cards of Identity*, there is Beckettian economy in the narrow focus of Dennis's *A House in Order* (1966) in which a prisoner-of-war is confined to a greenhouse and a small yard, and his aspirations and frustrations, fastened on whatever can be done in this limited microcosm, have symbolic significance. The fable is powerful.

The critique of contemporary values implicit in Dennis, Burgess, and Wilson suggests a common distrust of liberal humanism to be set beside the rejection of the values of liberal humanism in Christian orientated writers such as Golding and Mrs Spark. There appears to be a convergence of Christian and secular judgment on the once fashionable Forsterian ethic. There is, however, a refreshing outburst of confidence in the old Shavian Life Force and in the reliability of instinct in the pronouncements of the novelist, Brigid Brophy (1929–), who has managed to harness the spirit of Shavian reformism alongside Firbankian lightness of touch in *Hackenfeller's Ape* (1953), a fable about the treatment of animals, and in *The Finishing Touch* (1963) which is set in a private girls' school run jointly by two lesbian headmistresses. In both novels the sense of a writer enjoying herself is strong.

Nina Bawden (1925–) too gives the impression of easy accomplishment, but her terrain is suburbia and the authorial *persona* is more like Jane Austen than Ronald Firbank. *Tortoise by Candlelight* (1961) explores the child mind perceptively within the context of dimly glimpsed adult upsets. In *A Woman of My Age* (1967) Elizabeth Jourdelay faces a marital crisis in middle life and there is some subtlety in the interplay in her mind of immediate thought and hypothetical third-person commentary on it. Ironic dimensions of this kind give quality to the writing. *The Birds in the Trees* (1971) studies the personal and social problem of the teenager who becomes a heroin-addict at the age of sixteen. The repercussions on the parents and on the younger brother and sister are imaginatively registered. Nina Bawden's polish and native psychological discernment put her in line with Elizabeth Taylor.

An older woman who takes a broader canvas is Sybille Bedford (1911–). Having chronicled the story of two German families, Jewish and Catholic respectively, in *A Legacy* (1957), she turned in *A Favourite of the Gods* (1963) and *A Compass Error* (1968) to chronicle the lives of three generations in the persons of Anna Howland, an American born in the 1870s, her daughter Constanzia, and her grand-daughter Flavia. Anna's unsuccessful marriage to an Italian prince brings the scene to Italy and England, but the historical and political background of the passing decades is only thinly hinted at. The emphasis is upon the shift in methods of upbringing and in moral values and sexual *mores* from generation to generation, and the collisions they cause.

Public events impinge altogether more centrally on the personal lives of the characters of the *Balkan Trilogy* of Olivia Manning (1918–80), whose husband was a British Council Lecturer in Bucharest at the outbreak of war. The couple were driven successively to Athens and to Egypt as the Germans advanced. The novels of the trilogy, *The Great Fortune* (1960), *The Spoilt City* (1962), and *Friends and Heroes* (1965), record the gradual encroachment of war upon English residents in the Balkans. Most of them are watchers on events rather than participants. They eat meals in cafes and talk about the 'news' while disaster approaches a country corruptly governed and reeking of inequality. What gives the trilogy its inner vitality is Miss Manning's probing analysis of the relationship of Guy Pringle and his wife, Harriet. Private life is incidental to Guy. His fulfilment is in the outside world, and Harriet is irritated by 'the amount of mental and physical vitality he expended on others', which seems to leave no room for her. He is all things to all men — but does he really know anyone? His simplistic pro-Russian ideology also irritates her. The ordering of historic events around this telling registration of domestic tension gives cohesion to the work. A second sequence of novels, the Levant Trilogy, takes the Pringles on to Cairo at the time of the desert war: *The Danger Tree* (1977), *The Battle Lost and Won* (1978), and the posthumous *The Sum of Things* (1980).

Frank Tuohy (1925—), another portrayer of English colonies abroad, wrote of life in Brazil in *The Animal Game* (1957) and *Warm Nights of January* (1960), and of life in Poland in *The Ice-Saints* (1964). He defines perceptively the sense of being set apart endured by expatriates. Attitudes and conversational expressions long outdated at home are fossilised in English colonies abroad. Talk lacks the 'tiny adjustments, pressures, and ironies that an English background imposes on the expression of feeling and moral attitudes'. Habits and minor social obligations which fill up life at home, when withdrawn, leave a void, a moral vacuum which can suck the unwary into corruption. Tuohy's exploration of the problems of relationship and adjustment in racial and cultural melting-pots is made with analytical acumen.

The novelist whose appeal lies substantially in his evocation of foreign countries may answer a public hunger comparable to that satisfied by travel books. Francis King (1923—), who was brought up in Switzerland and India, and worked for the British Council in Italy, Greece, Egypt, Finland, and Japan, set *The Dividing Stream* (1951) in Florence and used Grecian backgrounds for *The Dark Glasses* (1954), *The Firewalkers* (1956), and *The Man on the Rock* (1957). It has been suggested that just as Byron brought to the public at home welcome news of the Mediterranean after the Napoleonic wars shut off contact, so books such as those of Francis King gained popularity in the 1950s with a British public starved of travel after the war by lack of foreign currency and by the difficulty of obtaining visas. Pure travel literature is of course

a many-stranded *genre*. There is the tradition of companion-
able personal reminiscence and reflection found in Hilaire
Belloc's jaunty record *The Path to Rome* (1902) and Norman
Douglas's engaging volumes about Italy. There are also records
of intrepid ventures into the unknown. Freya Stark (1893–),
an explorer in the mould of C. M. Doughty, journeyed into
the remoter areas of Arabia and Persia, and her books include
A Winter in Arabia (1940) and *Traveller's Prelude* (1950).
Lawrence Durrell, the novelist, celebrated the three islands
Corfu, Rhodes, and Cyprus respectively in *Prospero's Cell*
(1945), *Reflections on a Marine Venus* (1955), and *Bitter
Lemons* (1957), while his brother Gerald Durrell (1912–),
a zoologist, wrote entertainingly of collecting animals in
Africa and South America. His *My Family and Other Animals*
(1956) is an account of his childhood. Just as many recent
poets and novelists have found a useful second string in writing
stories for juveniles, so others have turned to writing travel
books. The poet David Wright (1920–), for instance, has
published authoritative travellers' guides to Portugal.

Nearer home a novelist who brought painstaking powers of
observation to bear on odd and sensitive people, and on the
grey areas of experience where the idiosyncratic overlaps
with the bizarre, was William Sansom (1912–76). His imaginative exactness in describing people and places can both tickle
the sense of humour and fix the curiosity. The London scenery
of *The Body* (1959) has been especially praised. ('Now it
contrived a mixed appearance of mediterranean courtyard,
derelict garage, and pixie glen.') The novel tells the story of
a middle-aged husband who becomes jealous of a neighbour's
attention to his wife and precipitates conditions for infidelity
by his desperate search for confirmation of it. ('This was to
drink the cup dry, to be deceived by one's best friend, it put
one somehow more in the right.') But though Sansom continued to write novels, such as *The Cautious Heart* (1958)
and *The Last Hours of Sandra Lee* (1961), and to investigate
in them just such behavioural byways, it is his short stories
which won most acclaim. *Fireman Flower* (1944), stories of
the London blitz in which Sansom served as a fireman, was
the first of a series of collections extending over the next
quarter of a century from which a selection was made in 1963,
The Stories of William Sansom, and introduced by Elizabeth

Bowen. In the descriptive precision, the dry humour, the subtly contrived dialogue, and the instinct for sensing the extraordinary beneath the superficially humdrum, Sansom held readers with tales immensely varied in substance and setting, in mood and atmosphere.

Rhys Davies (1909–78) had been publishing short stories for some seventeen years when Sansom began, and his prolific output of fiction ultimately spanned nearly fifty years, from *The Song of Songs* (1927) to *The Honeysuckle Girl* (1975). Having escaped from the Rhondda valley to the penurious circles of literary London in the 1920s, he remained permanently concerned with Welsh life. 'My carnal little stories were long-trousered productions, a Welsh mining valley their background, family avarice and brutal sex their themes,' he said of his first collection. Thereafter he carried on the tradition of Caradoc Evans without Evans's sourness. He was early dubbed 'the Welsh Chekov'. D. H. Lawrence admired his work and invited him to visit him at Bandol. The last episode in the friendship between the two, when Davies accompanied the now dying Lawrence on a trip to Paris, is vividly recalled in Davies's autobiography, *Print of a Hare's Foot* (1969). *Collected Stories* (1955) reveals a high level of narrative craftsmanship. Though it has been suggested that Davies's delight in registering idiosyncrasies of Welsh character and behaviour smacks of staging his own people for the entertainment of the English public, he manages to convey that it is essentially his own wry relish of quirkiness that is the source of his amusement, and that it could not but be applied to the people he knows best. Davies was by no means negligible as a novelist. *The Painted King* (1954) portrays in Guy Aspen an actor—composer seemingly modelled on Ivor Novello, trapped in the make-believe world of the theatre. *The Perishable Quality* (1957) portrays a Welsh girl who strikes gold as a London prostitute (reading Surtees novels while sitting naked for a voyeur at £5 a time).

Davies's view of Wales was that of a man who lived largely in exile from it. Glyn Jones (1905–), novelist and short-story writer, for long a schoolmaster, wrote from inside. He knew the seamy life of Merthyr Tydfil where he was brought up and he knew peaceful Cardiganshire. Industrial and agricultural Wales provided contrasting settings for his fiction. His range takes in the extremes of realism and fantasy: they are bound together by the sincerity of Jones's personal attachment to his people. His collections of short stories include *The Blue Bed* (1937) and *The Water Music* (1944). It is Jones's novels that belong to the 1950s and 1960s. *The Valley, the City, the Village* (1956) is autobiographical fiction alive with homely Welsh portraiture and anecdote, and rich in throwaway squibs like the one about the man who thought *Daniel Deronda* was a novel about Treorchy. *The Learning Lark* (1960) is a rollickingly good-tempered account of bribery in the educational career-structure in a mining valley. *The Island of Apples* (1965), a myth retold, recounts the arrival of a handsome young hero in a Welsh valley. Jones's verbal mastery of the squalid and the idyllic, the grotesque and the rhapsodic, is given full play. The sheer poetry, the high spirits, and the fun are infectious. ('Dragon Mills. Great Reductions. Davies's Trousers Down Again.')

V English and Welsh poets

Glyn Jones has paid tribute to the work of R. S. Thomas (1913–), parish priest in the Church of Wales and poet. His *Song at the Year's Turning* (1955) includes poems from earlier volumes and work dating back to 1942. Subsequent volumes include *Poetry for Supper* (1958), *The Bread of Truth* (1963), *Selected Poems 1946–1968* (1973), and *Frequencies* (1978). Thomas has been incumbent of rural parishes and has taught himself Welsh in order to be closer to his people. Disciplined yet illusionless dedication to his duties shines through his poetry. Glyn Jones applied to him a felicitous phrase from Alun Lewis, 'within the parish of my care': 'The parish of R. S. Thomas's care is the Wales of the small farms, and his achievement has been to give his themes and characters, limited and remote, by his passionate concern, universal significance.' The lucidity and spareness of R. S. Thomas's style has been contrasted with the obscurity and metaphorical prodigality of Dylan Thomas's. 'W. B. Yeats seems to have been the only recent writer to have made an acknowledged impression on R. S. Thomas's style,' John Betjemen observed in his Introduction to *Song at the Year's Turning*, adding that Thomas 'thinks that poetry should be read to oneself not out loud and that it is heard by an inner ear.'

Thomas has Yeats's gift for sucking the reader into the heart of a dialogue, whether an outer dialogue with the country people he serves, or an inner dialogue of scrupulous self-questioning. In either case he wrestles with contradictions whose roots lie deep. He is worried by the decay of rural life, the creeping erosion of Wales's culture and identity, but there is no sentimentalisation of the human reality. No one could have portrayed the hill farmers with more distaste for the brutishness of their ways — or with more compassion. The farmer's uncouthness has no kinship with the healing earth, with the grace and light of the hills.

> You stopped your ears to the soft influence
> Of birds, preferring the dull tone
> Of the thick blood, the loud, unlovely rattle
> Of mucous in the throat, the shallow stream
> Of neighbour's trivial talk.   ('Valediction')

But equally Nature herself is not only grace and light and beauty. The earth is a brown bitch fawning about man's feet and dragging him down to her level.

> My clothes stink, where she has pressed
> Her body to me, the lewd bawd,
> Gravid as an old sow, but clawed.   ('The Slave')

The dual influence of Nature in healing and brutalising evident to Thomas in his daily round is an aspect of man's ambiguous relationship to the natural order, and thus his commentary reflects not only on the specific condition of the Welsh peasantry as such, but on tensions inherent in human status.

In the same way Thomas has universalised his personal dilemma as an educated priest trying to teach, comfort, and bring spiritual realities to bear on fellow-creatures locked up in unresponsiveness. The dilemma is acute because there is a reverse side to the coin of resistant peasant savagery.

> You are lean and spare, yet your strength is a mockery
> Of the pale words in the black Book.
> And why should you come like sparrows for prayer crumbs,
> Whose hands can dabble in the world's blood?
>   ('A Priest to his People')

It would be no more adequate to describe Thomas as a 'regional' poet than it would be to describe Wordsworth or Hardy thus. The writer gets to the centre by digging deeply into his own locality. Norman Nicholson (1914–) has also learned this lesson. Born in Millom, Cumberland, he has spent most of his life there and mined from his home terrain topographical books about West Cumberland and the Lake District as well as books of poems that include *Five Rivers* (1944), *Rock Face* (1948), *The Pot Geranium* (1954), and *A Local Habitation* (1972). Nicholson has told in his autobiography, *Wednesday Early Closing* (1975), how he was brought up behind a draper's shop in an area which suffered badly from the depression. He noted in verse how, after the desolation of the slump years, the Second World War brought new life back to the decayed coal and iron industries of West Cumberland. The first harvest of these industries had corseted the land with railway lines. But now the miners dig for death.

> Every knuckle of soft ore
> A bullet in a soldier's ear.   ('Cleator Moor')

Nicholson played a part in the revival of verse drama at the Mercury Theatre when he gave freshness and sturdiness to the story of Elijah by locating it in Cumberland in *The Old Man of the Mountains* (1946), and later plays include a study of the Old Testament prophet, Hosea, in *A Match for the Devil* (1953), and an updating of the story of Elisha in *Birth by Drowning* (1960). Nicholson's verse is never slack or flaccid. He never assumes a vatic air or wraps a minstrel's mantle about him. Conversely he never cheapens his craft by easy vulgarities. His homeliest lines are, when weighed, his heaviest. He has always been able to find in his chosen, immediate environment — 'the fells, dales, farms, sea-shore and estuaries of the English Lake District, and from the houses, streets, blast furnaces, mines etc of the small industrial town of Millom' — imagery in which what he wanted to say about man's personal, social, and natural condition could be said with clarity and with plenty of resonance for the sensitive ear. But a growing control of colloquial directness and an increasingly subtle awareness of human personality has enriched his later work, so that in *A Local Habitation* he emerges as a master of relaxed, unhurried reminiscence and reflection, picking and choosing from a lifetime's affectionate memories, grave and cheerful, nostalgic and elegiac. And the initially most light-hearted of the pieces are often the richest both in quirky personal warmth and in hidden reverberations. (See 'Have You Been to London?' or 'The Tune the Old Cow Died Of'.)

An influential new poetic voice of the 1950s, that of Philip Larkin (1922–), directed delicious mockery at that rooted-ness in home town and childhood memories that are the stuff of Nicholson's verse. 'I remember, I remember' (the title echoing Thomas Hood's sentimental poem) ridicules the auto-biographical claims of celebrated writers by negating typical fictions of early days. The poet's train has stopped in Coventry, his birthplace.

> A whistle went:
> Things moved. I sat back, staring at my boots.
> 'Was that,' my friend smiled, 'where you have your roots?'
> No, only where my childhood was unspent,
> I wanted to retort, just where I started . . .

He goes on to deny that any of the significant prophetic inci-dents that other writers record took place there. But he lays no blame on the place. 'Nothing, like something, happens anywhere,' he concludes. The sardonic deflation of pose or gesture, the aborting of sentiment before it has time to breathe, the refusal to substitute anger for romanticism, and the final shrug of the shoulders in acceptance of negativity all character-ise a poet who confesses that he found sudden relief in dis-covering from the work of Thomas Hardy that being a poet need not involve screwing himself up to purposes external to his own life. 'One could simply relapse back into one's own life and write from it.' Larkin indeed believes that Hardy's is the finest body of poetry our century has produced. The implicit devaluation of Yeats and Eliot is notable because both poets assumed a vatic authority in commentary upon their age and both were innovators in poetic technique. Larkin is neither seer nor innovator, though his neo-Georgian crafts-manship does allow for the ready assimilation of colloquial vocabulary and rhythms, and for the cunning accumulation of impressionistic detail.

When *The Less Deceived* (1955), Larkin's third volume of poems, was published, it met with immediate acclaim. Subsequent volumes, *The Whitsun Weddings* (1964) and *High Windows* (1974), have confirmed the impression of a poetic integrity which, if it is narrow in its range, is narrow with the narrowness of a familiar contemporary constriction of thinking and feeling. His dry underestimate of life was congenial to a generation of educated young people who were dissatisfied enough to enjoy gentle carping at things without being conceited enough to turn angry or self-indulgent enough to plunge into *angst*. Moreover Larkin's recipe for poetry, 'verbal pickling' that preserves an experience indefinitely, is pleasingly unpretentious. In his case the pickling bottles not only moods of diffidence and extreme emotional caginess, of tolerant amusement and interrogative deliberation, but also sometimes moods of melancholy stoical realism that only just skim the waters of despair.

In the celebrated poem, 'Church Going', Larkin questions not only the continuing purpose of the church he visits but the compulsive motive that drew him there. Correspondingly he goes behind the question of what will happen when belief has gone to the question 'And what remains when disbelief has gone?', and behind the frail positive consolatory conclusion that 'a serious house on serious earth' can perhaps never become obsolete, to a final, sly, denigratory explanation of man's interest in seriousness. The practice of thus undercutting rueful observation with more rueful critique of it represents the domestication of escalating Beckettian irony into spiralling deflation. The poem is a specimen of Larkin's Indian-rope-trick model in which the poetic questioner climbs aloft from probe to probe until he finally disappears in thin air. The act achieves its effect by the curiosity it arouses before the sight of the empty stage reminds the audience that it is time to applaud. But the pickled experience keeps its flavour here no less than does the seemingly more positive account of the wedding-parties encountered *en route* by a stopping-train in the title poem of *The Whitsun Weddings*, where the problematical note is reserved for the conclusion and effects no devaluation of what has gone before.

Larkin, who edited *The Oxford Book of Twentieth-Century English Verse* (1973) with a marked tenderness towards slick balladry and cheerful trifling, himself gave temporary respectability to knowing dalliance with the wan and the bleak as a cosy between-meals substitute for passion and protest. His appearance in *New Lines* (1957), an anthology edited by Robert Conquest (1917–) which specifically reacted against modernism and excess in favour of traditional comeliness and clarity, caused him to be regarded as leader of what came to be called the 'Movement'. Other poets represented in the anthology have long marked out separate courses for themselves, and 'Movement' more satisfactorily defines a poetic tendency than a group of writers. But among the *New Lines* poets D. J. Enright (1920–) has retained the habit of pickling experiences without too much excitement. He has held university posts abroad and at home, and his habit has been to minute what he encounters in neat verses that carry the stamp of an intelligent and sensitive response to the needs of real people, and especially of foreigners, whose oddities are relished without patronisation. A dozen volumes of poems (including *Bread rather than Blossoms*, 1956; *Addictions*, 1962; and *Sad Ires*, 1976) contain a lively *corpus* that glosses a career of academic activity with chatty anecdotal marginalia easy on the eye and the ear. Enright's preference for patently lucid and unpretentious poetry is evident again in his editing of *The Oxford Book of Contemporary Verse 1945–1980* (1980).

Donald Davie (1922–), another university teacher, has never been content to jot down current impressions and has set no value on the illusion of immediacy or on a man-to-man familiarity achieved by being slipshod. Rather he has registered experience and reflection in studied lines and moulded stanzas. His *Collected Poems 1950–1970* (1972) has been succeeded by *The Shires* (1974) and *In the Stopping Train* (1977). Davie's choicely sculpted poems carry a load of wit and cerebral complexity which the transparency of early 'Movement' poetry scarcely allowed for. In elegance and decorum he has consciously learned from late Augustan models. The tentativeness of Larkin is as foreign to him as the free-wheeling chattiness of Enright. He has criticised 'Movement' poetry for the absence from it of 'outward and non-human things apprehended crisply for their own sakes' and for the way the poet failed to go out of himself in response to his experience so 'as not to be aware of the attitudes he is taking up'. The criticism might well apply to Kingsley Amis's off-the-cuff verse disclaimers to poetic pretension which studiously convert non-posturing into a strenuous posture. It might apply to John Wain's imposition of compact forms like *terza rima* and villanelle on intimate personal musings. Self-consciously being a poet is as dangerous as self-consciously not being a poet. The attempt by metronomic regularity to convey the feel of quiet understatement too readily teeters on the edge of banality. Wain's *A Word Carved on a Sill* (1956) was followed by *Weep Before God* (1961). The latter contains 'A Song about Major Eatherley', which ponders the subsequent troubled history of an American pilot who dropped a nuclear bomb on Nagasaki.

> Good news. It seems he loved them after all.
> His orders were to fry their bones to ash.
> He carried up the bomb and let it fall.
> And then his orders were to take the cash . . .

One of the influences behind the revival of interest in elaborate verse forms and the move to restore metaphysical wit was that of William Empson (1906–) whose *Collected Poems* came out in 1955. Through his critical work, *Seven Types of Ambiguity* (1930), and his poetry he explored the resources of verbal ambiguity in a way which made him a much-read mentor and a much-praised but little-read practitioner. There is a line beyond which the riddling metaphysical poet argues himself out of effective contact with his reader, and Empson's poetry, clotted with recondite allusions, kept him on the wrong side of the line. The reader who struggles finds his reward; but though 'Movement' poetry was identified with Empsonianism to such an extent that some critics tagged the poets the 'University Wits', the New Liners' rejection of obscurity made the link a tenuous one.

Elizabeth Jennings (1926–) came to regret her identification with the 'Movement'. Poetry from a series of volumes beginning with *Poems* (1953) was gathered in her *Collected Poems* (1967), and later volumes have included *Lucidities* (1970) and *Relationships* (1972). Miss Jennings is a lyricist with a contemplative mind whose quietness is not the quietness of contrived dramatic design but of an inner search for order.

Miss Jennings's directness rings true. In the early poem, 'Song at the Beginning of Autumn', she broods on the groping forward of autumn upon summer.

> But every season is a kind
> Of rich nostalgia. We give names —
> Autumn and summer, winter, spring —
> As though to unfasten from the mind
> Our moods and give them outward forms.
> We want the certain solid thing.

By giving the stamp of respectability to readily understand-able verse no doubt *New Lines* helped to create the public mood that turned *Collected Poems* (1958) by John Betjeman (1906–) into a best-seller. Betjeman had been publishing 'light verse' since the 1930s. Auden had edited a selection of Betjeman's verse and prose, *Slick but not Streamlined* (1947). An expert in the field of historical architecture, an enthusiast for Victorian buildings, an Anglo-Catholic with a keen eye for what is good and what is absurd in the Church of England, Betjeman has written about what he likes and dislikes with frankness and clarity, sometimes with mockery, and often with a powerful tug at the feelings. The secret of his popular appeal lies partly in his shameless relish of firm rhyme-schemes and rhythmic patterns. Traditional metrics have been exploited in great variety as only a highly skilled technician could exploit them. Betjeman has conceded that for him the composition of a poem begins when some pattern starts hammering inside his head. But the swinging rhythms of some of his comic and satiric portrayals of upper- and middle-class types have perhaps played too large a part in forming the popular image of Betjeman, who has too a vein of melancholy and a sense of tragedy.

> The heavy mahogany door with its wrought-iron screen
>   Shuts. And the sound is rich, sympathetic, discreet.
> The sun still shines on this eighteenth-century scene
>   With Edwardian faience adornments — Devonshire Street.
>
> No hope. And the X-ray photographs under his arm
>   Confirm the message. His wife stands timidly by.
>   ('Devonshire Street W.1')

Betjeman's long autobiographical poem, *Summoned by Bells* (1960), tells his story from infancy, through schooldays when he had T. S. Eliot for teacher, to a socially exciting if academically inglorious year at Oxford from where he was sent down. Blank verse is fitfully interspersed with lyrics in a delightful exercise in self-exposure.

While Betjeman sold like Byron, an even older poet, Basil Bunting (1900–), had to wait until the late sixties for modest recognition. A Northumbrian who has lived in Europe and North America, and who was in contact with major writers in the inter-war period, he was most strongly influenced by Pound. His free-range metres, packed allusiveness, and his brusque, businesslike incisiveness create a formidable poetic *persona*. Bunting's no-nonsense air has nothing of the voguishly relaxed off-duty tone or of fashionably slapdash garrulity. Verbal sleeves are rolled up. If a thing is worth saying it is worth hammering home with as few blows as possible.

> Poetry? It's a hobby,
> I run model trains,
> Mr Shaw here breeds pigeons.
>
> It's not work. You don't sweat.
> Nobody pays for it.
> You *could* advertise soap.
>
> ('What the Chairman told Tom')

Briggflatts (1966), an autobiographical poem, was acclaimed by Cyril Connolly as 'perhaps the most distinguished long poem to have been published since *Four Quartets*'. The rigorous artistry and the construction of the poem in quasi-musical movements give the comparison some validity. Other critics have pointed to the influence of Hopkins, while the inter-weaving of historical with personal memory also recalls David Jones.

While Bunting roamed widely before returning to his native Northumbria, Jack Clemo (1916–), no less a foe to easy self-accommodation to the demands of the age, has struggled through life in his native Cornwall, stone deaf for most of his adult life and blind since 1955. The china-clay industry has pock-marked rural Cornwall as physical deprivations have marred Clemo's life. He has found in the threatened environ-

ment and in the constrictions of personal deprivation a reflection of man's tortuously riven affiliations to the order of
nature and the order of grace. His two prose works, the novel,
Wilding Graft (1948), and the autobiography, *Confessions of
a Rebel* (1949), define the need for redemptive grafting of
spiritual grace into the instinctual and passional life of man.
This theme, with its recognition of the violence implicit in
spiritual demand as well as the aggressive element in the erotic,
informs much of his poetry. Successive volumes, from *The
Clay Verge* (1951) to *Broad Autumn* (1975), reveal, however,
a steady mellowing of mood and an extension of interests.

Clemo has been proclaimed 'one of the finest landscape
poets of his generation' by his fellow-Cornishman, Charles
Causley (1917–). Causley, a poet more akin to Betjeman,
had wartime service in the Navy behind him when *Farewell,
Aggie Weston* (1951) came out. The numerous successive
volumes up to *Collected Poems* (1975) reveal him as the
jaunty balladier whose rolling rhythms and bold images helped
to create a public for readings of popular poetry.

> You must take off your clothes for the doctor
> And stand as straight as a pin,
> His hand of stone on your white breast-bone
> Where the bullets all go in.

('Recruiting Drive')

Such transparencies hark back to Kipling and Housman.
Christopher Logue (1926–) on the other hand, author of
A Song for Kathleen (1958), took poetry to a larger audience
by rejecting traditional forms and metrics and interesting
himself in poetry-with-jazz, night-club songs, and poems
designed for posters. A poet of social, political, and cultural
protest, Logue has been too prolific. James Kirkup (1923–)
too has been apt to fall victim to his own facility, though the
title poem of *A Correct Compassion* (1952), a description of
heart surgery observed in the operating theatre, told how he
found in the disciplined correctness of the surgeon's dexterity
a ruling principle for life-giving acts.

A wartime experience lay dormant for years in the mind
of Vernon Scannell (1922–) who served in the Gordon High-
landers from 1941 to 1945 and was wounded in Normandy.
A visual memory haunted him thereafter until it struggled

through eleven versions to become his most celebrated poem, the title piece of *Walking Wounded* (1965). It was not accurate reproduction of the scene that worried him. 'I had to see what allegorical or symbolic meaning the image possessed. And slowly I came to see that the Walking Wounded represented the common human condition: the dramatically heroic role is for the few. Most of us have to take the smaller wounds of living . . .' (See James Gibson (ed.), *Let the Poet Choose* (1975).) Scannell's poetic eye has since been fixed on incidents and characters sharply representative of the world we observe through our media and our common life.

> She holds her chuckling baby to her bosom
> And says, 'My honey-pie, my sugar bun,
> Does Mummy love her scrumptious little darling?
> You're lovely, yes, you are, my precious one!'
> But when the little perisher starts bawling
> She says, 'For God's sake listen to your son.'

War service in the Navy and the death of comrades played their part in producing the sense of dislocation in the poetry of T. H. Jones (1921–65). The consuming demand for love, mental and physical exile from his native Wales in Australia, and escalating alcoholism intensified an alienation that is expressed with increasing lyrical power in his later volumes (*The Beast at the Door*, 1963; and *The Colour of Cockcrowing*, 1966), where simple wording is sometimes given a complex aural patterning.

> Only the stink around the grave
> Says, Here was one we could not save.
> ('Lines from the Death of an Alcoholic')

The literature of addiction has its own sad function as a record of twentieth-century life. In a novel, *The Feast of the Wolf* (1971), Thomas Blackburn (1916–77) portrayed the tragedy of an alcoholic English professor. Blackburn told in his autobiography, *A Clip of Steel* (1969), how he 'won free of the appalling alcoholic blackouts of my early twenties'. Volumes of poetry published in the 1950s were heavily influenced by Yeats, but in *A Smell of Burning* (1961) and *A Breathing Space* (1964) Blackburn achieves an individual style in autobiographical self-analysis. Imagery contributes to a compulsive exploration of experience in which acute emotional dilemmas are examined with hag-ridden thoroughness. One of Blackburn's most moving poems, 'Hospital for Defectives', a prayer with a hint of Wildean pastiche, arose from witnessing brutality by a warder in charge of mental defectives. It calls the 'Lord of Images', whose love is expressed in the language of 'eyelid and rose', to explain the insane silence of the men working together in the turnip-field.

> And yet between the four of them
> No word is ever said
> Because the yeast was not put in
> Which makes the human bread.

To turn to the poetry of Charles Tomlinson (1927–) is to enter a less confined world. 'The poems appeal outside of themselves only to the world perpetually bodied against our senses. They improve that world.' So Donald Davie wrote, introducing Tomlinson's collection, *The Necklace*, in 1951. Since then Tomlinson has been a productive poet. What critics have called an 'Augustan' mentality has been enriched by the influence of French symbolist poets and modern American poets; and Tomlinson sees himself writing 'phenomenological poetry with roots in Wordsworth'. Accuracy of observation, beauty of rhythm and pattern, and a remarkable gift for fixing in words rare moments of sharply awakened relationship to people and to nature make his output distinctive amid the poetry of the 1950s and 1960s. (See *Selected Poems 1951–74*, 1978.) The total absence of intrusive authorial temperament as well as of clamant tone or florid gesture frees the reader to read his own world for himself anew.

> Two cups,
> a given grace,
> afloat and white
> on the mahogany pool
> of table. They unclinch
> the mind, filling it
> with themselves.   ('A Given Grace')

VI Scottish and Irish poets

Among a number of highly individual poets from north of

the border, George Mackay Brown (1921–) is an Orcadian who has spent most of his life in Orkney. Comparisons have been made with Edwin Muir, but in fact Brown's rootedness in his locality, his identification with the local people in their struggle against the harsh realities of external nature and of their own earthiness, is strangely reminiscent of R. S. Thomas. There is the same sad story of the peasant going down to town with money in his pocket on his day off in Thomas's 'Out of the Hills' and in Brown's 'Hamanvoe Market' (*The Year of the Whale*, 1965).

> Johnston stood beside the barrel.
> All day he stood there.
> He woke in a ditch, his mouth full of ashes.

The fingers of the old fisherman plucking the guitar are the fingers that cut from the net the 'crab-eaten corpse of Jock washed from a boat / One old winter' ('Old Fisherman with Guitar'). Brown, a Roman Catholic convert, has Thomas's deep compassion for his people, his sense of a transcendent pattern subsuming their arduous life-spans and the rhythm of the natural order, and perhaps resolving the mystery of tragedy and its healing. While Brown, like Thomas, gets to the centre by the depth of his local penetration, his range of human interest is more various than Thomas's. Moreover Brown involves the present with the past, and daily experience with ancient symbol and religious ritual, in a manner more reminiscent of David Jones. Present and past, legend and reality, blend to give rare textural richness to Brown's novel of Orcadian life, *Greenvoe* (1972). It is a poet's novel.

Edward Lucie-Smith has compared, not Brown, but Iain Crichton Smith (1928–) with R. S. Thomas. Born in the Isle of Lewis in a Gaelic-speaking community, a schoolmaster in Oban, Smith has shown himself at once master of the colloquial manner yet fond of metaphorical plumage ('the moon's implacable sea / of hammered light'). He portrays Hebridean or Highland people and their settings with less personal commitment than Brown, with a more disturbed metaphysical unease.

> Your thorned back
> heavily under the creel
> you steadily stamped the rising daffodil.

Your set mouth
forgives no-one, not even God's justice
perpetually drowning law with grace.

('Old Woman')

For Smith human isolation and deprivation, like natural life, merit record but defy full assimilation by the interpretive mind. 'For the unknown seamen of the 1939—45 war Buried in Iona Churchyard' begins:

One would like to be able to write something for them . . .

But 'One simply doesn't / know enough . . .' *The Notebooks of Robinson Crusoe* (1974), however, contains poems of crisp, lively portraiture ('My Uncle') and others simmering with hidden passion ('In the Glen').

Edwin Morgan (1920—), a university lecturer at Glasgow, has caught aspects of human life there in sharply etched pieces. His human portraiture is too warmly conceived to allow Smith's ruminative withdrawals. Smith's old woman is finally 'alone'. Morgan's blind old man of 'In the Snack-bar' (*The Second Life*, 1968) engages the help of the poet to get down the steps to the lavatory.

Wherever he would go it would be dark
and yet he must trust men . . .
His life depends on many who would evade him.

The detachment is shot through with compassion. 'Many things are unspoken / in the life of man' Morgan has written, and his poems of the city, of love and loss, of popular celebrities, in their directness and their impressionable attentiveness betray a concerned magnanimity. Morgan's technical versatility has lured him to experiment, as did his fellow-Scot, Ian Hamilton Finlay (1925—), with 'concrete poetry' which rejects established modes of expression, syntax, and patterning in favour of a visual arrangement on the page that treats 'graphic space as structural agent' and words as units in a construction kit.

Perhaps closer to the standard Sassenach conception of the tough, outspoken, sardonic, down-to-earth Scottish poet is Alexander Scott (1920—), an Aberdonian and an academic whose most vigorous writing has been done in Scots. His fourth collection, *Cantrips* (1968), established his reputation. By its sinewy gusto, rumbustious satire, and vernacular vividness Scott's verse hits the reader in the eye, and the good-humoured overstatement is heart-warming. Tom Scott 1918–), a Glaswegian and a Scottish nationalist, stands like Alexander Scott in the tradition of the Makars and is himself a specialist in mediaeval Scots literature. In his editorial Introduction to the *Penguin Book of Scottish Verse* (1970), Scott confesses that after losing direction during the war he found it again 'partly by an involuntary upswelling of Scots in me, and partly thanks to Eliot and MacDiarmid'. Eliot encouraged him to make his Scots translation, *Seven Poems o Maister Francis Villon* (1953). MacDiarmid's dictum, 'Not Burns – Dunbar', encouraged him to find his own voice in Scots. The title poem of *The Ship* (1963) and *At the Shrine o the Unkent Sodger* (1968) are sturdy attempts to revitalise the long poem on the larger issues of civilisational decline and war.

To turn from Scottish voices of the period to Irish voices is to raise the question whether the achievement of nationalistic aspirations brings assurance to native poetry. There is a baffling sense of bafflement in the poetry of Thomas Kinsella (1928–), Irish civil servant who has tussled with acute personal issues of love and death and the artistic vocation, and extended his troubled explorations to his country's public life, bureaucratic and commercial. Kinsella subjects the contemporary scene to the kind of unhappy piecemeal analysis employed by the Eliot of *The Waste Land*. In the title poem of *Nightwalker* (1967) the ethos of the new and prosperous republic is under scrutiny. 'Productive investment . . . beckons the nations . . . let my people serve them / Bottled fury in our new hotels . . .' A metaphysical density in descriptive writing and in the brooding threaded through it detracts from the accessibility of some of Kinsella's poetry prior to *Nightwalker*, while in subsequent volumes of the 1970s he has plunged more teasingly and darkly into the inner life.

In the work of another Irish public servant, who rose to ambassadorial rank, Valentin Iremonger (1918–), there is much greater directness and lucidity but scarcely perhaps more inner ease. His widely spaced volumes, *On the Barricades*

(1944), *Reservations* (1950), and *Horam's Field* (1972), contain a minimal total output, yet to read them through leaves a dozen poems imprinted on the memory, nothing finer than the comparison in 'Icarus' between the modern pilot plunging to death and 'star-chaser . . . charmer Icarus', lying on the sea, while Daedalus, 'too busy hammering another job, / Remembered him only in pubs'. Again the comparatively small output of Richard Murphy (1927–), though less intense in feeling and more tenuous in texture, has sustained firmness of substance, notably perhaps the two family portraits of his father ('The God Who Eats Corn'), a British colonial governor, and his grandmother ('The Woman of the House'), an Irish *grand dame*, 'Mistress of mossy acres and unpaid rent'. (See *Sailing to an Island*, 1964.) A more vigorous work, 'The Cleggan Disaster', is a narrative poem about a storm in 1927 in which twenty-five fishermen lost their lives off the west coast of Ireland.

9

Recent voices
The 1960s and 1970s

I Introduction

IN literary terms the 1950s and 1960s belong together in that many dominant writers of the sixties, such as Beckett and Pinter, Golding and Larkin, had made their first impact in the fifties; but in social terms the sixties have acquired a distinct identity, coloured by associations of vital break-out like those of the twenties. The decade saw independence granted to numerous former imperial territories, it saw a massive swing from conservatism to socialism and back again, it saw the opening of new universities, the rapid development of comprehensive education, the expansion of computerisation, and the construction of motorways. President Kennedy was assassinated and the American astronauts landed on the moon, while at home the decade witnessed the great train robbery, the Profumo scandal, the thalidomide births, the growth of pop culture, the advent of the hippies and drop-outs. The decade also saw the abolition of theatre censorship, the legalisation of adult homosexual practices, and general acceptance of the contraceptive pill.

The coming of the boutique and the revolution in clothes made an enormous impact on the external scene. The influence of Paris and *haute couture* crumbled as the youth revolution against convention turned Art students such as Mary Quant into fashion-designers who decked out teenage trendies in a variety of extravagant and novel styles. Meanwhile Carnaby Street catered for the 'mod' young man whose attitude to male fashion brought back the taste for finery and colour of the Regency buck and the Elizabethan gallant. The Art schools also threw a challenge to the staid and the solemn into the world of painting. The decade ended with an exhibition in

London of ten years' paintings, prints, and drawings by the English pop-artist, David Hockney, an exponent of the new 'visual irony' which gave aesthetic status to banal objects such as tins of beans.

Pop culture did not thrive at the expense of the soberer arts. Michael Tippett, a composer who writes his own libretti and describes T. S. Eliot as 'my artistic father', followed his richly poetic opera, *The Midsummer Marriage* (1955) with a second, musically more austere opera, *King Priam* (1962). William Walton, whose opera, *Troilus and Cressida* (1954), had a libretto derived from Chaucer by the poet and literary biographer, Christopher Hassall (1912–63), wrote a one-act opera based on Chekhov, *The Bear* (1967), for the Aldeburgh Musical Festival established by Benjamin Britten in his East-Anglian home town. Britten's own output of opera, as of choral works, links him with a number of major literary figures. Of the late productions *A Midsummer Night's Dream* (1960) was based on Shakespeare and *Owen Wingrave* (1971), like the earlier *The Turn of the Screw* (1954), was based on material from Henry James.

There are those who speak of the 'violent seventies'. Back in 1965 the Pennine Moors murders, involving the torture and sexual molestation of children, seemed to reveal new depths of peace-time cruelty. In 1969 disturbances between the Unionist and Republican populations in Northern Ireland initiated a decade of violence, a decade which has witnessed throughout Europe the development of urban terrorism, kidnapping, hijacking, hooliganism and wilful vandalisation of private and public property. No doubt the violence of the seventies helped to weaken the sense of a civil polity over which rational man exercises control. At the same time hyperinflation, by impoverishing and enriching fortuitously and haphazardly without respect for human prudence, thrift, and hard work, strengthened the sense of meaninglessness at large. The intrusion of this sense, here and there, into the literature of the period, and the cultivation of answering moods — cynical, ironic, escapist, or nihilistic — was inevitable.

II The theatre

There was one new dramatist of the period, Tom Stoppard

(1937–), who spoke at first with the voice of the past. One of the marks of the Modernism of Joyce and Eliot, and indeed later of Beckett, was the practice of re-minting the coinage of past literature and utilising verbal currencies from numerous branches of cultural and social life. Pinter, on the other hand, disinfected his drama of recognisably bookish affiliations by pinning his ear to the keyholes of basement flats and public bars. Stoppard reverted to an extreme, even parasitical dependence on the literary tradition in his play, *Rosencrantz and Guildenstern are Dead* (1966). The contrast between the mind of a Hamlet and the minds of the two stooges trapped between the mighty opposites has great dramatic potential, and Stoppard's decision to put Beckettian gropers after something-or-other into the shoes of Rosencrantz and Guildenstern was a cunning one. He then turned to satirise abstract studies in the world of academic philosophy in *Jumpers* (1972). To stage a murder in the house of an academic philosopher obsessed with metaphysical speculation about ultimate values and the reality of evil was again an imaginative *coup de grâce*. The 'jumpers' are members of a school of philosophy who find in gymnastics the objective correlative of philosophical enquiry. The theme is the relativity of truth and the inadequacy of reason. *Travesties* (1975) is set in Zurich in 1918, where Joyce is working on *Ulysses*, Lenin on his revolution, and Tzara on Dadaism. Extravagant action is a vehicle for the display of verbal pyrotechnics, including a clever parody of the 'Ithaca' episode in *Ulysses*. *Night and Day* (1978) aims to compel the audience to thoughtful reflection on a current issue. It is set in a fictitious African country at a time of rebellion against a tyrannical President. British journalists arrive, whose behaviour, attitudes, and conversation constitute a dramatic enquiry into Fleet Street's methods and motives.

Peter Shaffer (1926–) won theatrical acclaim by a more conventional route in *The Royal Hunt of the Sun* (1964), a historical play chronicling episodically the Spanish conquest of Peru. This large-scale spectacular makes an ambitious attempt to represent the immensity of the enterprise, the perils of plunging into the centre of the Inca empire, and the collision of culture with culture: but, in the study of Pizarro, the perils inherent in costuming the clichés of fashionable theatrical *angst* are not happily negotiated. Shaffer's later play, *Equus* (1973), examines the case of a stable boy who sticks a metal spike in the eyes of horses. The psychiatrist who treats him finds his own bearings dislocated. In *Amadeus* (1981) Shaffer takes up dramatically the story that when Mozart (whose Christian names were 'Wolfgang Amadeus') died he accused a rival composer, Antonio Salieri, of having poisoned him.

The dislodgement of accepted norms and the championing of aberration became a convention of drama in the 1960s and 1970s. The establishment of aberrance itself as a theatrical norm deprives drama of the capacity to shock. Displacement of the values of morality and rationality by anarchic relativism removes the fulcrum on which the see-saw of tears and laughter is balanced. David Mercer (1928–80), for instance, whose early television plays tackled problems of social displacement and political disillusionment, became predominantly concerned with neurotic and lunatic eccentricity as representative of positive personal assertion. Implicit denigration of the submission of ordinary folk to acceptable behavioural norms will, if it is earnest, lead either to the assertion of valid alternative principles or to pessimistic acquiescence in futility. If the safety-valve of farce and wit is opened widely enough, of course, the dilemma can be resolved in laughter. Mercer, at his best, has a sharp ear for dialogue and a touch of Beckettian panache in epigrammatic embroidery. His stage play, *Flint* (1970), portrays an eccentric Anglican parson hilariously uninhibited in notions and conduct, and Mercer's gift for verbal acerbities that ring wittily in the ear is entertaining. *After Heggarty* (1970) is comparably lively, but Mercer's subsequent plays have shown increasing obsession with gloom and doom.

The negative evangelism of dramatists whose fulminations against contemporary society are counterbalanced by no valid social or moral recommendations invites the charge of naivety or irresponsibility. Edward Bond (1934–) has been worried about the quality of life in a consumer society dependent on avarice and a technological society destructive of community. In *The Pope's Wedding* (1962), a rural dialect play set in East Anglia, mental withdrawal overtakes a farm-worker, while in *Saved* (1966) urban delinquents murder a baby obscenely. Bond's dialogue is strong and so is his sense of humour, but he later succumbed to surrealistic extravagance, turning pop-shocker at the expense of easy targets such as Queen Victoria and Florence Nightingale in *Early Morning* (1968) and making a cad of Shakespeare in *Bingo* (1974). By contrast a real problem is tackled realistically by Peter Nichols (1927–) in *A Day in the Death of Joe Egg* (1967). Brian and Sheila have to live with their hopelessly damaged daughter, Joe, who is little more than a vegetable. They take refuge from the agony in imaginative acting between themselves, assuming self-defensively a skin of callousness towards Joe that stifles feeling. Thus they offset the dismal reality with back-chat and clownery that give Joe's predicament joke-status. The impact of the bitter-sweet foolery is harrowing. There is verbal adroitness here and again in *The National Health* (1969), but in the latter play the episodes from hospital life and the burlesque of a doctor–nurse romance lack human substance. *Chez Nous* (1974) has some vitality as a farcical exploration of the dilemma of a pediatrician whose anti-authoritarian study of secondary education has been marketed by an unscrupulous publisher as a trendy recommendation of teenage sex and become a best-seller. His own family is hit by the effects of the permissiveness he advocates. *Born in the Gardens* (1979), a study of a newly widowed old lady in the author's home city of Bristol, whose middle-aged children gather for their father's funeral, recaptures something of the pathos, the humour, and the human reality of *A Day in the Death of Joe Egg*, but *Passion Play* (1981), a hot-house sexual imbroglio, is a hotch-potch of theatrical contrivances, including a clumsy projection of dual *personae* for the two main characters.

In the plays of David Storey (1933–), the novelist, neurotic tensions and madness impinge on the domestic scene. The hero of *The Restoration of Arnold Middleton* (1967), a schoolmaster, acts out the tricks of the ham classroom performer in the home in sheer self-protection against his mother-in-law, and does it so zestfully that madness takes over. The sons of a Yorkshire miner return home in *In Celebration* (1969) for their parents' wedding anniversary, and hidden inadequacies in the lives of the educated sons boil up to the surface, reinforced by the psychological after-effects of the parental misalliance. In *Home* (1970) it gradually becomes clear that the old people on stage are in a mental asylum, and the total dislocation of utterance from felt content is eloquent of a wider human dilemma.

While despair drives the British to the madhouse, it sends the Irish to America. Brian Friel (1929–) brought his play, *Philadelphia, Here I Come*, from Dublin to London in 1967. It portrays a young Irishman, Gareth O'Donnell, on the eve of emigration to the USA. Friel analyses the frustrations and pressures behind Gareth's decision to leave. By projecting Gareth in two characters representing his public and private *personae* Friel gives the play a textural richness compounded of humour, irony, and sentiment. *The Freedom of the City* (1973), a moving record of the troubles in Northern Ireland, is set in Londonderry in 1970. Two young men and a mother, fleeing from CS gas used by the army in dispersing a Civil Rights demonstration, accidentally rush for shelter into a back door of the Town Hall and find themselves in the Mayor's Parlour. Outside rumour inflates them into forty armed rebels, the hall is ringed by tanks, and they are riddled with bullets as they go out to surrender. Time shifts allow a variety of running commentaries including a post-mortem tribunal of enquiry into the blunder and a broadcast of the requiem Mass held in their memory. Subsequent plays include *Faith Healer* (1979) and *Translations* (1980). The latter is set in Irish-speaking Donegal in the 1830s and examines the process of Anglicisation brought about by the Ordnance Survey of the country. The poet Seamus Heaney has declared Friel's fifteen plays to date the most significant dramatic achievement of today's Irish writers for the way in which they help Ireland to know herself. Another compatriot, Hugh Leonard (pseudonym of John Keyes Byrne) (1926–), has also been called 'the best living Irish dramatist' but his play, *The Patrick Pearse Motel* (1971), with its application of hare-brained logic to wildly improbable situations did not make a great impact in London.

The English public, however, received with increasing acclaim the comedies of the English dramatist, Alan Ayckbourn (1939–). By 1976 he had five plays running in London. He countered fashionable trends in having no political or social axe to grind and in deliberately setting out to write well-made plays. Careful theatrical craftsmanship, a nice ear for dialogue, and a prodigal command of the comic in character and situation proved the recipe for popular success in many countries. Ayckbourn has shown great ingenuity in contriving novel, or re-minted, situational quandaries rich in explosive potential. In *How the Other Half Loves* (1969) two socially contrasted living-rooms share the stage, and the interlinked marital adventures of two couples come to crisis when two separate dinner parties are fused in one riotous, if implausible, ensemble. A more testing feat was brought off in *The Norman Conquests* (1974), a linked sequence of three plays, *Table Manners, Living Together,* and *Round and Round the Garden,* which originated in the impulse to write the off-stage action play to end all off-stage action. This domestic comedy covers an eventful week-end for a family gathering of six characters, and the two later plays gradually fill in off-stage developments new to the audience. Thus the action of the first play takes place in the dining room between Saturday and Monday, while the second and third plays reveal what has transpired meanwhile in the sitting room and the garden respectively. The comic punch weakens towards the end but in sheer mechanical terms the achievement is a dexterous one. Subsequent successes have included *Just Between Ourselves* (1976), a comedy which stretches to new tautness the tightrope of comic over tragic incongruity. In a suburban household a harrassed, neurotic wife is driven into a catatonic trance by her affectionate but misguided husband and mother-in-law, who live mentally where a sense of her true condition need never impinge.

What Ayckbourn has provided refreshment and escape from may be gathered from the work of playwrights who wave flags of commitment or protest. Trevor Griffiths (1935–), another dramatist of considerable theatrical dexterity, directed Marxist judgment at our educational system in *Sam Sam* (1972), and in *The Party* (1973) gave a firm Trotskyist veteran a platform at a domestic gathering held in 1968 at the time of student riots in Paris. *Comedians* (1975) puts comics in their place whose humour appeals to supposed racist or sexist prejudice. The theme of middle-class insulation from reality implicit in *The Party* recurs in a de-politicised context in *The Philanthropist* (1970) by Christopher Hampton (1946–), a study of a university philologist. A more political protest is made in Hampton's *Savages* (1973), an indictment of United

States support for Brazilian dictatorship and native genocide in the 1960s; but in impact the play falters, the form being half-mosaic and half-chronicle, and the whole lacking substance.

Evidence that there is theatrical expertise abroad hungry for appropriate subject-matter is provided by the case of Alan Bennett (1934–) who made a vigorous portrayal of a verbally self-mesmerising Labour Member of Parliament in *Getting On* (1971) and then, after a lapse into tasteless farce in *Habeas Corpus* (1973), found a fit situation for exercise of his engaging literary fluency in *The Old Country* (1977). Set in a country house outside Moscow, it portrays an English expatriate, a Philby-style spy, and his wife at a point when relations take advantage of a trip to Moscow to look up their long-lost black sheep. In spite of patches of evident redundancy, a complex character and the personal and public ramifications of his past are convincingly projected. Bennett has wittily and observantly captured the qualities of Yorkshire home life and Yorkshire character in *Enjoy* (1980), a study of an old couple inhabiting the last back-to-back house in Leeds and the victims of over-caring and over-inquisitive attentions from social welfare agencies. Bennett has learned from Joyce and Beckett how to mingle the realistic idiom of the provincial working class with the jargon of the media and other public influences that play upon them, and to do it to highly comic and satiric effect.

III The novel

Friel apart, Irish dramatists have not impinged significantly on the English literary scene since Beckett, but Irish novelists have. William Trevor (William Trevor Cox) (1928–) from County Cork settled in England and *The Old Boys* (1964) brought his sardonic objectivity to bear on a group of aged oddities fixated on the past, lapped in seediness, ill-humour, and pernicketiness. 'The world is the School gone mad,' avers Mr Dowse, the eccentric, perverted housemaster. Trevor's terse, poised dialogue is meaty with humour. And the curtly dry treatment is meted out to another assembly of cranks, rogues, and misfits to equally comic effect in *The Boarding House* (1965). *Mrs Eckendorf in O'Neill's Hotel* (1970) is a more expansive study of various Dublin aberrants. Greater complexity of organisation is evident in Trevor's later work and sheer humour is increasingly tempered with compassion, but the attempt to focus more earnestly on a group of fairly ordinary women in *Elizabeth Alone* (1973) is too mechanically contrived. There is more naturalness in the laconically comic studies of human dilemmas and frustrations made in the collections of short stories, *Angels at the Ritz* (1975) and *Lovers of their Time* (1978). The latter includes 'Broken Homes', the story of a dear old octogenarian widow whose peace and happiness, as well as her flat, are devastatingly wrecked when she is bullied into being at the receiving end of social work by teenagers.

Trevor has been equally happy with Irish and English settings and portraiture. John McGahern (1934–) has done his best work in reproducing Irish life. In *The Barracks* (1964) the second wife of a testy, frustrated policeman has three stepchildren to look after. An invalid, she broods on her past Irish childhood and her experience as a nurse in the London blitz, and the nursing experience makes her aware of her true condition, that she is dying of cancer. *The Dark* (1965) traces a motherless boy's struggle to educate himself while struggling also against a brutal father. Exact presentation of provincial life as an ordeal of conflict with privation, disease, and the preying of man upon man, is effected with sombre, claustrophobic intensity. But neither *The Leavetaking* (1974) nor *The Pornographer* (1979) lives up to the immense promise of the earlier novels. More moving and sensitive are the short stories, *Getting Through* (1978), even the non-Irish ones like 'A Slip-Up', about a retired farmer who relives a working life on his farm as he waits daily for his wife, holding the shopping-bag outside Tesco's, and loses himself to the London world around him.

William Trevor has written in generous critical appreciation of the novels of his fellow expatriate, Edna O'Brien (1932–) from County Clare, a spokeswoman for protest against the treatment meted out to her sex in Ireland. Certainly *The Country Girls* (1960) gives a vivid feminine account of upbringing to match the boyhood records of such writers as McGahern, Kavanagh, and Joyce. In pursuing the subsequent careers of her two girl companions in further novels (*Girl with Green Eyes*, 1962; and *Girls in their Married Bliss*, 1968) and in later studies of frustrated and lonely women, the concern with rebellious sexual discontent and attempts to appease it become an uncomfortably central obsession.

A finer talent has emerged in the novels of Jennifer Johnston (1930–), daughter of the Irish playwright, Denis Johnston. A stylist of rare precision and economy, she evokes the feel of the Irish scene with magnetism and with authority, and analyses both the graver and lighter oddities of human character with compassion and humour. *The Gates* (1973) centres on a family home of the fading, impoverished Anglo-Irish gentry whose master declines into alcoholic decay while his orphaned niece can find warm companionship only with a local peasant boy. *How Many Miles to Babylon?* (1974) calls up in authentic detail not only the Ireland of the landed gentry at the beginning of the century but also the battlefield of Flanders to which a young heir and a local peasant boy from his estate are whisked as officer and private in the First World War. Their friendship withstands the assault of military regulations just as it transcends the barriers of social class and political allegiance, but at a fatal cost.

J. G. Farrell (1935–79), English-born of an Irish mother, spent his boyhood in Ireland. He found his feet as a novelist in his fourth book, *Troubles* (1970), which makes a decaying Irish hotel, the Majestic, a microcosm of the historic slide towards ruin of the Anglo-Irish ascendancy during the years 1919 to 1921. Relics of lost splendour form an ironic background to the grotesque antics of current residents. 'This was the history of the time. The rest was merely the "being alive" that every age has to do,' Farrell observes of the summer of 1919. This 'being alive' became Farrell's special preoccupation in exploring further historic episodes of Imperial decline. *The Siege of Krishnapur* (1973) is a finely researched account of the daily life of Europeans caught up in the Indian Mutiny. In terms of what is usually called 'history' it is the off-stage preoccupations, the personal and domestic day-to-day concerns of characters compulsorily passive in respect of the 'newsy' events around them that interest Farrell. His last book, *The Singapore Grip* (1978), turns to life in Singapore before the fall of the city to the Japanese in 1942.

Farrell argued that he preferred to write about the past

because people are more open-minded about it, while they 'have already made up their minds what they think about the present'. Paul Scott (1920–78) wanted to change people's thinking about the past. After spending some of the war years in India he became obsessed with the gigantic facts of Anglo-Indian rule, the sudden ending of a two-hundred-year-old British presence there, and the subsequent general ignorance at home of what it had all been about. Scott's major work, *The Raj Quartet* (1977), comprising *The Jewel in the Crown* (1966), *The Day of the Scorpion* (1968), *The Towers of Silence* (1972), and *A Division of Spoils* (1975), is a vast and intricate study of the closing years of the British Raj between 1942 and 1947. There is no bypassing of the big issues in Scott; they impinge urgently on daily life. The pressures of surrounding racial, social, and religious cross-currents are as much a part of the complex pattern of human affairs as is the personal psychological make-up of individuals. Fluency, mastery of organisation, a sense of humour, and a capacity to get under the skin of very various characters make the work eminently readable. Density of detail and patient analysis of finer points in the changing relationship between rulers and ruled are counterbalanced by vivid ironic strokes. The marriageable girls shipped out to India are 'so many young white well-bred mares brought out to stud for the purpose of coupling with so many young white well-bred stallions, to ensure the inheritance and keep it pukka'. Scott has naturally been compared with Kipling and E. M. Forster. 'Forster was of course right about the way people treated the Indians,' he observed. 'But he never showed them as full people. They lack one dimension — their work — a dimension that dignifies people.'

While Scott and Farrell investigated imperial decline, the regional novelists, David Storey (1933–) and Stanley Middleton (1919–), from Wakefield and Nottingham respectively, focused on the *minutiae* of personal life in the contemporary context they knew best. Storey is indebted to D. H. Lawrence for the way he links social tension caused by class-differentiation with discordances between man's physical, emotional, and cultural demands. *Flight into Camden* (1961) is a novel of break-out by a miner's daughter. *Radcliffe* (1963) projects in a pressurised homosexual relationship the tensions between the crude vitality of the working class and the faded former aristocracy that is somehow dependent on it for its wholeness. *Pasmore* (1972) probes the deeps in studying the human cost of a venture into middle-class adultery by a miner's son who is a university lecturer. The portrayal of growing up in a collier's home in *Saville* (1976) is unfortunately smothered in excessive social detail.

Stanley Middleton moves locally closer to Lawrentian territory in his studies of Nottingham life, but his social milieu is chiefly that of the professional middle class. In some eighteen novels published since *A Short Answer* (1958) Middleton has fastened on the commonplace ups and downs, crises and compensations of life in his locality. Infidelities, family problems, suicides, disease, and death take their toll; there is human loss that is irretrievable and there are human problems that are inherently insoluble, but there are consolations too, and in the general auditing of human happiness, if substantial profits do not accrue, bankruptcy can generally be kept at bay. There are no 'plots' in Middleton's novels. His method is to focus on a few months in the lives of men and women temporarily under stress in consequence of some perhaps long-standing dilemma. The suicide of his deranged and abandoned wife creates emotional problems for a prosperous businessman and his mistress in *Distractions* (1975). In *Two Brothers* (1978) an extrovert businessman long ago married the girl loved by his younger brother, an introvert, a schoolmaster, and a poet. The poet's accession to fame in his fifties and then his sudden death have repercussions on his brother's marital life.

Middleton works in imaginative monochrome. Melvyn Bragg (1939–), regional novelist from Cumbria, at first sight presents a more colourful canvas. His *For Want of a Nail* (1965) is a richly textured account of growing up in Wigton. Local portraiture is vivid. Exploration of the boy's mind is perceptive. The inner imaginative life is interwoven in the fabric of day-to-day events with skill. *The Second Inheritance* (1966), a study of a dour, oppressive Cumbrian farmer, Nelson Foster, and his suffering family is sharp in analysis and presentation. Bragg's is a moral world. His tragedy of village adultery, *Josh Lawton* (1972), brings conscience as well as cliché into play. *The Hired Man* (1969), a study of a Cumbrian agricultural

labourer, John Tallentire, and his wife in the early decades of
the century, has a sombre intensity. But Bragg's pursuit of
the history of the Tallentires in two subsequent novels, *A
Place in England* (1970) and *Kingdom Come* (1980), does
not add up to a cohesive or consistently authentic trilogy.

There is little evidence of a second wave of fantasists in the
tradition of Tolkien or Peake, or of hallucinationists in the
tradition of Lowry or Anna Kavan. Yet a curious desire to
tap the resources of the marvellous and then explain it all
away inspires the best-known, but not best, novel of John
Fowles (1926–), *The Magus* (1966). An English schoolmaster
on a Greek island, Nicholas Urfe, is confronted by breathtaking mystery and magic which turn out to be absurdly
elaborate displays devised by a wealthy arch-manipulator, the
'magus', who is playing at being God. Fowles has quoted Alain-
Fournier, the French novelist of wistful yearning for lost
wonder, in defining his taste for 'the marvellous inside the
real'. But the method is basically that of Ann Radcliffe in
The Mysteries of Udolpho, and Fowles has since conceded
that the book is 'a novel of adolescence written by a retarded
adolescent' (*The Times*, 28.5.77). Nevertheless the sheer
lavishness of technical and imaginative expenditure on this
book, its impact on the public, and Fowles's remarkable
perseverance in rewriting it in 1977, are symptomatic of a
taste coexisting with the taste for the realistic novel of contemporary life. Fowles had earlier published *The Collector*
(1958), a study of a psychopath who imprisons a girl he loves;
and he went on in *The French Lieutenant's Woman* (1969)
to reconstitute a Victorian love triangle in appropriate idiom
and with appropriate ethos and mental climate, and then to
impose upon it a twentieth-century perspective. The narrative
is equipped with alternative endings, Victorian and modern.
A later novel, *Daniel Martin* (1977), has a corresponding
dichotomy at its centre between a writer's own past and the
novel he is writing.

A highly popular success of the early seventies, *Watership
Down* (1972) by Richard Adams (1920–), took its origin
from a tale he began to tell his daughters on the way to school
in the car. Its setting precisely reproduces the topography of
an area in Berkshire. It is an odyssey of rabbits, whose adventures in search of a new settlement carry moral implications

for human beings. In his next book, *Shardik* (1974), Shardik, a twelve-foot-high bear, comes crashing through the jungle to an island outpost of an imaginary empire, where he is claimed by some as a divine restorer of power. ('Shardik requires of us all that we have.') He is drugged and caged, and escapes only to undergo the sufferings meted out to the ordained of God. Adams returns to a meticulously reproduced topography, the Lake District, for his canine adventure, *The Plague Dogs* (1977).

B. S. Johnson (1933–73), convinced that film and television had rendered such exercises in printed story-telling obsolete, experimented with new modes of presentation in *Travelling People* (1963) but displayed more ingenuity than inspiration. The heavy dependence on Joyce and Beckett in his *House Mother Normal* (1971), a collage of interior monologues by geriatrics, and in *Christie Malry's Double Entry* (1973), a ledgered credit-and-debit record of a psychopath's career of violence, scarcely represented a serious literary advance.

Johnson complained that 95 per cent of the novelists writing in his day wrote as though *Ulysses*, let alone *The Unnamable*, had never happened. But a number profitably recollected that *The Time Machine* had happened and serviced the continuing appetite for science-fiction with ingenious projections such as those of J. G. Ballard (1930–) in *The Drowned World* (1963) and *The Crystal World* (1966) which show vast geophysical cataclysms wiping out the civilisation we know. Ballard was continuing in the tradition of John Wyndham (pseudonym of John Benyon Harris) (1903–69) in projecting crises derived rather from natural or cosmic change than from any human agency. Wyndham had shown humanity under threat from a new form of sentient vegetable life in *The Day of the Triffids* (1946) and from a stirring submarine consciousness in *The Kraken Wakes* (1953).

The literary scene in the sixties and seventies began to reveal the full effect of educational developments in the post-war world. An increasing number of men and (more especially) women have taken university degrees, often in English Literature. Many have written novels — often of middle-class life — which lack neither intelligent insight into human thought and behaviour, nor technical proficiency in presentation. Sometimes they are funny too. Malcolm Bradbury (1932–), for instance, has directed comic satire at university life in England and in the USA in *Eating People is Wrong* (1960) and *Stepping Westwards* (1965) respectively. Sharper and funnier in his satiric touch is David Lodge (1935–) who has made hay of an exchange between two English faculty members at the American State University of Euphoria and the redbrick home University of Rummidge in *Changing Places* (1975). Yet in the absence of any unique illumination, any exciting stylistic finesse, or any acute recognition of values that transcend ephemeral fashion, such novels cannot be regarded as potentially significant in a nation's literature. They may nevertheless have interest as a record of current social attitudes. Margaret Drabble (1939–), for instance, produced a study of university-educated sisters full of brittle flippancy in *A Summer Bird-Cage* (1963), and in *The Millstone* (1965) made the most of the moral and social lessons to be learned by a scholarly young woman whose pregnancy shifts her from the library to the ante-natal clinic. Miss Drabble's later novels, *The Realms of Gold* (1975) and *The Middle Ground* (1980), are representative of a now modish class of fiction that focuses on the lives of writers, academics, journalists, media-men, and the like, usually London-based, and obsessed with problems peculiar to a social and intellectual class increasingly divorced from English, let alone British, life in the large. There is broader awareness and surer artistic control in the novels of Susan Hill (1942–). *A Change for the Better* (1969) makes two balancing studies of household tyrants, a mother whose interfering possessiveness has eroded her daughter's marriage, and a testily senile major. The unselfish victims, daughter and wife respectively, are freed by bereavement. Irony and humour give the book a richer texture than that of Miss Hill's *I'm the King of the Castle* (1970), a study of calculating cruelty practised by one boy on another with tragic consequences, but *In the Springtime of the Year* (1974) is a very sensitive record of a young wife's struggle to come to terms with sudden widowhood.

Much current fiction registers an uneasy conflict between sexual permissiveness and self-discipline. Fay Weldon (1935–) has injected into her amusing running commentaries on the struggle between the sexes and that within her sex a piquant note of wounded aggressiveness. Chloe, the heroine of *Female*

Friends (1975), guileless, affectionate, loyal, bewildered, the imposed-upon victim alike of life-long friends, of self-centred seducer, and of bullying husband, wins the reader's sympathy for not being liberated and yet seems to learn at the end that it's time to break out. Mrs Weldon's narrative style is distinctive. It interweaves the subjective and the objective. Disjointed and peremptory, it crackles with wit, punch-lines, and knock-out surprises. Scooped-up jottings in the present tense give the impression of breathless speed and irresistible vitality. Quick shifts of angle over different life-stories and different decades bring illumination homing in through a magnifying glass on to the burning present. Yet technique, like liberation, is not enough. *Little Sisters* (1978) follows Fowles into coy enclosure of the marvellous inside the real and fails to convince.

It is dangerous to generalise about the recent past, yet the 1970s ended with acclamation for a novelist, Barbara Pym (1913–80), whose books had been ignored in the 1950s and could surely never have appealed to the mood of the swinging 1960s. Her earlier novels, *Excellent Women* (1952) and *A Glass of Blessings* (1958), were reissued and new titles followed: *The Sweet Dove Died* (1978), *Quartet in Autumn* (1978), and *A Few Green Leaves* (1980), the last posthumously. A quiet-voiced writer, Miss Pym has a gift for delicately refined prose, and her world is that of femininity scarcely attuned to the crudities of modernity, let alone of liberation. Gentle humour simmers above registration of the thought and talk of often harrassed but never obstreperous women whose interests do not exclude the local church, the parish priest, and the spiritual and social demands they make.

IV Poetry

In poetry a dominant voice, that of Ted Hughes (1930–), suddenly made understatement and genteel versification seem insipid. Hughes brought a new stridency, a rasping sinewiness, to replace the formal graces of 'Movement' poets, a new awareness of untameable energy and rawness in the natural world to replace their suburban intimacy with bars and shops, trains and hospitals. Hughes was acclaimed for his first collection, *The Hawk in the Rain* (1957). Subsequent volumes include

Lupercal (1960), *Animal Poems* (1967), *Woodwo* (1967), *Crow* (1970), *Crow Wakes* (1971), *Eat Crow* (1972), *Season Songs* (1976), and *Gaudete* (1977), as well as radio plays and stories for children. The physical violence that erupted in Hughes's poems, the harsh landscape of the West Riding, and the creation in his numerous animal studies of what has been called a modern bestiary, have given individuality to his work. Tortuous angularity of idiom and metre, celebration of the instinctual and the brutal, and the vivid depiction of cataclysmic or desolate scenery — these are potent ingredients in poetry which fastens on to the animal world a cartoonery of human struggle and destiny. Hughes's descriptive technique is unnervingly apt.

> Skinfull of bowls, he bowls them,
> The hip going in and out of joint . . .
> At every stride he has to turn a corner
> In himself and correct it . . .
>
> ('Second Glance at a Jaguar')

So he portrays the caged jaguar. But the animal world does not exist to be stared at. In the celebrated *Crow* poems, which have been called a 'parody of all creation myths' and which Hughes presented as passages from 'what was to have been an epic folk tale', Crow gets on, sometimes mockingly, sometimes guiltily, with the business of surviving, devouring, and indulging his taste for savage antics, while God wrings his hands or goes to sleep. Great claims have been made for Crow as a new hero and certainly some of the poems are powerful in impact; but there are others where the reader is asked to assume that an insignificant act becomes profound if attributed to a bird and a commonplace shout amusing if attributed to God.

Partly because he was paired with Hughes in *Selected Poems* (1962), Thom Gunn (1929–) was early associated with him. A common interest in violence seemed to suggest a common Lawrentian gesture against suburbanism and intellectualism. But Gunn's concern with movement and action is not so much a direct celebration as a starting-point for inquiry. In 'On the Move' reflection is sparked off by the Boys thundering by on their motor bikes, goggled, jacketed, and strapped.

One is not necessarily discord
On earth; or damned because, half animal,
One lacks direct instinct, because one wakes
Afloat on movement that divides and breaks.

In Gunn's successive volumes, *Fighting Terms* (1954), *My
Sad Captains* (1961), *Touch* (1967), *Moly* (1971), and *Jack
Straw's Castle* (1976), the theme of the individual's isolation
as a stimulus to seemingly meaningless action is increasingly
philosophised.

Fashionable distrust of posture perhaps reaches its ultimate
in some of the poems of Philip Hobsbaum (1932–), who has
delighted in knocking the pretensions, romantic or metaphysical, into which poethood lures the practitioner. (See
Coming Out Fighting, 1969.) The poet is encountered at his
most undignified, making love to a student on the tutorial-
room floor ('A Lesson in Love') or slipping into bed with a
casual pick-up ('A Secret Sharer'). Hobsbaum came under
Leavis's influence at Cambridge and then was a leading figure
in what came to be called the 'Group', a gathering of poets
who subjected each other's work to scrutiny in poetry 'work-
shops'. Hobsbaum's readiness to debunk his own *persona* is
an aspect of his pursuit of candour. He brings the drabness
and clumsiness of experience into poetry which sometimes
vividly reproduces the atmosphere of familiar urban environments. He was joint editor of *A Group Anthology* (1963)
with Edward Lucie-Smith, himself a poet of more overtly
conscious artistry than Hobsbaum: his work tends to wear an
air of literary contrivance. Lucie-Smith's Penguin anthology,
British Poetry Since 1945 (1970), is an admirably representative collection.

Another member of the 'Group', George MacBeth (1932–),
has been prolific in output, versatile in range, and is gifted
technically with a professionalism that makes less copious
and inventive writers look amateurish. But fluency has its
dangers, especially when it is consciously aimed at a big public.

Your cowboy
politicians march on their stomachs into
the supermarkets of mercy
without their credit cards . . .

('The Bamboo Nightingale')

So MacBeth sings in his 'Funeral-song to America, for her
negro dead in Vietnam', one of many poems on burning public
issues. In *Collected Poems 1958—1970* (1971) there are
violent and gruesome poems, poems of playful artifice (like
'Scissor-Man') and negative absurdity (like 'When I am Dead')
which seem to say 'How clever I am!', and poems of deeply
felt personal reflection (like 'The Miner's Helmet' and 'On
the Death of Mary Street') chastely free of flamboyance or
mockery. 'No poet writing today has put so much of the
touchable surface of life into his poetry,' Peter Porter (1929—)
has said. And Porter himself, another member of the 'Group',
who came from Australia and settled in England, has surveyed
contemporary vanities and idiocies with a scathing satirical
acuteness. The crisp radio announcement of a nuclear strike,
with accompanying instructions for immediate action, contained in 'Your Attention Please', is an ironic master-
stroke.

> Leave the old and bed-
> ridden, you can do nothing for them . . .
> All flags are flying fully dressed
> On Government buildings — the sun is shining.

Porter has immersed himself in European culture, has celebrated poets, painters, and musicians in verse, and has written
moving poems of personal bereavement in *The Cost of Seriousness* (1978). By sheer intensity of substance and sustained
energy of style Porter achieves a compulsiveness often lacking
from 'Group' poetry.

During a period in which there are poets who have poured
out exuberant verse prodigal of imagery but self-indulgently
extravagant it is refreshing to encounter the disciplined self-
restraint of Geoffrey Hill (1932—). Not that self-restraint
always guarantees ready communication. Hill teases the reader
with complex, even tortuous, turns of thought compressed in
verse that wrestles with the realities of faith and love, pain
and death, and does so with a seemingly electric passion for
exactness. In 'Genesis', from his early volume, *For the Unfallen*
(1959), Hill surveys the six days of Creation in images of rare
imaginative resourcefulness and with spare economy.

> And the third day I cried, 'Beware
> The soft-voiced owl the ferret's smile,
> The hawk's deliberate stoop in air,
> Cold eyes, and bodies hooped in steel,
> Forever bent upon the kill.'

Hill is closer to Ted Hughes than to the 'Group', but he transcends Hughes's vision in thoroughness of intellectual awareness and in sensitivity to historic dimensions. The collection, *King Log* (1968), contains in 'Funeral Music' a cycle of sonnets on bloody events in the Wars of the Roses that are rich in symbol and texture. *Mercian Hymns* (1971) moves between past and present, Offa's Mercia and the terrain of the M5 motorway and of Hill's own childhood, in a verse-prose that is vigorously alive. At this point Hill looks like a poet isolated from contemporary groupings but capable of wearing the vatic mantle naturally. *Tenebrae* (1978), more consonant in form with earlier volumes, contains two new sonnet sequences: the form is peculiarly appropriate to Hill's taste for tight structure, taut cadences, and packed fabric.

Anthony Thwaite (1930–) has described Hill's *Mercian Hymns* as 'complex, rich, many-layered, an intricately worked meditation on history, power, tradition, order, and memory', and Thwaite is himself a poet who has written with consistent technical polish over a wide variety of subjects, immediate and remote both in time and space. He is one of those rare poets to be found represented in anthologies by poems widely different in kind. Compare the popular 'Mr Cooper' (from *The Owl in the Tree*, 1963), with its surprise confrontation with death between drinks in a Manchester pub, or the quizzically resonant dialogue between poet and bird on the sea-shore in 'The Plausible Bird' (from *Home Truths*, 1953) with the speculation on the Donatist schism sparked off by the mass martyrdom of butterflies on the windscreen in a hundred-mile drive through the desert in 'Butterflies in the Desert'.

> At the end of the journey we see the juggernaut
> Triumphant under their flattened wings, crushed fluids.
> Innocent power destroys innocent power.
> But who wins, when their bloody acid eats through chrome?
> In the competition for martyrs, Donatus won.
> But the stout churches of his heresies now stand
> Ruined, emptied of virtue, choked with sand.

Stones of Emptiness (1967) contains many poems deriving thus from experience in Libya where Thwaite held a professorship at Benghazi. It also contains a captivating sequence of poems, 'Letters of Synesius'. Synesius, a native of Cyrene, born about 370, who studied at Alexandria and eventually became Bishop of Ptolemus, left letters illuminating life in Africa under imperial Rome. A more exacting exercise is Thwaite's part-verse, part-prose commentary on St Augustine, *New Confessions* (1974), which combines gloss on Augustine with private meditation. The collection *A Portion for Foxes* (1977) is a more accessibly relaxed body of pieces on homelier personal matters. *Victorian Voices* (1981) is a fascinating collection of dramatic monologues in the manner of Browning by less than distinguished nineteenth-century characters. It includes a felicitous rejoinder to George Meredith's sequence of poems on the break-up of his marriage, *Modern Love*. In Thwaite's 'A Message from Her', Meredith's wife, Mary Ellen, gives her version of events in ironically comparable form.

Another poet whose profound sensitivity to the immediate and the local has sent him digging down to the past is Seamus Heaney (1939–), one of a group of Ulster poets whose work represents a minor renaissance. Heaney, to whom the overworked label, 'the best Irish poet since Yeats', has been duly applied, portrayed Irish scenes and people in *Death of a Naturalist* (1966) with a freshness, a full-bloodedness, and an accuracy of impression that won immediate acclaim. Determination was evoked by the sight of his father and the memory of his grandfather toiling with their spades.

> Between my finger and my thumb
> The squat pen rests.
> I'll dig with it.   ('Digging')

This was the beginning of a disciplined excavation in words of the Ireland he knows. In 'Bogland' (from *Door into the Dark*, 1969) he sees Irish pioneers striking inwards and downwards:

> Every layer they strip
> Seems camped on before.

And he has written of this poem that it is 'an attempt to

make the preserving, shifting marshes of Ireland a mythical landscape, a symbol of the preserving, shifting consciousness of the Irish people. History is the soft ground that holds and invites us into itself, century after century'. (See James Gibson (ed.), *Let the Poet Choose* (1975).) Heaney's output includes *Wintering Out* (1972), *North* (1975), and *The Watchman's Flute* (1978). It shows rare patience and simplicity practised in decoding landscape and human portraiture, the public 'troubles' and the most intimate of personal experiences.

None of the other new Ulster poets has yet achieved, except fitfully, the emotional pressure and imaginative intensity that Heaney has sustained, yet there is plenty of technical accomplishment both in winning human portraiture and in reflection on the 'troubles'. Derek Mahon (1941–), in *Night-Crossing* (1968) and in *Lives* (1972), reveals these qualities without convincing the reader that he has entered deeply into what is often adroitly presented. An older poet, John Hewitt (1907–), a polished craftsman, born in Belfast but distanced by residence in England for much of his life, has celebrated the Ulster landscape and Ulster characters with affection and has mused on the 'colonial' situation (see 'The Colony') in steady, conversational idiom. Michael Longley (1939–), in *An Exploded View* (1973), summed up the long agony of Ulster with a poem, 'Wounds', which sets the long-delayed death of his father from the after-effects of wounds received on the Somme alongside the recent murder of three teenage soldiers and a bus-conductor, shot through the head –

> By a shivering boy who wandered in
> Before they could turn the television down
> Or tidy away the supper dishes.
> To the children, to a bewildered wife,
> I think 'Sorry Missus' was what he said.

Seamus Deane (1940–) from Derry city has written with powerful directness of the background of continuing violence in *Gradual Wars* (1972).

> Night after night we consume
> The noise as an alcoholic
> Drinks glass after glass until his voice
> Is hurled like a flaw
> Into his numbed palate.   ('Elegy 3')

The youngest of this group, Paul Muldoon (1951–) from County Armagh, differs from the rest in lacking verbal transparency. A dexterous manipulator of images and contriver of conceits, he broods enigmatically on the mystery of things. The poetic *persona* is withdrawn and inacessible. A more established figure, John Montague (1929–), who was brought up in New York by an Irish father movingly remembered in 'The Cage', and who returned to Ireland to teach, has written verse equally strong in intellectual substance, sensual awareness, and lyrical refinement. Editor of the *Faber Book of Irish Verse* (1974) and author of over a dozen volumes of poetry, he has written of Ireland, Ulster especially, with a fervour that is never myopic or sentimental. He sees the destruction of the small area from which he derives as only part of the larger theme of 'continually threatened love. We must warn and warm ourselves against a new ice age.'

Another academic, Brendan Kennelly (1936–) from County Kerry, Professor of Modern Literature at Trinity College, Dublin, has been publishing poetry steadily since 1959 (*Cast a Cold Eye*) and edited the *Penguin Book of Irish Verse* in 1970 (revised 1972). He frankly seeks poetry in everyday life, accepting that 'the poem is born the moment one sees into and through one's world', and selects the right words to express the insight. Kennelly has a fine economic touch in describing places and people, at once outlining them sharply, giving them substance, and yet seeing them wrapped in the larger mysteries. 'The Limerick Train' from *Good Souls to Survive* (1967) musingly characterises his home country.

> From my window now, I try to look ahead
> And know, remembering what's been done and said
> That we must always cherish, and reject, the dead.

The sixties saw the growth in England of what was called 'pop' poetry, a movement entangled both with the new pop-music cults and with radical protest among students. Easily assimilated placard-vocabulary, populist jingles, bold satire, and vivid images all geared to instant communication, such as are exploited in the celebrated poem by Adrian Mitchell (1932–), 'To Whom It May Concern', with its refrain, 'Tell me lies about Vietnam', provided heady entertainment when performed live before mass audiences. Roger McGough

(1937–) and Brian Patten (1946–), both from Liverpool, and Adrian Henri (1932–) from Birkenhead, had the requisite facility for working this vein with some éclat. Euphoria spread by the initial pop-protest-poetry alliance encouraged in some poets an anti-élitist bias which led to the literary dead-end of trying to appeal to a non-literary audience.

But there are poets who seem to have quietly taken stock of the merits of voguish unpretentiousness without losing sight of literary values and have focused intelligently on matters of personal or public concern without recourse either to soap-box declamation or to stand-up clowning. Jon Stallworthy (1935–) grappled in 'The Almond Tree' from *Root and Branch* (1969) with a father's response to the birth of a mongol son. Tony Connor (1930–) has quietly enriched an initially conventional technique in moving from family and local portraits in his home city of Manchester (*Lodgers*, 1965) to the less naturalistic *Memoirs of Uncle Harry* (1974). Another quiet and careful craftsman, Peter Scupham (1935–), is happy to work at poetry as a word-game, but his sense of history and awareness of time give depth to his vision. A sequence of sonnets, the title piece of *The Hinterland* (1977), measures the sombre weight of the First World War, as well as of the Second, pressing on subsequent decades of our century with a sensitivity which anyone who has surveyed the century's literature is bound to respond to.

Indeed insights which seem to give shape to the body of our century's literature naturally appeal to the literary historian. Working through that literature, he acquires a sense of its distinctiveness from previous literature that is perhaps not wholly illusory. For even the writers of the early decades are still strangely close to us in some respects. While the greater of them exercise living influence through their place in academic studies and on examination syllabuses, a glance at television and radio programmes, or at the book and feature pages of Sunday newspapers, will show that many of the lesser writers of those early days are also alive in their work and fascinate us personally in themselves. And indeed they all have their place in embodying the experience of the age to which we belong, registering its public and private agonies, its spiritual and moral disquietudes, its saving graces of humour and hope.

Further reading

ALLEN, WALTER: *Tradition and Dream: The English and American Novel from the Twenties to Our Time* (London: Phoenix House, 1964); as *The Modern Novel in Britain and the United States* (New York: Dutton, 1964).

BERGONZI, BERNARD: *The Situation of the Novel* (London: Macmillan, 1970).

BERGONZI, BERNARD (ed.): *The Twentieth Century*, vol. 7 of *History of Literature in the English Language* (London: Sphere Books, 1970).

BLAMIRES, HARRY (ed.): *A Guide to Twentieth-Century Literature in English* (London: Methuen, 1982).

_____ *A Short History of English Literature* (London: Methuen, 1974).

BRADBURY, MALCOLM: *The Social Context of Modern English Literature* (Oxford: Basil Blackwell and New York: Shocken Books, 1971).

BURGESS, ANTHONY: *The Novel Now: A Student's Guide to Contemporary Fiction* (London: Faber, 1967, revised 1971; New York: Norton, 1967).

DONOGHUE, DENIS: *The Third Voice* (Princeton: Princeton University Press and London: Oxford University Press, 1966) — on modern poetic drama.

ESSLIN, MARTIN: *The Theatre of the Absurd* (London: Eyre and Spottiswoode, 1962; revised and enlarged edn, Harmondsworth: Penguin, 1968).

FORD, BORIS (ed.): *The Modern Age*, vol. 7 of the *Pelican Guide to English Literature* (Harmondsworth: Penguin, 1961).

FRASER, G. S.: *The Modern Writer and His World* (London: Verschoyle, 1953; New York: Criterion Books, 1955; revised and enlarged, London: Deutsch, 1964; New York: Praeger, 1965).

GILLIE, C.: *Movements in English Literature (1900–1940)* (London: Cambridge University Press, 1975).

GRIGSON, GEOFFREY (ed.), *The Concise Encyclopedia of Modern World Literature* (London: Hutchinson, 1963; revised, 1970).

HALL, JAMES: *The Tragic Comedians: Seven Modern British Novelists* (Bloomington, Indiana: Indiana University Press, 1963; new edn, Westport: Greenwood Press, 1978).

ISAAC, JACOB: *An Assessment of Twentieth-Century Literature* (London: Secker and Warbourg, 1951).

JOHNSTONE, J. K.: *The Bloomsbury Group* (London: Secker and War-bourg, 1954).

KARL, FREDERICK R.: *A Reader's Guide to the Contemporary English Novel* (London: Thames and Hudson, 1961).

KITCHIN, LAURENCE: *Drama in the Sixties: Form and Interpretations* (London: Faber, 1966).

LEAVIS, F. R.: *New Bearings in English Poetry* (London: Chatto and Windus, 1932; new edn, 1950; new impression, Harmondsworth, Penguin, 1972).

MAXWELL, D. E. S.: *Poets of the Thirties* (London: Routledge and Kegan Paul, 1969).

MORRISON, BLAKE: *The Movement: English Poetry and Fiction of the 1950s* (Oxford: Oxford University Press, 1980).

NEWBY, P. H.: *The Novel, 1945–50* (London: Longman, 1951).

O'FAOLAIN, SEAN: *The Vanishing Hero: Studies in Novelists of the Twenties* (London: Eyre and Spottiswoode, 1956).

ORR, PETER (ed.): *The Poet Speaks: Interviews with contemporary poets* (London: Routledge and Kegan Paul, 1966).

PRESS, JOHN: *A Map of Modern English Verse* (London and New York: Oxford University Press, 1969).

ROBSON, W. W.: *Modern English Literature* (London: Oxford University Press, 1970).

ROSS, ROBERT H.: *The Georgian Revolt: Rise and Fall of a Poetic Ideal, 1910–1922* (Carbondale: Southern Illinois University Press, 1965; London: Faber, 1967).

SCANNELL, VERNON: *Not Without Glory: Poets of the Second World War* (London: Woburn Press, 1976).

SCHMIDT, MICHAEL & LINDOP, GREVEL: *British Poetry Since 1960* (Oxford: Carcanet Press, 1972).

SCULLY, JAMES (ed.): *Modern Poets on Modern Poetry* (London: Fontana, 1977) originally published as *Modern Poetics* (New York: McGraw Hill, 1965).

SILKIN, JON: *Out of Battle: Poetry of the Great War* (London and New York, Oxford University Press, 1972).

SISSON, C. H.: *English Poetry 1900–1950, An Assessment* (London: Hart Davis, 1971).

SPENDER, STEPHEN: *World Within World, The Autobiography of Stephen Spender* (London: Hamish Hamilton, and New York: Harcourt Brace, 1951).

STEWART, J. I. M.: *Eight Modern Writers* (vol. XII of the *Oxford History of English Literature*) (Oxford: Clarendon Press, 1963).

SWINNERTON, FRANK: *The Georgian Literary Scene* (London: Heine-mann, 1935).

TAYLOR, JOHN RUSSELL: *Anger and After: Guide to the New British Drama* (London: Methuen, 1962).

THWAITE, ANTHONY: *Poetry Today 1960–1973* (London: Longman, 1973).

——————— *Twentieth-Century English Poetry: An Introduction* (London: Heinemann, 1977) – a rewritten and updated version of *Contemporary English Poetry* (London: Heinemann, 1959).

TINDALL, WILLIAM YORK: *Forces in Modern British Literature 1880–1946* (New York: Knopf, 1947).

TREWIN, J. C.: *The Theatre Since 1900* (London: Andrew Dakers, 1951).

WILLIAMS, RAYMOND: *Drama from Ibsen to Brecht* (Harmondsworth: Penguin, 1973).

Bibliographies

WILLISON, I. R. (ed.): *The New Cambridge Bibliography of English Literature* (ed. G. WATSON) Volume 4: *1900–1950* (London: Cambridge University Press, 1972).

ETHRIDGE, JAMES M. (ed.): *Contemporary Authors: A Bio-Bibliographical Guide to Current Authors and their Works* (Detroit, Michigan: Gale Research Company, 1964).

GASTER, ADRIAN- (ed.): *The International Authors and Writers Who's Who* (Cambridge: International Biographical Centre, 8th edn, 1977).

VINSON, JAMES (ed.): *Contemporary Novelists (Contemporary Writers of the English Language)* (London: St James's Press and New York: St Martin's Press, 1972).

———————— *Contemporary Dramatists (Contemporary Writers of the English Language)* (London: St James's Press and New York: St Martin's Press, 1973).

———————— *Contemporary Poets (Contemporary Writers of the English Language)* (London: St James's Press and New York: St Martin's Press, 1975).

Selected Bibliographies can be found in certain concise studies of individual authors. *Writers and their Work*, a series of booklets published for the British Council by Longman, includes studies of many major twentieth-century English writers. *Columbia Essays on Modern Writers*, a series of booklets published by the Columbia University Press, New York and London, includes a limited number of outstanding twentieth-century English writers. *Twayne's English Authors* series, edited by Sylvia E. Bowman and published by Twayne Publications Inc. New York, has a wide coverage of twentieth-century writers.

See also

DAICHES, DAVID (ed.): *British and Commonwealth Literature* (vol. 1 of *The Penguin Companion to Literature*) (Harmondsworth: Penguin, 1971) — generally generous in space to twentieth-century writers.

BATESON, F. W.: *A Guide to English Literature* (London: Longman, 1965; revised, 1970).

Chronological table

Abbreviations: (D.) = drama, (P.) = prose, (V.) = verse

DATE	AUTHOR AND TITLE	EVENT
1900	Conrad (1857): *Lord Jim* (P.)	Richard Hughes (*b.*)
	Shaw (1856): *You Never Can Tell* (D.)	Sean O'Faolain (*b.*)
	Wells (1866): *Love and Mr Lewisham* (P.)	Elgar: *The Dream of Gerontius*
1901	Conrad (1857) and Ford (1873): *The Inheritors* (P.)	L. Grassic Gibbon (*b.*)
	Kipling (1865): *Kim* (P.)	James Hanley (*b.*)
		Queen Victoria (*d.*)
		Accession of King Edward VII
1902	Barrie (1860): *The Admirable Crichton* (D.)	Stevie Smith (*b.*)
	Bennett (1867): *Anna of the Five Towns* (P.)	Salisbury succeeded Balfour as PM
	Hardy (1840): *Poems of the Past and the Present* (V.)	Boer War ended
	James (1843): *The Wings of the Dove* (P.)	Education Act made local authorities responsible for secondary education
	Yeats (1865): *Cathleen ni Houlihan* (D.)	*Times Literary Supplement* started
1903	Childers (1870): *The Riddle of the Sands* (P.)	Rhys Davies (*b.*)
	Conrad (1857): *Typhoon* (P.)	George Orwell (*b.*)
	James (1843): *The Ambassadors* (P.)	Evelyn Waugh (*b.*)
	Masefield (1878): *Ballads* (V.)	

DATE	AUTHOR AND TITLE	EVENT
1904	Barrie (1860): *Peter Pan* (D.)	C. Day Lewis (*b.*)
	Conrad (1857): *Nostromo* (P.)	Graham Greene (*b.*)
	Hardy (1840): *The Dynasts I* (D.)	Puccini: *Madam Butterfly*
	James (1843): *The Golden Bowl* (P.)	Chekhov: *The Cherry Orchard*
	Shaw (1856): *Candida* (D.)	
1905	Granville-Barker (1877): *The Voysey Inheritance* (D.)	Henry Green (*b.*)
	Ford (1873): *The Fifth Queen* (P.)	Arthur Koestler (*b.*)
	Forster (1879): *Where Angels Fear to Tread* (P.)	Anthony Powell (*b.*)
	Wells (1866): *Kipps* (P.)	C. P. Snow (*b.*)
		Einstein propounded the Special Theory of Relativity
		Automobile Association founded
1906	Galsworthy (1867): *The Man of Property* (P.)	Samuel Beckett (*b.*)
	Galsworthy (1867): *The Silver Box* (D.)	John Betjeman (*b.*)
	Hardy (1840): *The Dynasts II* (D.)	T. H. White (*b.*)
	Shaw (1856): *The Doctor's Dilemma* (D.)	Liberal Government returned under H. Campbell-Bannerman
1907	Belloc (1870): *Cautionary Tales* (V.)	W. H. Auden (*b.*)
	Hodgson (1871): *The Lost Blackbird* (V.)	Christopher Fry (*b.*)
	Joyce (1882): *Chamber Music* (V.)	Louis MacNeice (*b.*)
	Synge (1871): *The Playboy of the Western World* (D.)	Boy Scout movement founded by Baden-Powell
1908	Barrie (1860): *What Every Woman Knows* (D.)	Kathleen Raine (*b.*)
	Bennett (1867): *The Old Wives' Tale* (P.)	Ford started the *English Review*
	Chesterton (1874): *The Man Who Was Thursday* (P.)	Old Age Pensions introduced
	Hardy (1840): *The Dynasts III* (D.)	Epstein's 'Figures' on the BMA building in the Strand caused a furore

DATE	AUTHOR AND TITLE	EVENT
1909	Galsworthy (1867): *Strife* (D.)	Malcolm Lowry (*b.*)
	Hardy (1840): *Time's Laughing-stocks* (V.)	Stephen Spender (*b.*)
		J. M. Synge (*d.*)
	Wells (1866): *Ann Veronica* (P.)	Bleriot flew the Channel
1910	Bennett (1867): *Clayhanger* (P.)	Norman McCaig (*b.*)
	Forster (1879): *Howards End* (P.)	Death of Edward VII and accession of George V
	Synge (1871–1909): *Deirdre of the Sorrows* (D.)	Post-Impressionist Exhibition held in London
	Wells (1866): *The History of Mr Polly* (P.)	Marie Curie: *Treatise on Radiography*
1911	Brooke (1887): *Poems* (V.)	Delhi Durbar
	Chesterton (1874): *The Ballad of the White Horse* (V.)	Lloyd George's National Health Insurance Act
	Lawrence (1885): *The White Peacock* (P.)	Amundsen reached the South Pole
	Masefield (1878): *The Everlasting Mercy* (V.)	
	Moore (1852): *Ave* (P.)	
	Walpole (1884): *Mr Perrin & Mr Traill* (P.)	
1912	Marsh (ed.): *Georgian Poetry I* (V.)	Laurence Durrell (*b.*)
	De la Mare (1873): *The Listeners* (V.)	Roy Fuller (*b.*)
		William Sansom (*b.*)
		The *Titanic* sank
	Moore (1852): *Salve* (P.)	Militant agitation for Women's Suffrage
	Saki (1870): *The Unbearable Bassington* (P.)	
1913	Lawrence (1885): *Sons and Lovers* (P.)	George Barker (*b.*)
		R. S. Thomas (*b.*)
	Masefield (1878): *Dauber* (V.)	Angus Wilson (*b.*)
		Fr Rolfe (*d.*)
		Proust: *Du Côté de Chez Swann*

DATE	AUTHOR AND TITLE	EVENT
1914	Hardy (1840): *Satires of Circumstance* (V.) Joyce (1882): *Dubliners* (P.) Moore (1852): *Vale / Hail and Farewell* (P.) Shaw (1856): *Pygmalion* (D.)	Ronald Duncan (*b.*) Norman Nicholson (*b.*) Dylan Thomas (*b.*) First World War began
1915	Aldington (1892): *Images* (V.) Brooke (1887): *1914 & Other Poems* (V.) Evans (1878): *My People* (P.) Ford (1873): *The Good Soldier* (P.) Lawrence (1885): *The Rainbow* (P.)	Alun Lewis (*b.*) Rupert Brooke (*d.*) J. E. Flecker (*d.*) Julian Grenfell (*d.*) Battles of Loos and Ypres Allied landings at Gallipoli Coalition Government formed under Asquith
1916	Bennett (1867): *These Twain* (P.) Buchan (1875): *Greenmantle* (P.) Joyce (1882): *A Portrait of the Artist as a Young Man* (P.)	Henry James (*d.*) Saki (*d.*) Battles of Verdun and the Somme Allies evacuated Gallipoli Lloyd George became PM Easter Rising in Dublin
1917	Barrie (1860): *Dear Brutus* (D.) Douglas (1868): *South Wind* (P.) Eliot (1888): *Prufrock* (V.) Firbank (1886): *Caprice* (P.)	Anthony Burgess (*b.*) John Whiting (*b.*) Edward Thomas (*d.*) Battle of Passchendaele Russian Revolution Bolsheviks took control
1918	Brooke (1887–1915): *Collected Poems* (V.) Wyndham Lewis (1884): *Tarr* (P.) Sassoon (1886): *Counter-Attack* (V.) Strachey (1880): *Eminent Victorians* (P.)	P. H. Newby (*b.*) Muriel Spark (*b.*) Wilfred Owen (*d.*) Isaac Rosenberg (*d.*) Armistice ended the war Lloyd George's Government return in 'Coupon' Election

DATE	AUTHOR AND TITLE	EVENT
1919	Eliot (1888): *Poems* (V.) Firbank (1886): *Valmouth* (P.) Sassoon (1886): *The War Poems* (V.) Yeats (1865): *The Wild Swans at Coole* (V.)	Doris Lessing (*b.*) Treaty of Versailles Lady Astor became the first woman MP
1920	Macaulay (1881): *Potterism* (P.) Owen (1893—1918): *Poems* (V.) Shaw (1856): *Heartbreak House* (D.) Thomas (1878—1917): *Collected Poems* (V.)	Keith Douglas (*b.*) Paul Scott (*b.*) League of Nations formed Civil War in Ireland Oxford University admitted women to degrees
1921	Huxley (1894): *Crome Yellow* (P.) Lawrence (1885): *Women in Love* (P.) Strachey (1880): *Queen Victoria* (P.) Yeats (1865): *Michael Robartes and the Dancer* (V.)	George Mackay Brown (*b.*) Irish Free State established Birth Control Clinic opened in London Prokofiev: *The Love of the Three Oranges*
1922	Eliot (1888): *The Waste Land* (V.) Galsworthy (1867): *The Forsyte Saga* (P.) Gerhardie (1895): *Futility* (P.) Joyce (1882): *Ulysses* (P.) E. Sitwell (1887): *Facade* (V.)	John Braine (*b.*) Philip Larkin (*b.*) W. H. Hudson (*d.*) Lloyd George's Coalition Government succeeded by Conservative Administration under Bonar Law BBC(ompany) started regular broadcasting
1923	Bennett (1867): *Riceyman Steps* (P.) Huxley (1894): *Antic Hay* (P.) Lawrence (1885): *Kangaroo* (P.)	Brendan Behan (*b.*) Hitler's Nazi *putsch* at Munich failed Baldwin became PM

DATE	AUTHOR AND TITLE	EVENT
1924	Ford (1873): *Some Do Not* (P.) Forster (1879): *A Passage to India* (P.) O'Casey (1880): *Juno and the Paycock* (D.) T. F. Powys (1875): *Mr Tasker's Gods* (P.) Shaw (1856): *St Joan* (D.)	Conrad (*d.*) Brief Labour Government under Ramsay Macdonald superseded by Conservative Government under Baldwin after 'Zinoviev Letter' affair
1925	Compton-Burnett (1892): *Pastors and Masters* (P.) Ford (1873): *No More Parades* (P.) MacDiarmid (1892): *Sangschaw* (V.) Woolf (1882): *Mrs Dalloway* (P.)	John Wain (*b.*) Locarno Treaties Kafka: *Der Prozess* ('The Trial')
1926	Ford (1873): *A Man Could Stand Up* (P.) T. E. Lawrence (1888): *The Seven Pillars of Wisdom* (P.) MacDiarmid (1892): *A Drunk Man Looks at the Thistle* (V.) O'Casey (1880): *The Plough and the Stars* (D.)	Ronald Firbank (*d.*) John Fowles (*b.*) Elizabeth Jennings (*b.*) General Strike in May J. L. Baird demonstrated television
1927	Bowen (1899): *The Hotel* (P.) Mottram (1883): *The Spanish Farm Trilogy* (P.) T. F. Powys (1875): *Mr Weston's Good Wine* (P.) Woolf (1882): *To the Lighthouse* (P.)	Charles Tomlinson (*b.*) BBC(orporation) established Trades Disputes Act made General Strikes illegal
1928	Blunden (1896): *Undertones of War* (P.) Huxley (1894): *Point Counter Point* (P.) Lawrence (1885): *Lady Chatterley's Lover* (P.)	Thomas Hardy (*d.*) William Trevor (*b.*) Votes given to women as fully as to men. First 'talkie' (sound) films shown

DATE	AUTHOR AND TITLE	EVENT
	Sassoon (1886): *Memoirs of a Fox-hunting Man* (P.)	
	Waugh (1903): *Decline and Fall* (P.)	
1929	Aldington (1892): *Death of a Hero* (P.) Graves (1895): *Goodbye to All That* (P.) Hughes (1900): *A High Wind in Jamaica* (P.) Sherriff (1896): *Journey's End* (D.)	John Osborne (*b.*) Labour Government formed under Ramsay Macdonald New York Stock Exchange collapsed
1930	Eliot (1888): *Ash Wednesday* (V.) Priestley (1894): *Angel Pavement* (P.) Sackville-West (1892): *The Edwardians* (P.) Waugh (1903): *Vile Bodies* (P.)	Robert Bridges (*d.*) D. H. Lawrence (*d.*) John Arden (*b.*) Ted Hughes (*b.*) Harold Pinter (*b.*) 107 Nazis were elected to the Reichstag
1931	Day Lewis (1904): *From Feathers to Iron* (V.) Powell (1905): *Afternoon Men* (P.) Sassoon (1886): *Memoirs of an Infantry Officer* (P.) Woolf (1882): *The Waves* (P.)	Arnold Bennett (*d.*) National Government formed under Macdonald Statute of Westminster gave independence to the Dominions Walton: *Belshazzar's Feast*
1932	Cary (1888): *Aissa Saved* (P.) Grassic Gibbon (1901): *Sunset Song* (P.) Hanley (1901): *Boy* (P.) Huxley (1894): *Brave New World* (P.)	Harold Munro (*d.*) Lytton Strachey (*d.*) Geoffrey Hill (*b.*) Hunger March of unemployed to London Shakespeare Memorial Theatre opened at Stratford Nazis became largest party in Reichstag

DATE	AUTHOR AND TITLE	EVENT
1933	Greenwood (1903): *Love on the Dole* (P.) Spender (1909): *Poems* (V.) Waddell (1889): *Peter Abelard* (P.) Yeats (1865): *The Winding Stair* (V.)	John Galsworthy (*d.*) George Moore (*d.*) David Storey (*b.*) Hitler became German Chancellor Reichstag fire: Communists blamed
1934	Eliot (1888): *The Rock* (D.) Graves (1895): *I, Claudius* and *Claudius the God* (P.) Dylan Thomas (1914): *Eighteen Poems* (V.) Waugh (1903): *A Handful of Dust* (P.)	Elgar, Delius, and Holst (*d.*) Hitler purged followers in the 'Night of the Long Knives'. Peace Pledge Union formed. Mersey Tunnel opened
1935	Compton-Burnett (1884): *A House and its Head* (P.) Eliot (1888): *Murder in the Cathedral* (D.) Greene (1904): *England Made Me* (P.) Hanley (1901): *The Furys* (P.) MacNeice (1907): *Poems* (V.) Yeats (1865): *A Full Moon in March* (V.)	T. E. Lawrence (*d.*) J. G. Farrell (*b.*) Baldwin succeeded Macdonald as PM ('National' Government) Italy invaded Abyssinia First British National Park established in Snowdonia
1936	Eliot (1888): *Burnt Norton* (V.) J. C. Powys (1872): *Maiden Castle* (P.) Roberts (ed.): *Faber Book of Modern Verse* Sassoon (1886): *Sherston's Progress* (P.) E. Sitwell (1887): *Selected Poems* (V.) Yeats (ed.): *Oxford Book of Modern Verse*	G. K. Chesterton (*d.*) A. E. Housman (*d.*) Rudyard Kipling (*d.*) George V died Accession and abdication of Edward VIII Accession of George VI Spanish Civil War began Purges in Russia

DATE	AUTHOR AND TITLE	EVENT
1937	Jones (1895): *In Parenthesis* (V.)	Sir James Barrie (*d.*)
		Tom Stoppard (*b.*)
	Wyndham Lewis (1884): *Blasting and Bombadiering* (P.)	Neville Chamberlain succeeded Baldwin as PM
	Tolkien (1892): *The Hobbit* (P.)	
	Williams (1886): *Descent into Hell* (P.)	
1938	Beckett (1906): *Murphy* (P.)	Hitler annexed Austria
	Bowen (1899): *Death of the Heart* (P.)	Munich Agreement signed
	Greene (1904): *Brighton Rock* (P.)	
	White (1906): *The Sword in the Stone* (P.)	
1939	Cary (1888): *Mister Johnson* (P.)	Ford Madox Ford (*d.*)
	Eliot (1888): *The Family Reunion* (D.)	W. B. Yeats (*d.*)
		Alan Ayckbourn (*b.*)
	Joyce (1882): *Finnegans Wake* (P.)	Seamus O'Heaney (*b.*)
		Nazi–Soviet Pact signed.
	MacNeice (1907): *Autumn Journal* (V.)	Hitler invaded Poland
		Second World War began
	O'Brien (1911): *At Swim-Two-Birds* (P.)	
1940	Eliot (1888): *East Coker* (V.)	W. H. Davies (*d.*)
	Greene (1904): *The Power and the Glory* (P.)	Winston Churchill became PM
		B.E.F. evacuated from Dunkirk
	Koestler (1905): *Darkness at Noon* (P.)	Battle of Britain
	Snow (1905): *Strangers and Brothers* (P.)	
1941	Cary (1888): *Herself Surprised* (P.)	James Joyce (*d.*)
		Hugh Walpole (*d.*)
	Eliot (1888): *The Dry Salvages* (V.)	Virginia Woolf (*d.*)
		Hitler invaded Russia
	Gunn (1891): *The Silver Darlings* (P.)	Churchill met Roosevelt: Atlantic Charter signed
	Warner (1905): *The Aerodrome* (P.)	

DATE	AUTHOR AND TITLE	EVENT
1942	Cary (1888): *To be a Pilgrim* (P.)	Montgomery's victories in North Africa
	Eliot (1888): *Little Gidding* (V.)	RAF bombing raids in Germany
	Alun Lewis (1915): *Raiders' Dawn* (V.)	Siege of Stalingrad. Beveridge *Report on Social Security & National Insurance*
	C. S. Lewis (1898): *The Screwtape Letters* (P.)	
1943	Bridie (1888): *Mr Bolfry* (D.)	Sidney Keyes (*d.*)
	Gascoyne (1916): *Poems 1937–1942* (V.)	Beatrix Potter (*d.*)
	Green (1905): *Caught* (P.)	German army surrendered at Stalingrad.
		Churchill—Roosevelt meeting at Casablanca demanded 'Unconditional Surrender'
1944	Cary (1888): *The Horse's Mouth* (P.)	Keith Douglas (*d.*)
	Connolly (1903): *The Unquiet Grave* (P.)	Alun Lewis (*d.*)
	Eliot (1888): *Four Quartets* (V.)	Allied invasion of Normandy
	Hartley (1895): *The Shrimp and the Anemone* (P.)	Butler Education Act established secondary education for all
1945	Auden (1907): *For the Time Being* (V.)	Caradoc Evans (*d.*)
	Keyes (1922): *Collected Poems* (V.)	Charles Williams (*d.*)
	Mitford (1904): *The Pursuit of Love* (P.)	Yalta Conference
		Defeat of Germany
	Orwell (1903): *Animal Farm* (P.)	Atomic bombs dropped on Japan
	Waugh (1903): *Brideshead Revisited* (P.)	Labour Government returned under Clement Attlee
1946	Fry (1907): *A Phoenix too Frequent* (D.)	H. Granville-Barker (*d.*)
	Muir (1887): *The Voyage* (V.)	H. G. Wells (*d.*)
	Peake (1911): *Titus Groan* (P.)	Nuremberg War Trials
	Dylan Thomas (1914): *Deaths and Entrances* (V.)	1927 Trades Disputes Act repealed
		BBC inaugurated Third Programme

DATE	AUTHOR AND TITLE	EVENT
1947	Compton-Burnett (1892): *Man-servant and Maidservant* (P.) Hartley (1895): *Eustace and Hilda* (P.) Lowry (1909): *Under the Volcano* (P.)	India Independence Act First British nuclear reactor built at Harwell Britten's *Peter Grimes* at Covent Garden Camus: *La Peste*
1948	Auden (1907): *The Age of Anxiety* (V.) Fry (1907): *The Lady's Not for Burning* (D.) Green (1905): *Concluding* (P.) Greene (1904): *The Heart of the Matter* (P.)	Gandhi assassinated Russians blockaded West Berlin Allies responded with air-lift
1949	Bowen (1899): *The Heat of the Day* (P.) Eliot (1888): *The Cocktail Party* (D.) Muir (1887): *The Labyrinth* (V.) Orwell (1903): *Nineteen Eighty-Four* (P.)	Ireland Act recognised the Republic of Ireland as outside the Commonwealth First Russian atomic explosion recorded North Atlantic Treaty signed
1950	Barker (1913): *True Confessions* (V.) Fry (1907): *Venus Observed* (D.) C. S. Lewis (1898): *The Lion, the Witch, and the Wardrobe* (P.) Peake (1911): *Gormenghast* (P.)	George Orwell (*d.*) G. B. Shaw (*d.*) Labour Government re-elected without overall majority Korean War began
1951	Beckett (1906): *Malone Dies & Molloy* (P.) Greene (1904): *The End of the Affair* (P.) Powell (1905): *A Question of Upbringing* (P.) Snow (1905): *The Masters* (P.)	Festival of Britain Conservative Government returned under Churchill Burgess and Maclean defected to the USSR

DATE	AUTHOR AND TITLE	EVENT
1952	Hanley (1901): *The Closed Harbour* (P.)	Norman Douglas (*d.*)
		Death of George VI
	Jones (1895): *The Anathemata* (V.)	Accession of Elizabeth II
	Lessing (1919): *Martha Quest* (P.)	Contraceptive pill manufactured
	Powell (1905): *A Buyer's Market* (P.)	
	Wilson (1913): *Hemlock and After* (P.)	
1953	Amis (1922): *Lucky Jim* (P.)	Hilaire Belloc (*d.*)
	Beckett (1906): *Watt* (P.)	T. F. Powys (*d.*)
	Cary (1888): *Except the Lord* (P.)	Dylan Thomas (*d.*)
	Hartley (1895): *The Go-Between* (P.)	Hillary and Tensing climbed Everest
		Korean War ended
1954	Golding (1911): *Lord of the Flies* (P.)	US Hydrogen bomb tested at Bikini Atoll
	Dylan Thomas (1914—1953): *Under Milk Wood* (D.)	
	Tolkien (1892): *The Fellowship of the Ring* (D.)	
	Whiting (1917): *Marching Song* (D.)	
1955	Beckett (1906): *Waiting for Godot* (D.)	Anthony Eden succeeded Churchill as PM
	Behan (1923): *The Quare Fellow* (D.)	Commercial television introduced
	Golding (1911): *The Inheritors* (P.)	Albert Einstein (*d.*)
	Larkin (1922): *The Less Deceived* (V.)	
	R. S. Thomas (1913): *Song at the Year's Turning* (V.)	
	Tolkien (1892): *The Two Towers* (P.)	

DATE	AUTHOR AND TITLE	EVENT
1956	Conquest (ed.): *New Lines* (V.) Golding (1911): *Pincher Martin* (P.) Osborne (1929): *Look Back in Anger* (D.) Tolkien (1892): *The Return of the King* (P.)	Max Beerbohm (*d.*) W. de la Mare (*d.*) Suez crisis Anglo-French invasion of Egypt called off Kruschev denounced Stalin Russian tanks crushed Hungarian rising
1957	Braine (1922): *Room at the Top* (P.) Durrell (1912): *Justine* (P.) Powell (1905): *At Lady Molly's* (P.) Waugh (1903): *The Ordeal of Gilbert Pinfold* (P.)	Joyce Cary (*d.*) Wyndham Lewis (*d.*) Malcolm Lowry (*d.*) Harold Macmillan succeeded Eden as PM Wolfenden Report on Homosexual Offences Walton: Cello Concerto
1958	Behan (1923): *The Hostage* (D.) Pinter (1930): *The Birthday Party* (D.) Spark (1918): *Robinson* (P.) R. S. Thomas (1913): *Poetry for Supper* (V.) White (1906): *The Once and Future King* (P.)	Rose Macaulay (*d.*) CND launched Aldermaston march Notting Hill race riots European Common Market formed De Gaulle restored to power in France
1959	Arden (1930): *Serjeant Musgrave's Dance* (D.) Golding (1911): *Free Fall* (P.) Peake (1911): *Titus Alone* (P.) Spark (1918): *Memento Mori* (P.)	Edwin Muir (*d.*) Middleton Murry (*d.*) Conservative Government returned under Macmillan First section of M1 motorway opened
1960	Betjeman (1906): *Summoned by Bells* (V.)	Macmillan made 'wind of change' speech in Capetown

DATE	AUTHOR AND TITLE	EVENT
	Durrell (1912): *Clea* (P.)	Publishers of *Lady Chatterley's Lover* prosecuted unsuccessfully under the Obscene Publications Act
	Hughes (1930): *Lupercal* (V.)	
	Larkin (1922): *The Whitsun Weddings* (V.)	
	Pinter (1930): *The Caretaker* (D.)	
1961	Greene (1904): *A Burnt-Out Case* (P.)	S. Africa left the Commonwealth
	Osborne (1929): *Luther* (D.)	Seven new universities set up
	Storey (1933): *Flight into Camden* (P.)	Thalidomide drug was withdrawn
	Waugh (1903): *Unconditional Surrender* (P.)	
1962	Beckett (1906): *Happy Days* (D.)	Richard Aldington (*d.*)
		Ralph Hodgson (*d.*)
	Burgess (1917): *A Clockwork Orange* (P.)	Peak of Commonwealth immigration reached, Bill to restrict it enacted
	Lessing (1919): *The Golden Notebook* (P.)	New Cathedral at Coventry opened
	Spark (1918): *The Prime of Miss Jean Brodie* (P.)	
1963	Arden (1930): *The Workhouse Donkey* (D.)	Aldous Huxley (*d.*) C. S. Lewis (*d.*)
	Clarke (1896): *Flight to Africa* (V.)	Louis MacNeice (*d.*) J. C. Powys (*d.*) Profumo scandal.
	Hobsbaum & Lucie Smith (ed.): *A Group Anthology* (V.)	Alec Douglas-Home succeeded Macmillan as PM
	Storey (1933): *Radcliffe* (P.)	Kim Philby defected to Moscow
		President Kennedy was assassinated
1964	McGahern (1934): *The Barracks* (P.)	Brendan Behan (*d.*)
	Shaffer (1926): *The Royal Hunt of the Sun* (D.)	Sean O'Casey (*d.*) Edith Sitwell (*d.*)
	Snow (1905): *Corridors of Power* (P.)	T. H. White (*d.*)
	Trevor (1928): *The Old Boys* (P.)	Labour Government returned under Harold Wilson
		Growth of 'pop culture'

DATE	AUTHOR AND TITLE	EVENT
1965	Bragg (1939): *For Want of a Nail* (P.) Golding (1911): *The Spire* (P.) Heaney (1939): *Eleven Poems* (V.) Pinter (1930): *The Homecoming* (D.) Trevor (1928): *The Boarding House* (P.)	T. S. Eliot (*d.*) Helen Waddell (*d.*) Winston Churchill (*d.*) Pennine Moors murders involved torture and sexual molestation of children The era of 'Swinging London', Carnaby Street, and mini-skirts
1966	Fowles (1926): *The Magus* (P.) Heaney (1939): *Death of a Naturalist* (V.) Scott (1920): *The Jewel in the Crown* (P.) Stoppard (1937): *Rosencrantz and Guildenstern are Dead* (D.)	Flann O'Brien (*d.*) Evelyn Waugh (*d.*) Labour Government returned with increased majority Homosexual acts between consenting adults were legalised
1967	Hughes (1930): *Woodwo* (V.) O'Brien (1912): *The Third Policeman* (P.) Storey (1933): *The Restoration of Arnold Middleton* (D.) Thwaite (1930): *The Stones of Emptiness* (V.)	Patrick Kavanagh (*d.*) John Masefield (*d.*) Siegfried Sassoon (*d.*) Revolution in (often 'unisex') clothes Use of cannabis increased Era of 'hippies' and of student unrest
1968	Bunting (1900): *Collected Poems* (V.) Hill (1932): *King Log* (V.) O'Connor (1903–1966): *My Father's Son* (P.) Scott (1920): *The Day of the Scorpion* (P.)	Mervyn Peake (*d.*) Herbert Read (*d.*) Theatre censorship abolished Rapid expansion of motorway system
1969	Enright (1920): *Selected Poems* (V.) Fowles (1926): *The French Lieutenant's Woman* (P.)	Ivy Compton-Burnett (*d.*) Osbert Sitwell (*d.*) USA Moon landing

DATE	AUTHOR AND TITLE	EVENT
	Susan Hill (1942): *A Change for the Better* (P.)	Disturbance started in Northern Ireland
	Upward (1903): *The Rotten Elements* (P.)	
1970	Farrell (1935): *Troubles* (P.)	E. M. Forster (*d.*)
	Hughes (1930): *Crow* (V.)	Bertrand Russell (*d.*)
	Mercer (1928): *Flint* (D.)	De Gaulle (*d.*)
	Trevor (1928): *Mrs Eckendorff in O'Neill's Hotel* (P.)	Conservative Government returned under Edward Heath
1971	Mackay Brown (1921): *Fishermen with Ploughs* (V.)	A. P. Herbert (*d.*)
	Hill (1932): *Mercian Hymns* (V.)	Stevie Smith (*d.*)
		Igor Stravinski (*d.*)
	MacBeth (1932): *Collected Poems 1958–70* (V.)	US space capsule landed on Mars
	Storey (1933): *The Changing Room* (D.)	Further violence in Northern Ireland
1972	Davie (1922): *Collected Poems 1950–70* (V.)	C. Day Lewis (*d.*)
	Nicholson (1914): *A Local Habitation* (V.)	L. P. Hartley (*d.*)
		Ezra Pound (*d.*)
	Scott (1920): *The Towers of Silence* (P.)	Former King Edward VIII (*d.*)
		President Nixon re-elected
	Stoppard (1937): *Jumpers* (D.)	
1973	Hampton (1946): *Savages* (D.)	W. H. Auden (*d.*)
	Kinsella (1928): *Selected Poems 1956–1968* (V.)	Noel Coward (*d.*)
		Elizabeth Bowen (*d.*)
	Larkin (ed.): *Oxford Book of Twentieth-Century English Verse* (V.)	Henry Green (*d.*)
		Neil Gunn (*d.*)
	Storey (1933): *A Temporary Life* (P.)	Nancy Mitford (*d.*)
		William Plomer (*d.*)
		J. R. R. Tolkien (*d.*)
		Great Britain joined the Common Market
		Vietnam War cease-fire

DATE	AUTHOR AND TITLE	EVENT
1974	Ayckbourn (1939): *The Norman Conquests* (D.)	Edmund Blunden (*d.*)
		Austin Clarke (*d.*)
	Susan Hill (1942): *In the Springtime of the Year* (P.)	David Jones (*d.*)
	R. S. Thomas (1913): *Selected Poems* (V.)	Ernest Raymond (*d.*)
		Labour Government returned (twice) under Wilson
	Thwaite (1930): *New Confessions* (V.)	President Nixon resigned after Watergate scandal
1975	Causley (1917): *Collected Poems 1951–75* (V.)	R. C. Sherriff (*d.*)
		Sydney Goodsir Smith (*d.*)
	Heaney (1939): *North* (V.)	Elizabeth Taylor (*d.*)
	Powell (1905): *Hearing Secret Harmonies* (P.)	P. G. Wodehouse (*d.*)
	Stoppard (1937): *Travesties* (D.)	
1976	Ayckbourn (1939): *Just Between Ourselves* (D.)	Agatha Christie (*d.*)
		Richard Hughes (*d.*)
	Gunn (1929): *Jack Straw's Castle* (V.)	William Sansom (*d.*)
		Benjamin Britten (*d.*)
	T. H. Jones (1921–65): *Collected Poems* (V.)	Harold Wilson resigned. James Callaghan succeeded him as PM
	Storey (1933): *Saville* (P.)	
1977	Bennett (1934): *The Old Country* (D.)	Thomas Blackburn (*d.*)
		William Gerhardie (*d.*)
	Scupham (1933): *The Hinterland* (V.)	Henry Williamson (*d.*)
	Tolkien (1892–1973): *The Silmarillion* (P.)	Queen Elizabeth II's Silver Jubilee
	Upward (1903): *The Spiral Ascent* (P.)	Jimmy Carter became US President
1978	Hill (1932): *Tenebrae* (V.)	Rhys Davies (*d.*)
	Middleton (1919): *Two Brothers* (P.)	Hugh MacDiarmid (*d.*)
		Paul Scott (*d.*)
	Porter (1929): *The Cost of Seriousness* (V.)	S. Townsend Warner (*d.*)
	Tomlinson (1927): *Selected Poems 1951–1974* (V.)	Publication of the *Times* temporarily suspended
	Trevor (1928): *Lovers of their Time* (P.)	Pope John Paul II elected

DATE	AUTHOR AND TITLE	EVENT
1979	Golding (1911): *Darkness Visible* (P.)	J. G. Farrell (*d.*).
	Heaney (1939): *Field Work* (V.)	Conservative Government returned under Margaret Thatcher
	Hughes (1930): *Moortown* (V.)	USSR invaded Afghanistan
	Middleton (1919): *In a Strange Land* (P.)	Anthony Blunt revealed as former spy
1980	Enright (ed.): *Oxford Book of Contemporary Verse 1945–1980* (V.)	Olivia Manning (*d.*)
		C. P. Snow (*d.*)
	Golding (1911): *Rites of Passage* (P.)	
	Greene (1904): *Dr Fischer of Geneva* (P.)	
	Trevor (1928): *Other People's Worlds* (P.)	

Index